A Marketplace Book

BIG TRENDS IN TRADING

Strategies to Master Major Market Moves

Founded in 1807, John Wiley & Sons is the oldest independent publishing company in the United States. With offices in North America, Europe, Australia and Asia, Wiley is globally committed to developing and marketing print and electronic products and services for our customers' professional and personal knowledge and understanding.

The Wiley Trading series features books by traders who have survived the market's ever changing temperament and have prospered—some by reinventing systems, others by getting back to basics. Whether a novice trader, professional or somewhere in-between, these books will provide the advice and strategies needed to prosper today and well into the future.

For a list of available titles, please visit our Web site at www.WileyFinance.com.

A Marketplace Book

BIG TRENDS IN TRADING

Strategies to Master Major Market Moves

PRICE HEADLEY

John Wiley & Sons, Inc.

Published by John Wiley & Sons, Inc., New York
Published simultaneously in Canada.

This publication is designed to provide accurate and authoritative information in regard to the subject matter covered. It is sold with the understanding that the publisher is not engaged in rendering professional services. If
professional advice or other expert assistance is required, the services of
a competent professional person should be sought.

ISBN 0-471-41269-4

Printed in the United States of America.

10 9 8 7 6 5 4 3 2 1

To Kimberlyn, my wonderful wife:
Though markets may fluctuate, your support and
encouragement have been ever-present.
You have given me a world of true happiness and joy.

CONTENTS

ACKNOWLEDGMENTS

I am grateful for the support and assistance of many individuals in the creation of this book, including:

Kimberlyn, my wife, who has endured many lost hours and been cheerful from the beginning to the end of the process. I thank you for your patience and devotion.

My mother, Miller Harper, my father, Price Headley, and my stepfather, Charles Harper, whose love and support these many years have allowed me to truly flourish.

My dedicated associates at BigTrends.com, who have made this journey more rewarding for knowing them, and working side-by-side with them. First, Bill Wade, who has been my friend for many years, and has worked tirelessly to serve our customers. John Buzzard, who has done an outstanding job of aligning our vision of placing customers first with constant innovations in the BigTrends.com web site and in various channels of product placement. And Ken Rogers, who has worked steadily with me to develop unique content based on in-depth research and analysis.

I also want to thank Larry McMillan of McMillan Analysis Corp., who has been a good friend and taught me many lessons about doing business with the long-term in mind since I founded BigTrends.com in 1999.

My thanks also go out to Chris Myers of Traders Library, who was instrumental in helping me get the ball rolling on this book project, and to Pamela van Geissen of John Wiley & Sons, who helped guide me through to the book's completion.

And finally, thanks to TradeStation Technologies for the permission to use the excellent TradeStation charting software for the many charts and performance summaries used throughout this book.

Price Headley
September 2001

INTRODUCTION

Big trends and trading—some might call these a contradiction in terms. Traditionally, trading involves scalping quick gains, darting in and out, while big trends and big profits are made by buying a sound fundamental value and holding for the long haul, right? Wrong. That may be one way to profit from big trends, but it is certainly not the only way. As a trader for over a decade, I have adjusted with the markets as the time frames have become shorter for moves to occur, yet the markets are still seeing similar magnitudes of trends occurring, both on the upside and the downside. The incredible speed and intensity of both the bull market in the Nasdaq in 1999 and early 2000, and the bear market that followed through the fall of 2001, offer a compelling example of this compression. We saw moves happen in two years that would have taken well over a decade to play out in the past. Big trends are relative—if you owned a slow-moving stock earning 10 percent per year, and it managed to make 50 percent, that is what I call a big trend. Similarly, on a three-day trade where you usually make 8 percent and instead you profit 30 percent, that is a big trend, too. This book documents my search for above-average returns, across all time frames, which can serve both traders and investors. This book gives you flexible tools, so you can adapt with the market, and stay with big trends as they develop. I will show you how my time-tested indicators and systems have produced favorable results in both bull and bear markets.

I learned early in my life to study past patterns of performance. My initial recollections of such patterns began at Keeneland racetrack in Lexington, Kentucky, where my family has long been involved in the thoroughbred horse business. I particularly noticed how the crowd would become enthralled with one particular horse, which would become the "chalk," or the favorite. But I also noticed that the chalk would often lose (roughly one-third of the favorites win), and when the favorite did happen to win, the chalk would offer only a meager payoff since the crowd had expected the victory. A similar phenomenon happens in the stock market, as expectations become too high for a stock, and even though the underlying company may be very sound, the high expectations create too much risk if things do not go as well as most investors had hoped. I carried those lessons into my career as a market technician, as I wanted to look not only at the price action in the market, but also at the sentiment of the crowd toward the market at any given time. I monitor sentiment indicators that track investor behavior for extreme readings in fear or greed among investors. It is at these emotional extremes that many of the best buying and selling opportunities occur. Sentiment indicators will tend to be early; that is, they are leading indicators as a rule. The best sentiment readings will allow you to enter and exit just before the trend has actually turned and the crowd starts to rush in. I find that most investors are reacting to price action, while sentiment indicators allow you to be proactive regarding the next likely trend.

Technology has sped up the time period in which traders will react to short-term swings in price action. Even in choppy trading range markets, I see excellent swings in fear and greed which provide traders with more opportunities over shorter periods of time. The goal here is to take what the market is giving, rather than trying to pre-define labels like "day trader," "swing trader" or "buy-and-hold investor." Many individuals ask me whether they should focus their efforts as a short-term trader or a longer-term investor. In my view, these distinctions are becoming less relevant in today's markets. The more important question is: what opportunities are available to achieve the best profits for an acceptable level of risk?

I believe there are opportunities across many markets. Given the success of my market timing model (*Timer Digest* in Greenwich, Connecticut rated me as the sixth-highest ranked stock market timer for the calendar year 2000), I prefer leveraged vehicles to get the best bang for my buck. This includes buying and short selling growth stocks or other fast-moving shares, as well as using leveraged mutual funds. However, my favorite vehicle is options. Options give you the ability to control the underlying shares in a company for a fraction of the cost of the stock, often as little as 5 to 10 percent of the cost of the shares. With market volatility continuing to increase, I believe options will become the vehicle of choice for both active traders and investors with up to a three-year time frame. Options give you the ability to participate in both uptrends and downtrends. Just as importantly, options give you the ability to control your dollars at risk. As volatility rises, options allow you to protect more of your nest egg in safer investments, while giving you the opportunity to still participate in more aggressive growth by controlling the underlying shares of stock for a defined period of time.

I have found that in today's volatile markets, a more active approach has produced attractive profits over time, while also allowing me to sell out of the markets in periods of above-average risk.

THE CASE FOR A MORE ACTIVE TRADING APPROACH

1. Commission costs on stocks and options are way down. High trading costs used to be a major drawback of active trading, but with many brokers offering round trip stock or options trades for under $40, commissions become the last of the worries for all but the most active day traders. You should care much more about the quality of your broker's executions than the commissions in the current day and age.

2. The bid/ask spread on stocks has also dropped substantially. Decimalization has helped force bid/asked spreads on stocks to be tighter, as the market now shows most of the active stocks quoting bid and asked prices within pennies.

3. If markets are volatile but in a trading range, the active trader can wring out gains while the longer-term investor moves sideways. I believe you are going to see markets get even more volatile in the coming years, since information access is so evenly distributed that swings in fear and greed that used to take weeks to play out often happen in a few days now. If markets are swinging widely, you owe it to yourself to look for more ways to profit from them, instead of sitting on a stock on a road to nowhere over time.

CHALLENGES OF SHORT-TERM TRADING

1. An issue in the options market is that, although stocks and options were converted to decimalization in 2001, you still have options on many of the active stocks trading at a bid/asked spread of 20 cents or even 50 cents. That is the one thing I see that is holding the options industry back. Groups like the International Securities Exchange (ISE), which now offer electronically-traded options on about 600 highly-liquid stocks, have the potential to tighten those spreads over time, thanks to increasing competition in the market for customer orders. If options spreads tighten, you could see the options business explode with even more interest. If I thought a stock was going to have a short-term move, I would rather buy an in-the-money option, which could give me 3 to 10 times the leverage of the underlying stock. But right now, the wide spreads eat into my return.

2. Return on your time. One of the issues I have with day trading exclusively is the return you get should be commensurate with the time you invest. If a day trader is spending six hours per day for the one hour per day that a position trader is spending, should there not be a higher return on investment to justify the extra time spent? I believe so. Some

may say they have no better way to spend their time than day trading. That is great, but then I wonder if such traders are trading too much for entertainment. I also legitimately enjoy trading, but I try not to let it entertain me so much that I lose my focus and edge.

3. Taxes are higher. An issue with my short-term approach is that it comes with a taxable income consequence, which causes high net-worth individuals to pay higher taxes. So far, the returns I have generated more than offset even the highest tax rates. But look at Table I.1 through Table I.3 to see what you need to produce as a short-term trader (closing positions in under 12 months) to beat the lower long-term capital gains tax rate (for positions closed after 12 months).

A capital gain or loss is considered "long-term" if you hold the asset for at least a year and a day before you sell it. You then receive a lowered long-term capital gain rate. In most cases the rate will be 20 percent (or 10 percent if the capital gain falls within the 15 percent bracket).

As you can see, the gap starts to widen for high net-worth individuals in the highest tax bracket. This is not to say short-term trading cannot make up more than this gap, especially in volatile but relatively directionless markets. It just means you need to evaluate your results on an after-tax basis, and make sure you are getting more than enough extra return to cover this tax effect.

I started this book as a sort of encyclopedia of technical indicators. However, I amassed far too much information on too many different indicators and ideas, and I realized that if I were trying to read it, I would be thoroughly confused. My experience over the last decade of testing systems and theories to see what works and what does not has determined "simpler is better." As a trader, you must put yourself in a position to take action. Perhaps my greatest weakness in past trades was to think too much, do too much research, and create so many opposing views that I became a victim of "analysis paralysis," unable to pull the trigger and make the trade. Amid this confusion I was reminded of the words of Henry David Thoreau in *Walden:* "Simplify! Simplify! Simplify!" By simplifying an investment approach to the indicators that work best, my aim is to reduce the brain clutter that immobilizes a trader from making the trade, as well as reducing the hesitation in cutting losses quickly without doubt or hope.

As a result, my goal in this book is to present my experience on what has worked best, in both bull and bear markets, as well as mistakes I have made and will share with you, so that you might also avoid the many traps that appear along the investing road.

What you will find in this book is the story of my search to find the best trends in the markets, and then develop strategies to capture profits

Table I.1   The Impact of Taxes on Long-Term versus Short-Term After-Tax Returns—10% Pre-Tax Return

Tax Bracket	Long-Term	Short-Term Equivalent
15%	9.00%	10.59%
28%	8.00%	11.11%
39.60%	8.00%	13.25%

Table I.2   The Impact of Taxes on Long-Term versus Short-Term After-Tax Returns—20% Pre-Tax Return

Tax Bracket	Long-Term	Short-Term Equivalent
15%	18.00%	21.18%
28%	16.00%	22.22%
39.60%	16.00%	26.49%

Table I.3   The Impact of Taxes on Long-Term versus Short-Term After-Tax Returns—30% Pre-Tax Return

Tax Bracket	Long-Term	Short-Term Equivalent
15%	27.00%	31.76%
28%	24.00%	33.33%
39.60%	24.00%	39.74%

from them. You will learn that when hunting for big game, there is an ever-present danger of getting trampled, so your strategies to manage risk must exist simultaneously with the effort to bag the big one. I have seen too many investors who were bragging about how rich they were in 1999 that were then whining about how they gave it all back and then some in the subsequent bear market of 2000 to 2001. The secret to success in up, down, or sideways markets is to have a trading plan that identifies the prevailing conditions correctly, seeks out situations with high Reward-to-Risk ratios, and judiciously deploys your capital into the best opportunities relative to risk.

My experience with trend spotting is that you can make very nice gains when the crowd has not yet recognized the trend, yet you can also lose big if you jump on an obvious trend where most investors are already on board. That is why it is so critical to monitor the sentiment of the crowd to determine if most investors have caught on. What has always surprised me is how some trends will be recognized, while occasionally investors and the media will actually bet against certain trends that appear "overdone." It is the synthesis of technical analysis (which forecasts trends) and sentiment analysis (also known as behavioral finance) which will allow you to ride trends while also having an exit point when crowd opinion starts to bubble up in recognition of the trend.

Technical analysis focuses on price action, believing that the trend in prices reflects the nature of the news to come and the outlook ahead for a stock, before the news actually becomes fully known. Price action rules how people feel, especially in the short term. As I stated earlier, the market cycles have become more compressed and more volatile over shorter time frames, and this puts added weight on the importance of technical analysis. At the most basic level, I compare the current technical situation for a stock with the corresponding investor sentiment, which measures the behavior of investors to see if they are doubting the trend or piling on board.

Sentiment is widely misunderstood, so let me explain this concept further. Many investors have experienced the pain of the bear market in 2000 and 2001. So when I show people that my firm actually made money for my subscribers in 2000, and have continued to strongly outperform the indexes in 2001, they ask me "How did you do it?" The answer is one that took me many years to figure out, but has proved incredibly rewarding. The answer is "Sentiment." *Barron's* called me "Mr. Sentiment" in an article on September 11, 2000, where I explained how my sentiment indicators showed extreme complacency and predicted major problems for the Nasdaq when it was still over 4,000.

What is sentiment? Sentiment is the market's mood. How fear and greed interact in the markets is the most critical factor to evaluate. Why? Because sentiment determines whether most investors have already bought (thus exhausting demand and setting the stage for a top), or if most investors have already sold (thus ending the selling pressure and setting the stage for a significant bottom). Most investors are often confused by what they read, especially if they witness how a stock or the market reacts differently. If the major media are negative on the market, yet the market starts to rally, most will be perplexed. However, that will be a major sign that the market is ready to rally further. Why? Because so many investors will have been told that the market will not rally, so their investments are in cash or other areas. Yet the market is already moving higher by early-stage buyers, and investors in later stages will drive it further upward as they gradually recognize that they need to be a part of a rising market. When the market rises despite heavy skepticism, there is an untapped reservoir of future buying power. Conversely, back on March 10, 2000, when the major media trumpeted the new high in the Nasdaq Composite over 5,000 and the crowd was showing an unprecedented euphoria, I told my subscribers to switch from bullish to neutral on stocks, as I exited the market. That decision to move to the sidelines saved my customers a lot of money, as did other subsequent indications of concern during the downturn of 2000 to 2001.

Finally, fundamentals make sure the stock has an underlying sustainable trend based on the company's growth prospects. Most trends are driven by some underlying fundamental driver. Factors like new products, a hot industry group, new management, or other fundamental factors are all important, but they tend to all show up in the most important fundamentals of all: sales and earnings growth rates. I will share my favorite strategies for finding fast-growing stocks and determining how to filter down from the thousands of stocks available to the best few you should be choosing at any point in time. However, I place fundamental considerations behind technical and sentimental indicators in order of importance. While this goes against the conventional wisdom, many accepted fundamental indicators have caused investors to lose big when a stock is proving them wrong. By the time these investors read or hear that the fundamentals have changed, it is too late! In contrast, technical analysis gives you evidence as to the trend in prices before all the news has been fully accounted for by the crowd, while sentiment indicators will often send early warning signals when the crowd has recognized the prevailing price action, suggesting that trend is about to end.

A big part of my success in trading came when I realized that trading was about generating results at the end of the month and year, not about how many trades I could make each day for the thrill of the game. It is this excitement angle that gets many traders into an activity-based mentality, when they need to convert to a results-based mindset. If your edge is not present on a given day, you are better off not trading until a clearer edge appears. One of the principles I established on the founding of BigTrends.com in 1999 was a focus on results, not on activity. This means that it is acceptable to make no trades if an edge is not clear. In fact, it is preferable, as there can be a frustration deep down inside of a trader that has a tendency to come out when a losing position occurs, especially if the trader never had a major conviction in the trade initially. The emotional impact of such losses is often greater than the financial impact, as it can devastate your confidence, which can in turn cause difficulty in sticking with a trading plan. Once you deviate from your plan, you will be riding an emotional roller coaster. You must have a plan to keep yourself balanced, never getting too high after a win or too low after a loss. My goal here is to help you create that plan, and to understand the psychological challenges that you must overcome to experience personal growth and move to a higher level as a trader.

I hope this book becomes a valuable resource for you on your path to investment profits.

Price Headley

Part I

GETTING THE MARKET RIGHT FIRST

Some strategists would have you believe that any focus on predicting the market would prove futile, since no one can predict where the market is headed next. I strongly disagree. The broader market's trend sets the tone for many of the most-actively traded stocks. Growth stocks were all the rage when the market was rising in 1999, but as the bear market of 2000 and 2001 hit, these growth stocks were hammered just as hard on the downside. Did these companies' prospects really change that much over the course of a year? No, it was the market environment that changed, making the growth leaders the most vulnerable to profit-taking and shorting when the general market trend turned for the worse.

The strategy of moving in and out of the market based on indicators is known as "market timing." Market timing has built a bad name, because it is true that *most* investors cannot time the market. They are simply too reactive, coming in after the move has already occurred. The ineffectiveness of the majority of investors does not mean you should also disparage market timing. In fact, if the majority of investors time the market poorly, you should look to do the opposite of the majority and turn their loss into your gain. This is exactly the philosophy I follow, and it defines why I watch the activity of the rest of the crowd. The crowd's behavior has proved, over many years of research, to be an effective contrarian tool.

During the past 15 years, if you had bought and held the market, you would have gained 13.00 percent annually. Those who say market timing does not work point to the fact that if you missed the best 20 days in the stock market (measured by the S&P 500 from January 1, 1986 to December 31, 2000), your average annual return would have dropped from 13.00 to 6.99 percent. If you missed the 40 best days, your average annual return would be 3.12 percent, which is not much better than T-Bills. However, if you missed the 40 best *and* 40 *worst* days in the stock market, your annual return would rise from 13.00 percent to 15.95 percent. And if you missed only the 40 worst days in the stock market, your annual return would more than double from 13.00 to 26.83 percent.

As a result, you can see that proper market timing adds value, both to reduce risk and exploit favorable periods via leveraged instruments like options. You can actually benefit from declines in stock prices. Most investors who buy stocks to hold them for the long term are typically stuck when the stock goes into a sideways or lower mode. When you correctly predict the downside potential in a stock, you can profit by selling short (by selling a stock at a higher level first and later buying it back at a lower level), or buying puts (options traded expecting a drop in stocks) as a hedge. In contrast, you can neutralize your bullish positions by finding bearish positions to offset your bullish exposure.

In this section, I will share my favorite indicators to monitor the crowd's behavior, and then I will show you the systems I created to profit from the wrong-way opinions of the crowd at major turning points.

1

THE CBOE EQUITY PUT/CALL RATIO—MY FAVORITE CONTRARY INDICATOR

*Most people would rather fail conventionally
than win unconventionally.*

—John Maynard Keynes

What does it mean to be a "contrarian"? Do you zig when everyone else zags, by necessity? No, you must define extremes in investor psychology as a first condition. I look for indicators that measure the crowd's level of fear or greed. Once this crowd opinion appears to be held by a wide number of market participants, I then look for the market to start proving that opinion wrong. If the crowd is overly optimistic, and the market starts to reverse to the downside, a lot of potential sellers are sitting in stocks. In contrast, a market that is seeing high fear after a sell-off suggests that there are potential buyers ready to come in once the market starts to turn to the upside. Typically, I look for some catalyst in the form of upcoming news or events, read the expectations for that news, and then look for the surprise against expectations as a catalyst.

Sentiment indicators show something that those who are following a price chart technically cannot see: how everyone else is reacting to that price chart. I find that by the time most traders recognize a trend, that trend is likely to end. Therefore, sentiment measures can give us a "heads up" as to the potential for continuation of a trend, or the risk of a coming reversal. While it takes some time to get comfortable trading as a contrarian, once you start to experience profits, you will learn the benefits of buying when others panic, and selling when everyone else wants in.

The basic principle here is Economics 101: the Law of Supply and Demand. If most players are bullish, this suggests they have already bought. Since most investors follow price as their indicator, this leads them to be too reactionary, resulting in a "pile on" effect after major rallies. If most players are bearish, sellers have already driven prices down, and it does not take much new buying to overcome the lack of selling pressure, thus swinging the pendulum of price back to the upside. Sentiment is a leading indicator, meaning that it can sometimes lead too far in front of price. You will need indicators that tell you when sentiment has truly reached an extreme. I use technical indicators as a filter to determine when the market is about to turn after extremes in sentiment.

The CBOE (Chicago Board Options Exchange) equity put/call ratio is my favorite sentiment indicator. The CBOE equity put/call ratio is a measure of the amount of bullish or bearish sentiment in the market. The "equity" only refers to this ratio's focus on stock options, not index options. Stock options give a better representation of the market's mood, in my experience. Index options include too much institutional hedging to be considered effective contrarian indicators on their own.

When options players rush to buy calls, they are making bullish bets, and the put/call ratio will drop as the crowd gets more optimistic. Similarly, when the crowd has become fearful, and conviction about lower prices is strong, many puts will trade as speculators expect to profit from a further decline. This will cause the put/call ratio to spike higher, usually right near major market bottoms. At major extremes in optimism and pessimism, the put/call ratio serves as an excellent contrarian indicator. Why? Because too many bulls (shown by a low put/call ratio) suggest that buying power has been exhausted, indicating a short-term top. Too many bears (a high put/call ratio) imply that many have sold out of the market already, which often occurs near bottoms as selling power evaporates.

How should the points at which the put/call ratio reaches such extremes be defined? The conventional approach to gauge such extremes has been to look for predetermined levels at which the put/call ratio might suggest the market is overbought or oversold. Specifically, let us look at the CBOE equity put/call ratio. I use the CBOE because the data is easily accessible on its web site at *www.cboe.com.*

Stated simply, the equity put/call ratio is the percentage of puts (options traded expecting a drop in stocks) that are trading relative to calls (options traded expecting a rise in stocks). When the percentage of puts to calls increases, it indicates rising fear in the market, which I interpret as a buy signal at extremes. One rule of thumb to gauge extremes suggests that if the CBOE equity options put/call ratio falls below 40 percent (4 puts trading for every 10 calls) the market is near a top, while a reading above 80 percent (8 puts trading for every 10 calls) suggests a market bottom. While these guidelines may have been more effective when the market was not so volatile, these fixed levels have become less meaningful in more rapidly changing market conditions. For example, when the market was nicely trending higher in 1999, my indicators adjusted to account for this strength by only selling on relatively massive spikes in greed. Otherwise a trader might exit a bull market prematurely. Similarly, in the more volatile trading range market in 2000, my indicators adjusted to pick up the extreme moves in very short periods of time, while also exiting the market during the higher risk corrective periods, like early March, mid-April, and mid-July, during which the Nasdaq dropped 15 percent or more in periods of three weeks or less. However, let us look at what happens in Figure 1.1 if we buy when the CBOE equity put/call ratio reaches 80 percent, followed within the next 10 days or less by a close above the highs of five trading days earlier, which would suggest a new technical uptrend coming off this fear spike. Similarly, we will look for sell signals at the 40 percent mark, confirmed by a close less than the lower of five days previously. See Figure 1.2 for a performance summary of the Nasdaq Composite's performance once the ratio's absolute levels are reached. The main statistics I look at in these performance

Figure 1.1   Nasdaq Composite versus CBOE Equity Put/Call Ratio 2001:
80 percent Readings Can Trigger Buys and 40 percent Readings
Can Trigger Sells

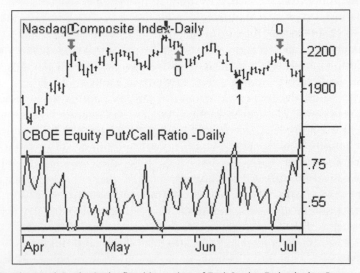

Chart created on TradeStation®, the flagship product of TradeStation Technologies, Inc.

Figure 1.2   Performance Summary—Nasdaq Composite versus CBOE Equity
Put/Call Ratio with 80 percent Buy and 40 percent Sell Triggers

```
Equity Put/Call 8040  Nasdaq Composite Index-Daily  01/02/1990 - 09/21/2001

                    Performance Summary: All Trades

Total net profit      $  1555.96    Open position P/L      $  -264.50
Gross profit          $  5475.36    Gross loss             $ -3919.40

Total # of trades         334       Percent profitable         54%
Number winning trades     179       Number losing trades       155

Largest winning trade $   734.63    Largest losing trade   $  -420.85
Average winning trade $    30.59    Average losing trade   $   -25.29
Ratio avg win/avg loss      1.21    Avg trade(win & loss)  $     4.66

Max consec. winners         7       Max consec. losers           7
Avg # bars in winners       3       Avg # bars in losers         3

Max intraday drawdown $  -913.74
Profit factor               1.40    Max # contracts held         1
```

Chart created on TradeStation®, the flagship product of TradeStation Technologies, Inc.

summaries are the "percent profitable" and the "ratio avg win/avg loss." How often you win and how often you win or lose will ultimately determine the profitability of a particular trading method.

Based on my desire to create an indicator which determined relative highs and lows in sentiment based on more recent data, I tested various indicators and found that using adaptive bands was best. I found the Bollinger Bands particularly effective on any data series that tends not to trend. Bollinger Bands (created by John Bollinger) are an excellent tool for defining extremes in a non-trending data series like the put/call ratio. Bollinger Bands are derived by taking a moving average (in this case, a 21-day moving average) to approximate the last month's trading activity, and then putting a band two standard deviations around each side of this moving average. Figure 1.3 shows how to calculate standard deviation.

Bollinger Bands are based around a simple moving average, usually plotted two standard deviations above and below the moving average. The distance the bands are placed away from the moving average is a function of how volatile that stock has been recently, which is also known as the standard deviation. Statistics show that these Bollinger Bands with two standard deviations should encompass about 95 percent of the price action between these bands. Therefore, I look for the other 5 percent of the time that something is happening outside of these Bollinger Bands.

I use the 21-day Bollinger Bands with two standard deviations above the 21-day moving average and two standard deviations below the moving average to better quantify the high and low points, allowing me to pinpoint new buy and sell signals from fear and greed extremes in CBOE equity

Figure 1.3   Standard Deviation Calculation

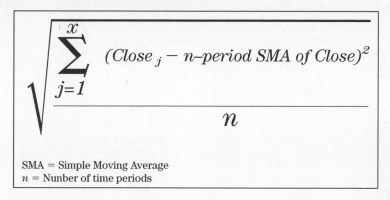

$$\sqrt{\dfrac{\sum_{j=1}^{x} (Close_j - n\text{-}period \; SMA \; of \; Close)^2}{n}}$$

SMA = Simple Moving Average
n = Nunber of time periods

put/call activity. This served to incorporate the volatility of the CBOE put/call ratio by placing a band above and below the 21-day simple moving average. So, when the put/call ratio climbs above the 21-day upper Bollinger Band and then falls back below, a peak in fear has occurred, and a buy signal is triggered. A close below the lower Bollinger Band and a return back above it suggests too much call buying, which results in a sell signal.

In Figure 1.4, the CBOE equity put/call ratio reaches peaks above the upper Band in January and February 2000, which experiences pain as the Nasdaq is in a nasty downtrend. Once the Nasdaq has technically recovered, the CBOE equity put/call ratio spikes up to the upper two standard deviation Bollinger Band signal, creating short-term bounces in a choppy market.

My goal in using 21-day Bollinger Bands is to make current sentiment readings more relevant to recent activity. Since 21 days is closest to the average number of days in one month of trading, I consider this a useful measure of the past month's volatility in a data series. I start by plotting the 21-day Bollinger Bands around a put/call reading or other sentiment indicator with two standard deviations on either side, implying that 95 percent of the price action should occur within those Bollinger Bands. This creates the upper and lower band boundaries you see around the put/call ratio chart. If there is a close above or below the bands, it signals an unusual event that should result in an important turn in the market once the indicator closes back into the band, which suggests a peak in fear or greed has occurred. The beauty of the Bollinger Bands is that they work very well on non-trending data, and sentiment measures like put/call ratios tend to be non-trending over time. The Bollinger Bands also adjust to more recent conditions, so if the market is getting less volatile this month than in prior months, the bands will be less wide and it will be easier to get a new signal. The key is that these bands form the basis to get a relatively high or low reading compared to the other recent data. In more volatile markets, the bands will

Figure 1.4   Nasdaq Composite versus CBOE Equity Put/Call Ratio with 21-Day Bollinger Bands, Not Factoring in Price Trend: January–June 2000

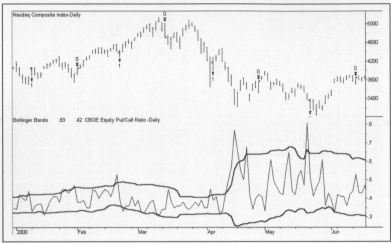

Chart created on TradeStation®, the flagship product of TradeStation Technologies, Inc.

stretch wider, so it will take more than just a noise-filled day to get a new signal. Therefore, the bands adjust for higher volatility and greater extremes in more volatile market conditions.

PUTTING THIS SYSTEM TO THE TEST

I like to test indicators like the CBOE equity put/call indicator for its effectiveness over time. In this test, I examine the buy and sell signals on the CBOE equity put/call ratio using the Bollinger Bands previously described, and then buy or sell the Nasdaq Composite when new signals are reached. On buy signals my tests show you should hold the Nasdaq Composite for 15 days (unless previously reversed by a new bearish trade). Since 1990, there have been 89 buy signals generated by this system, and 73 percent of the time these buy signals have resulted in a profit, with the average gain on wins besting the average drop on the losers by over 40 percent.

In contrast, sell signals have had a poorer showing in the last 10 years, thanks to a strongly uptrending bull market over most of that period. Still, bearish trades were profitable over this period despite fighting the bullish bias. Holding the bearish trades for eight trading days (or until a new buy signal was given) resulted in correct signals just 52 percent of the time, but when right, the average gain was more than 50 percent greater than the average loss. It is an encouraging sign that even against the broader trend, the CBOE equity put/call ratio can be effective in pointing out periods where the broader trend may experience a short-term reversal.

THE PUT/CALL RATIO SYSTEM: A CASE STUDY

Let us look at specific examples in 2000, using adaptive bands on the CBOE put/call ratio in Figure 1.5 to show buy and sell points within a volatile market environment.

Our first signal occurs on January 10th, the trading day after the market gets a relative extreme in pessimism on January 7th. The CBOE equity put/call (hereafter called the put/call) reading at 44 percent (or over .4 on the bottom half of the chart in Figure 1.5) has a close above the upper 21-day Bollinger Band on January 7th, followed by a close back below this band on the 10th. The buy signal occurs at the closing price on January 10th. Therefore, you implement your buy order on the following morning's opening price. As you can see in the chart, the market pulls back for two sessions, then rallies to create a small profit before the exit signal occurs after

Figure 1.5 Nasdaq Composite versus CBOE Equity Put/Call Ratio with 21-Day Bollinger Bands and 50-Day Moving Average Filter: January to June 2000

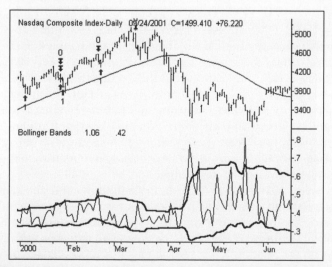

Chart created on TradeStation®, the flagship product of TradeStation Technologies, Inc.

two trading sessions. This buy signal was not held 15 trading days because a sell signal was subsequently received five trading days later on January 18th. This sell signal occurred because the put/call reading fell to 31 percent on the prior trading day (January 14th), pushing it under the lower 21-day Bollinger Band, and then returned back above the lower band the following trading day. This marked a relative extreme in optimism. The beauty of these adaptive bands is that they allow you to enter and exit the market more quickly if volatility causes sentiment to swing more rapidly than it previously did. So my sell signal occurs and the market trails higher for three more closes, then begins a nasty reversal for five sessions that causes a drop from my original short entry at 4,130.76 to the closeout date eight trading days later at 3,887.07, resulting in a 5.9 percent gain for my short position. At this point technicians may say I could have lowered my risk by waiting for the lower close before putting on the short or any number of other technical ideas to further improve this method. There are many ways a technician can add value, but for the purposes of this indicator, and for the sake of simplicity, I am focusing entirely on the pure sentiment buy and sell points.

The next put/call signal occurs on February 16th, when the put/call ratio crossed back below the upper band to register a 49 percent reading on February 16th, after a 55 percent number occurred the prior day (February 15th). What you notice in this example is that the put/call ratio then has another surge above the upper band two days later, on February 18th at 63 percent. What should be done in these situations? Since a bullish position is already established, you should seek to follow the indicator and stay with the signal until it is either reversed by a sell signal (which would only occur at the other extreme, below the lower band, usually after a rally) or if the time is up for the trade (in the bullish case, after 15 trading days). As you can see in this case, the trade is held for the 15 trading days, and then is exited on March 9th at what turns out to be within two points of the closing high on the Nasdaq Composite (the absolute high and closing high occur the following session). This trade was initiated at 4,427.65, and in just three weeks was exited at 5,046.86, resulting in a 14.0 percent gain. Such steady directional trends are what all traders dream about, and option buyers in particular benefit most from these trends. When you get strong directional moves in relatively short periods of time, option buying will be the most rewarding strategy in such environments.

As an aside, one thing I particularly liked about the fear that created this signal was that the market had been relatively strong when this buy signal was generated. As you can see, the Nasdaq had made a new high, then went sideways for five trading sessions. Yet fear rose substantially, despite the market consolidation. When I see such extreme fear in the face of a relatively strong market, it gets me particularly bullish. If the market drops sharply, you expect fear—it is a rational outcome of a declining market. But extreme fear in the face of a relatively strong market can be considered relatively irrational. Whether the worry is related to the Federal Reserve's posture on interest rates, an oil shock, a Presidential affair, and so on, it is of no concern to me as an analyst. All I see is a strong market with a lot of fear, which means many investors are on the sidelines. As this uncertainty is resolved, or as the market continues to blast higher in spite of this uncertainty, these sidelined investors will be forced back into the market. This serves as an indicator of future buying power.

In early March 2000, the system remained out of the market, awaiting the next buy signal. The market plunged after the March 9th exit, and the buy signal given after the April 4th panic caused the put/call reading to spike up to 55 percent. The subsequent drop back under the upper band on April 5th gives the buy signal, and the Nasdaq starts to recover sharply. The recovery is so swift that sentiment now takes a dramatic turn to the optimistic side in only three trading sessions. The relative optimism occurs at the close on April 7th, with a closing put/call number at 37 percent hitting the lower Bollinger Band. As a result, I switched from bullish to neutral on the close of trading on Friday, April 7th. This allowed me to avoid the next week's huge decline, which at the time was the worst week in Nasdaq history. On Monday of the next week, there was an upside reversal that finally caused a sharp spike top in fear and gave me the confidence to make a new switch from neutral to bullish at the close on April 17th, after the fear spike on April 14th at 92 percent was officially in place. This buy signal is then typically held 15 days, and results in a poor trade for the put/call ratio, as the purchase occurred near 3,793.57 and the exit after 15 days occurs at 3,384.73, resulting in a 10.8 percent loss. In contrast to my earlier point that I love to see high fear when the market is relatively strong, this trade showed high fear in a very weak market, which is to be expected. As a result, such high fear signals can be filtered by savvy traders who wish to only trade in periods where the trend is still relatively strong and likely to get stronger as this extreme pessimism is unwound. The reality of my action is that I officially stayed bullish on the market, as my other indicators (which will be discussed in the following three chapters) suggested fear was still incredibly high. The equity put/call ratio confirmed this fear by giving another buy signal on May 22nd at 3,364.21, thanks to the reversal of the prior day's fear spike at 89 percent on Friday, May 19th. As you can see, the market then starts with a headfake to the downside, testing as low as 3,042.66 two days later but then beginning a remarkably quick burst up to 3,821.76. In only nine trading days after entry, the trade made 13.6 percent before it was reversed by a new sell signal on June 5th, a day after the greed inflection point at 32 percent on June 2nd.

Note what is happening here. Investors are reacting to what the market is doing, and rushing out near the bottom and then rushing back in near the short-term top. The put/call ratio allows you to convert your approach from a reactive, rear-view mirror mentality to instead focus proactively on the reversals that are likely going forward. This allows you to be prepared for major turns in the road that will cause rear-view mirror players to wreck themselves financially. In the case of the June 5th sell signal at 3,821.76, you can see in Figure 1.6 that the market did not particularly drop while this position was held. Note that relative to the exit on June 15th at 3,845.74, it did not particularly rally either. This is very important information for option buyers, as option buyers want to avoid periods where little movement occurs and time elapses. Time is the enemy of the option buyer, so staying out of the market during such periods is very valuable indeed.

The next buy signal, at 3,863.10, occurs on July 5th, thanks to having the fear climax at 65 percent on July 3rd in place. This begins a quick rally in the Nasdaq to 4,174.85 on July 13th, resulting in an 8.1 percent gain in just six trading sessions. At that point a new sell signal is given, thanks to the 40 percent reading on July 12th falling below the lower band and then being reversed. There is one more reading below the lower band on July 14th,

Figure 1.6   Nasdaq Composite versus CBOE Equity Put/Call Ratio with 21-Day Bollinger Bands and 50-Day Moving Average Filter: June to December 2000

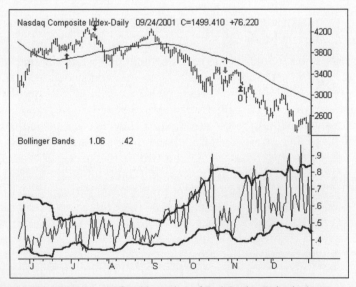

Chart created on TradeStation®, the flagship product of TradeStation Technologies, Inc.

after which the market carnage begins. The eight-day exit rule kicks in on July 25th at 4,029.57, allowing a 4.5 percent profit even though the market declines still further thereafter.

Surprisingly, as the market has a key reversal and begins to rally back in early August, sentiment becomes very optimistic, as most players appear to expect a market bottom. The sell signal is given on August 7th at 3,862.99, and while the market initially drops to just under 3,700 in four trading days intraday, the trade is closed after eight full days at 3,940.87 for a mild loss of 2.0 percent. Yet in a "bigger picture" view, my experience with such crowd optimism, even as the market is making lower highs, is that this optimism will need to be broken by another hard decline in the market, as such optimism is not rational in the face of a broader downtrend in the market.

The bottom line is that the concept of relative bands makes indicators like the CBOE equity put/call ratio more adaptive to more recent changes in market volatility. This allows traders to be more flexible and to adjust as the markets change, which can greatly increase trading profits over time. Figure 1.7 shows the total performance of the equity put/call ratio signals using the 50-day moving average as a trend filter.

Notice how the equity put/call ratio is incredibly effective when combined with the intermediate-term trend as a filter, in this case the simple 50-day moving average. In addition, I have found that, as a general rule, the price action should have turned into the profitable direction by no later

Figure 1.7 Performance Summary—Nasdaq Composite versus CBOE Equity Put/Call Ratio with 21-Day Bollinger Bands and 50-Day Moving Average Filter: 1990 to 2001

BollBand EQPC Nasdaq Composite Index-Daily 01/02/1990 - 09/21/2001

Performance Summary: All Trades

Total net profit	$ 3532.37	Open position P/L	$ 0.00
Gross profit	$ 4792.74	Gross loss	$ -1260.37
Total # of trades	114	Percent profitable	70%
Number winning trades	80	Number losing trades	34
Largest winning trade	$ 574.99	Largest losing trade	$ -187.36
Average winning trade	$ 59.91	Average losing trade	$ -37.07
Ratio avg win/avg loss	1.62	Avg trade(win & loss)	$ 30.99
Max consec. winners	11	Max consec. losers	4
Avg # bars in winners	9	Avg # bars in losers	11
Max intraday drawdown	$ -266.96		
Profit factor	3.80	Max # contracts held	1

Chart created on TradeStation®, the flagship product of TradeStation Technologies, Inc.

than five trading days after the put/call system's entry to prove this system right. Therefore, if a position is not profitable after five trading days or more, then it is usually better to exit the position at that point. And per my rule to typically hold positions that are aligned with the 50-day trend for 15 days, if I am stopped out on the fifth day or later, I make it a rule not to take any new contrarian signals until at least 15 days have passed since my original entry. Why? Because just as the signal works well most of the time for 15 days, when it is not working and I must stop out a position, I do not want to get right back in against that trend. I would rather give that trend time to play out, and in my experience it pays to use the remaining 10 or fewer days to wait for that trend to exhaust itself before taking new trades.

Here is the TradeStation® EasyLanguage® code for this put/call system:

```
Put/Call System:

Long Entry:

Close < BollingerBand(Close,21,2) and Close[1] >
BollingerBand (Close,21,2)[1] or Close[2] >
BollingerBand(Close,21,2)[2] or Close[3] >
BollingerBand(Close,21,2)[3]

Long Exit:

BarsSinceEntry=15

Short Entry:
Close[1] < BollingerBand(Close,21,2)[1] and Close[2] <
BollingerBand(Close,21,2)[2] OR Close[3] <
BollingerBand(Close,21,2)[3] and Close[4] <
BollingerBand(Close,21,2)[4] OR Close[5] <
BollingerBand(Close,21,2)[5]

Short Exit:

BarsSinceEntry=2
```

WEEKLY PUT/CALL READINGS—A LONGER-TERM INDICATOR

*If you torture the data sufficiently,
it will confess to anything.*

—Dean LeBaron

I like to look at different time frames, and I sometimes see patterns that appear very consistent, which later prove to play out in the opposite direction versus what the pattern suggests. This does not mean the analysis is no good, but rather that when a pattern breaks, you should be equally aware that something has gone wrong to change the pattern, which should result in a continuation move in the opposite direction as traders unwind prior bets and take new positions on the reversal of the trend.

I spotted a weekly chart pattern on the equity put/call ratio in early 2001 that had had outstanding historical success, which later proved to tell me something equally meaningful when the pattern broke down. Since I monitor the weekly chart of the equity put/call ratio in addition to the daily ratio, as it takes out some of the noise of the daily chart, I noticed the following pattern: when the weekly equity put/call ratio finished over 80 percent on a given week, there is an extreme in fear on a weekly closing basis. Once the market confirms this with a technical breakout as defined by a weekly close above the high of five weeks ago, you should buy. You hold this trade for 10 weeks at a minimum to avoid any initial noise, then trail with a 10-week moving average so that any weekly close in the Nasdaq Composite under the 10-week average after the first 10 weeks have passed will take you out of this trade. This trade happens on average about once per year. Figure 1.8 shows the results before the 2001 signal.

As you can see, this indicator had a remarkable string of seven out of seven winning trades headed into 2001, with most signals getting off to quick starts. Only the 1994 and 2000 signals sputtered at first before seeking

Figure 1.8   Nasdaq Composite Individual Trades Based on CBOE Weekly Equity Put/Call Ratio: 1990 to 2000

BollBand D2 EQPC>.80 Nasdaq Composite Index-Weekly 07/30/82 - 09/21/01							
Date	Time	Type	Cnts	Price	Signal Name	Entry P/L	Cumulative
11/16/90		Buy	1	350.850			
05/17/91		LExit	1	481.370		$ 130.52	$ 130.52
11/04/94		Buy	1	766.080			
10/06/95		LExit	1	1012.040		$ 245.96	$ 376.48
08/23/96		Buy	1	1143.050			
02/21/97		LExit	1	1334.320		$ 191.27	$ 567.75
01/23/98		Buy	1	1575.920			
05/22/98		LExit	1	1805.000		$ 229.08	$ 796.83
10/23/98		Buy	1	1693.860			
02/19/99		LExit	1	2283.600		$ 589.74	$ 1386.57
09/10/99		Buy	1	2887.030			
03/31/00		LExit	1	4572.830		$ 1685.80	$ 3072.37
06/16/00		Buy	1	3860.560			
09/08/00		LExit	1	3978.410		$ 117.85	$ 3190.22

Chart created on TradeStation®, the flagship product of TradeStation Technologies, Inc.

Figure 1.9   Nasdaq Composite versus CBOE Weekly Put/Call Ratio Buy Signals and Exits: 1999 to 2001

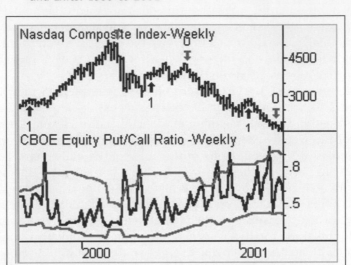

Chart created on TradeStation®, the flagship product of TradeStation Technologies, Inc.

to rally. The remarkable aspect of this system was that despite only being in the market 41 percent of the time, you made 50 percent more total points in the Nasdaq Composite! The stop rule designed to wait 10 weeks before considering an exit was a bit longer than I would usually prefer, but it had worked like a charm in the past, even managing a mild gain from the 2000 signal before the downside hit later that year. Therefore, when I received the new signal in January of 2001, the market figured to realistically see some short-term upside fireworks.

As you can see in Figure 1.9 and Figure 1.10, a perfect record does not guarantee eternal success. However, as I said before, if an indicator should usually work and now it does not, this is meaningful information. It tells us that conditions have changed in the short-term, and warns us to prepare for more price action in the opposite direction of the generally successful signals. In this case, the opposite direction theory said that the trend would be down for a while longer, and it was.

This scenario also reminds me of John Hill of Futures Truth, who said "Your worst drawdown is always in front of you." This system had experienced very minimal drawdowns before the 2001 trade, and it goes to show that you should plan for at least twice the prior worst drawdown, or even three times the worst drawdown if you want to play more conservatively, into your plan. This will then affect your money management decisions regarding how much capital to commit to each trade.

Figure 1.10 Updated Performance Summary with 2001 Trade Included

BollBand D2 EQPC>.80 Nasdaq Composite Index-Weekly 07/30/82 - 09/21/01							
Date	Time	Type	Cnts	Price	Signal Name	Entry P/L	Cumulative
11/16/90		Buy	1	350.850			
05/17/91		LExit	1	481.370		$ 130.52	$ 130.52
11/04/94		Buy	1	766.080			
10/06/95		LExit	1	1012.040		$ 245.96	$ 376.48
08/23/96		Buy	1	1143.050			
02/21/97		LExit	1	1334.320		$ 191.27	$ 567.75
01/23/98		Buy	1	1575.920			
05/22/98		LExit	1	1805.000		$ 229.08	$ 796.83
10/23/98		Buy	1	1693.860			
02/19/99		LExit	1	2283.600		$ 589.74	$ 1386.57
09/10/99		Buy	1	2887.030			
03/31/00		LExit	1	4572.830		$ 1685.80	$ 3072.37
06/16/00		Buy	1	3860.560			
09/08/00		LExit	1	3978.410		$ 117.85	$ 3190.22
01/26/01		Buy	1	2781.300			
03/30/01		LExit	1	1840.260		$ -941.04	$ 2249.18

Chart created on TradeStation®, the flagship product of TradeStation Technologies, Inc.

INTRADAY PUT/CALL READINGS

When things were looking ugly during the first half hour on July 17, 2001, with the Nasdaq testing down near the 2000 support mark, I noticed a surprising amount of fear in the CBOE intraday equity put/call ratio. At 10:00 AM ET, this ratio was at 90 percent, showing 9 puts trading for every 10 calls. This was a relatively high amount of fear, as the upper 21-day Bollinger Band designed to show relatively high fear on the put/call ratio was any reading over 87 percent. When expectations get this low, a positive surprise is usually the result as selling pressure has been exhausted, in this case on an intraday basis.

If you look at the intraday table in Table 1.1 and compare it to the intraday price chart in Figure 1.11, you will see how this big spike in fear led to the best move of the day in the Nasdaq 100 Trust (QQQ), rising from 41.50 to 42.50 between 10:15 and 10:48 AM ET (the table shows Central time, one hour behind Eastern time). From 11:30 AM ET on (10:30 Central on the table), the intraday put/call ratio reverted back to the 50 percent area, showing a more normal one put trading for every two calls. At that point, the sentiment extreme no longer existed, and traders could then follow the trend from a purely technical viewpoint for the rest of the session. This shows you how following sentiment closely intraday can give you an additional edge versus just looking at technical price action alone.

If you want to get these intraday updates every 30 minutes, you can find them posted under the "Market Statistics—Intraday Volume" link at the CBOE web site (*www.cboe.com*).

Table 1.1 CBOE Intraday Equity Put/Call Ratio—July 17, 2001

| Time | Equity Only | | |
	Call Volume	Put Volume	Put/Call Ratio
9:00 AM	43,795	39,519	0.902
9:30 AM	92,583	79,877	0.863
10:00 AM	147,885	108,141	0.731
10:30 AM	257,102	133,020	0.517
11:00 AM	293,146	153,927	0.525
11:30 AM	332,600	171,863	0.517
12:00 PM	366,856	189,006	0.515
12:30 PM	403,089	202,808	0.503
1:00 PM	441,048	231,064	0.524
1:30 PM	472,550	253,961	0.537
2:00 PM	506,820	280,324	0.553
2:30 PM	550,999	300,542	0.545
3:00 PM	614,662	325,808	0.530

Figure 1.11 Nasdaq 100 Trust (QQQ): Three-Minute Chart—July 17, 2001

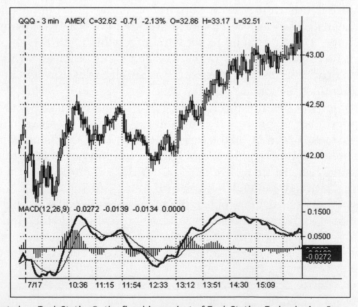

Chart created on TradeStation®, the flagship product of TradeStation Technologies, Inc.

THE TOTAL PUT/CALL RATIO GREATER THAN 1.00

Another useful signal that fear has reached a panic is when the total put/call ratio reaches 1.00. The total put/call ratio adds both the equity and the index options together. When more puts trade than calls, the put/call ratio will be greater than 1.00. This is a relatively rare occurrence, as the put/call ratio as a whole averages about 0.60 over time (6 puts trading for every 10 calls). A fear build-up that causes more puts to trade than calls is often a signal of a market bottom. Figure 1.12 and Figure 1.13 show what would happen if you bought the close on days where the CBOE total put/call ratio was greater than 1.00, and held the position for X days.

This indicator showed the market at the major bottoms in October 1998, October 1997, and July 1996. At the same time, this indicator also had difficulty in the bear market period of 2000 and 2001. It will help if the trend is factored in to make sure the system is buying high fear within a longer-term bull market, as opposed to buying into the teeth of a bear market. Figure 1.14 shows what happens when the system only takes trades when the total put/call ratio is above 1.00 and the closing price of the index is above its 200-day moving average.

As you can see, the maximum drawdown is substantially reduced from −1732.69 to −92.08 points by avoiding bullish trades when the long-term

Figure 1.12 CBOE Total Put/Call Ratio Greater Than 1.00: 1999 to 2001

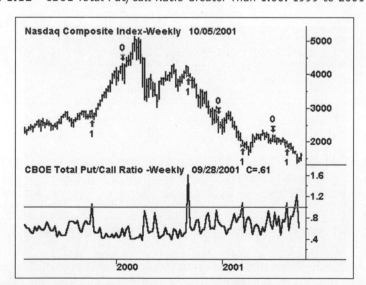

Chart created on TradeStation®, the flagship product of TradeStation Technologies, Inc.

Figure 1.13 Performance Summary—CBOE Total Put/Call Ratio Greater Than 1.00

```
CBOE Put/Call > 1.00  Nasdaq Composite Index-Weekly  12/23/1994 - 10/05/2001

                        Performance Summary: Long Trades

Total net profit        $  390.35    Open position P/L        $ -261.71
Gross profit            $ 1851.71    Gross loss               $ -1461.36

Total # of trades            6       Percent profitable          83%
Number winning trades        5       Number losing trades         1

Largest winning trade   $ 1155.26    Largest losing trade     $ -1461.36
Average winning trade   $  370.34    Average losing trade     $ -1461.36
Ratio avg win/avg loss       0.25    Avg trade(win & loss)    $   65.06

Max consec. winners          4       Max consec. losers           1
Avg # bars in winners       15       Avg # bars in losers        15

Max intraday drawdown   $ -1732.69
Profit factor                1.27    Max # contracts held         1
```

Chart created on TradeStation®, the flagship product of TradeStation Technologies, Inc.

Figure 1.14 Performance Summary—CBOE Total Put/Call Ratio Greater Than 1.00 and Close Greater Than 200-Day Moving Average

```
Put/Call>1 + New Hi  Nasdaq Composite Index-Weekly  12/23/1994 - 10/05/2001

                        Performance Summary: Long Trades

Total net profit        $ 1648.89    Open position P/L        $   0.00
Gross profit            $ 1648.89    Gross loss               $   0.00

Total # of trades            4       Percent profitable         100%
Number winning trades        4       Number losing trades         0

Largest winning trade   $ 1428.97    Largest losing trade     $   0.00
Average winning trade   $  412.22    Average losing trade     $   0.00
Ratio avg win/avg loss     100.00    Avg trade(win & loss)    $ 412.22

Max consec. winners          4       Max consec. losers           0
Avg # bars in winners       15       Avg # bars in losers         0

Max intraday drawdown   $  -92.08
Profit factor              100.00    Max # contracts held         1
```

Chart created on TradeStation®, the flagship product of TradeStation Technologies, Inc.

trend is no longer up. Total profitability is improved as well. Clearly factoring the trend in with sentiment measures can be a beneficial tool to reduce risk and potentially improve total net profits.

HIGH PUT/CALL READINGS ON RALLY DAYS OVER ONE PERCENT

I have always believed that defining the trend is important when looking at sentiment indicators, because knowing the trend helps define what you would normally expect the crowd reaction to be. In a bull trend, you expect to see more call activity than put activity, while in a bear trend put activity should pick up. These are rational expectations that must be accounted for. But more importantly, if the trend is up but fear is still high, that would suggest an irrational expectation. The crowd is betting against the trend, figuring it has to reverse. Just as you should follow the motto "the trend is your friend," so too should the crowd. When the consensus opinion is not following the trend, this implies that there is even more potential fuel for the trend as these opinions are eventually changed and additional money flows back in the direction of the trend.

For example, if the market rallies by more than 1 percent on a given day, yet the CBOE equity put/call ratio is 67 percent or greater (two puts for every three calls), the results would be similar to those in Figure 1.15 and Figure 1.16.

As you can see, the power of this indicator comes from the signal that there is too much fear even as the market is acting more bullishly. This indicator picks up on the potential extra buying power that is available to a prevailing uptrend. I like to use the "coiled spring" analogy. When the bears have pressed down on the market sufficiently hard, they are rewarded as long as the market continues to drop. But you will see bears keep pressing their good fortune, in which fear levels are high but the market stops dropping or even starts to reverse to the upside. In this situation, the spring has been compressed downwards, but there is all of this pent-up energy in the spring, which just needs a catalyst to be unleashed. As it is let loose, the spring explodes higher, using all of the compressed energy to shoot higher. Relaying this to the market, once the bears have taken a market sufficiently low enough, the market will stop dropping and start rising. When this occurs, all of the sideline

Figure 1.15 Performance Summary—CBOE Equity Put/Call Ratio 0.67 or Greater and Market Rises More Than 1 Percent

Hi P/C in Up Market Nasdaq Composite Index-Daily 01/02/1990 - 10/05/2001

Performance Summary: Long Trades

Total net profit	$ 908.73	Open position P/L	$ 0.00
Gross profit	$ 1263.41	Gross loss	$ -354.68
Total # of trades	14	Percent profitable	57%
Number winning trades	8	Number losing trades	6
Largest winning trade	$ 413.08	Largest losing trade	$ -184.55
Average winning trade	$ 157.93	Average losing trade	$ -59.11
Ratio avg win/avg loss	2.67	Avg trade(win & loss)	$ 64.91
Max consec. winners	3	Max consec. losers	2
Avg # bars in winners	16	Avg # bars in losers	7
Max intraday drawdown	$ -269.98		
Profit factor	3.56	Max # contracts held	1

Chart created on TradeStation®, the flagship product of TradeStation Technologies, Inc.

Figure 1.16   CBOE Equity Put/Call Ratio 0.67 or Greater and Market Rises More
Than 1 Percent

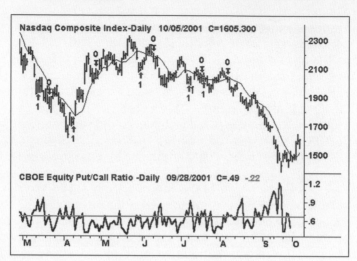

Chart created on TradeStation®, the flagship product of TradeStation Technologies, Inc.

cash and shorts will be put under pressure to buy the market to avoid the fear
of missing out on the up move. This brings in new energy in the form of new
buyers, which can drive the market higher. The high put/call ratio on a rally
day suggests the spring is loaded and there is plenty of energy that is waiting
to be unleashed on the market in the form of new buying power.

APPLYING A MOVING AVERAGE TO THE DAILY PUT/CALL RATIO

One of the biggest challenges I have found in using sentiment data is that it
can tend to be too much of a leading indicator in front of the price action.
As a result, you can occasionally think you see an extreme daily reading,
but the trend of the data may need to be effectively "lagged" to let the price
action catch up to the sentiment data. One method to accomplish this lag
effect is to apply a moving average to the daily put/call readings. Two of my
favorite time frames to lag the put/call data are 21 days (again, the last
month's activity on average) and 10 days (about half of one month).

The goal of these efforts to somewhat lag the sentiment data is to find
significant peaks and troughs in the moving average to signal a turning
point in sentiment and thus in the market itself. Looking at the charts in
Figure 1.17 and Figure 1.18, you will notice some nice peaks and valleys
that match up with important market highs and lows.

Figure 1.17 Nasdaq Composite versus 10-Day Moving Average of Equity Put/Call Ratio

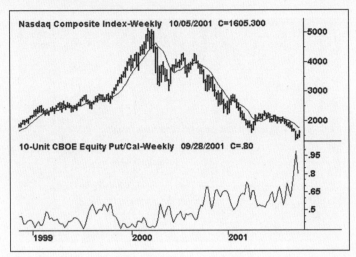

Chart created on TradeStation®, the flagship product of TradeStation Technologies, Inc.

Figure 1.18 Nasdaq Composite versus 21-Day Moving Average of Equity Put/Call Ratio

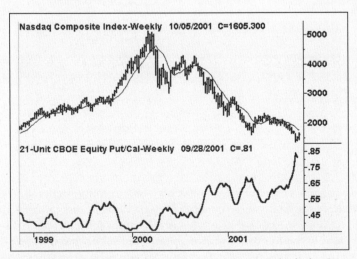

Chart created on TradeStation®, the flagship product of TradeStation Technologies, Inc.

Figure 1.19   Nasdaq Composite versus 10-Day Cross of the 21-Day

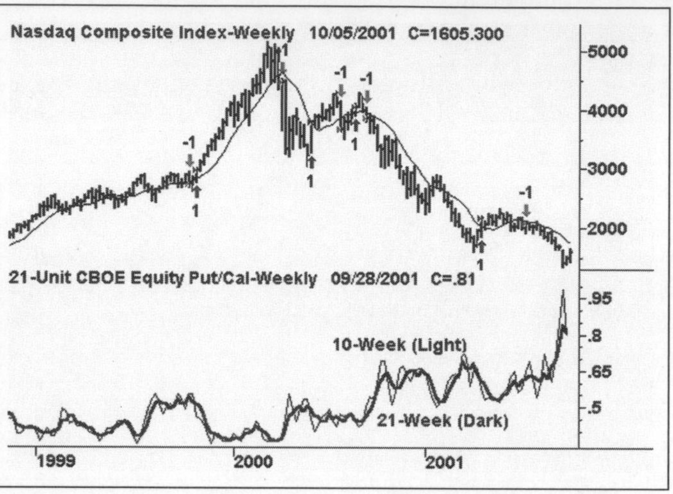

Chart created on TradeStation®, the flagship product of TradeStation Technologies, Inc.

Figure 1.20   Performance Summary—Nasdaq versus 10-Day Cross of the 21-Day

10-Unit <> 21-Unit Nasdaq Composite Index-Weekly 02/02/1990 - 10/05/2001			
Performance Summary: All Trades			
Total net profit	$ 4129.81	Open position P/L	$ 479.49
Gross profit	$ 6202.81	Gross loss	$ -2073.00
Total # of trades	39	Percent profitable	54%
Number winning trades	21	Number losing trades	18
Largest winning trade	$ 1671.85	Largest losing trade	$ -401.51
Average winning trade	$ 295.37	Average losing trade	$ -115.17
Ratio avg win/avg loss	2.56	Avg trade(win & loss)	$ 105.89
Max consec. winners	5	Max consec. losers	3
Avg # bars in winners	21	Avg # bars in losers	5
Max intraday drawdown	$ -784.61		
Profit factor	2.99	Max # contracts held	1

Chart created on TradeStation®, the flagship product of TradeStation Technologies, Inc.

While anyone can hand pick some very nice turning points on the chart, as a technical analyst I wish to quantify these turning points more objectively. What if a system plotted both averages, and then took signals once the 10-day average crossed the 21-day moving average after reaching a past historical extreme? Figure 1.19 and Figure 1.20 show the results, based on these variables.

I have always considered the 10-day moving average of the CBOE equity put/call ratio rising above 60 percent as one of my favorite put/call buy signals. When that happens, you should buy at the next morning's open. Our last signal occurred at the close on October 15, 1999 (the low close of the

Dow, and one day before the low close on the Nasdaq). This indicator is so bullish that it prompted me to write the following on October 15, 1999 with the Dow at 10,020 after a several month decline:

Major Long-Term Bottom in Stocks is Very Near!!!

While our ego tells us not to look stupid in proclaiming market bottoms in the midst of such carnage this past week, our market timing indicators say it's time to get up and shout as we must pound the table. Most investors throw in the towel on the market's outlook at just the wrong time (which makes sense, because stock prices are driven by supply and demand, and when most investors have sold based on gloomy sentiments, it takes fewer buyers to then turn stocks around and start a new uptrend).

Well, investors and traders are now doubting the market's prospects so heavily, we can only find four prior examples of such pessimism in the 1990s. Based on heavy equity option put trading over the last 10 trading sessions, the 10-day CBOE equity put/call ratio today registered a reading of 61 percent (61 puts traded for every 100 calls). In the 1990s, we have only moved up to the 60 percent threshold four other times:

1. January 14, 1991 (the day of the low, ahead of a 20 percent gain in 1 month)
2. April 23, 1997 (9 days after the low, but still a 20 percent gain over the next 3 months)
3. August 21, 1998 (7 days before absolute low in 1998, a 31 percent gain over 8-1/2 months)
4. October 6, 1998 (2 days before low on Dow, 45 percent gain over the next 7 months)

Only the August 21, 1998 buy signal did not play out favorably at first, while the other three signals were incredibly powerful from the start. Three prior signals were happening in the midst of global crises—the 1991 signal came the day before the Persian Gulf War broke out, and last year's [1998's] signals came amidst the LTCM hedge fund crisis that threatened much of the financial system here and abroad. While currently the crisis must be considered the Fed's future tightening given today's very strong PPI data, we cannot rate the current situation as stressful as these past signals, yet option traders are just as pessimistic.

The bottom line is that you have two choices: you can cost yourself money by panicking like the rest of the crowd, or you can use their panic to pick up quality stocks at what will appear to be bargain prices as we look back in future months. Our bet is for a panic sell-off Monday and/or Tuesday morning, with the potential intraday down to Dow 9650. Whether this target is reached or not, you want to be a buyer of

Table 1.2   Performance after 10-Day CBOE Equity Put/Call Ratio > 60%

	1 Month	3 Months	6 Months	12 Months
January 14, 1991	15.8%	18.1%	20.4%	30.7%
April 23, 1997	7.8%	18.7%	15.2%	34.2%
August 21, 1998	-7.0%	9.8%	11.9%	32.4%
October 6, 1998	15.9%	23.2%	28.6%	36.7%
Average	8.1%	17.5%	19.1%	33.5%

stocks on any such sharp pullbacks, and blow out any bearish positions you have. And the last thing you want to do is give up on this bull market right now—too many have, and they will only live to regret it.

Based on these past occurrences, plus the current signal's huge success thus far (with the Nasdaq up 24 percent and the Dow up 10 percent in one month after the mid-October signal), we can project the gains shown in Table 1.2 for the Dow over the next 11 months.

Based on average percentage gains, the latest signal at Dow 10,020 suggests targets of:

	1 month	3 months	6 months	12 months
October 15, 1999	10,835	11,772	11,929	13,378

In retrospect, this indicator proved highly accurate over the one, three, and six month time frames, as the Dow reached as high as 10,885 in one month, 11,908 in three months, and 11,908 in six months. This high at 11,908 proved to be just in front of the market top in March 2000, which I correctly forecast and exited the market. For traders who followed this 12-month horizon statically, the Dow finished the 12-month holding period at 10,238, generating a slight profit but not getting the upside follow-through due to the change in the bull trend to a bear market.

In conclusion, you now know a number of techniques using put/call ratios as an important gauge to determine upcoming turning points in the markets. One of the important aspects of all of these studies is defining true extremes in fear or greed according to the put/call ratio. Techniques such as Bollinger Bands, moving averages, and historically extreme levels all serve to help you mark important extremes in this valuable sentiment indicator.

2

RYDEX MUTUAL FUND FLOWS—
THE CROWD IS OFTEN WRONG
AT EXTREMES

The RYDEX (Nova + OTC)/Ursa ratio is a measure of how the crowd is thinking, determining whether the majority of mutual fund switchers are generally bullish, bearish, or somewhere in between. The RYDEX Fund Group was formed in 1993; RYDEX was the first fund family to offer a "short" fund, as well as the first mutual fund family to have a "leveraged" mutual fund. RYDEX encourages active fund trading, as a fund switcher at RYDEX can move between funds on a virtually unlimited basis, if desired, without penalty. Many fund groups limit switches to 6 to 12 per year, and some fund families place a redemption fee on funds that are sold in less than 30 days. RYDEX did away with these restrictions, and several other fund groups have followed their lead, like the ProFunds mutual fund family.

The three RYDEX funds I focus on to determine the prevailing sentiment among fund switchers are the Nova, OTC, and Ursa funds. I track daily asset flows in these key funds, and these three funds offer my price history going back to March 1994. RYDEX Nova provides 1.50 times the performance of the S&P 500 Index. RYDEX OTC provides 1.00 times the performance of the Nasdaq 100 Index. RYDEX Ursa provides −1.00 times the performance of the S&P 500 Index (seeking to act inverse to the S&P 500—if the S&P 500 drops 10 percent, Ursa should gain 10 percent). I add up the assets of the Nova and OTC funds, both of which are bullishly-oriented, and divide that total by the assets in the bearishly-oriented Ursa fund. This gives me a method to track market sentiment among fund switchers. Since RYDEX imposes no restrictions on the number of switches per year, this allows for a free-flowing reading on the bullish or bearish sentiment on any particular day.

The ratio is a valuable contrary indicator as it allows individuals to track investor fear—the lower the ratio, the lower the investors' confidence in the market, which becomes a buy signal at extremes.

For example, when the ratio hits relatively high levels (I define "relatively high" as levels at or above the upper 21-day Bollinger Band, the upper band in the bottom half of the chart), the market is seeing too much bullishness, as the

Figure 2.1 Nasdaq Composite versus RYDEX (Nova+OTC)/Ursa Ratio: 2000 to 2001

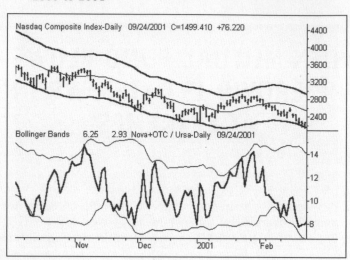

Chart created on TradeStation®, the flagship product of TradeStation Technologies, Inc.

assets in bullish Nova and OTC funds swell relative to the assets in the bearish Ursa fund. Such peaks in optimism were seen in early November 2000, the second week of December 2000, and late-January 2001. As you can see in Figure 2.1, all three of these instances marked very significant tops in the Nasdaq.

In contrast, readings at the lower Bollinger Band showed investors are relatively fearful, as assets in bullish funds dwindle and assets in bearish funds rise, causing the (Nova+OTC)/Ursa ratio to decline. Readings near the lower band in late-November 2000, the beginning of 2001, and the beginning of April 2001 all proved excellent short-term buying opportunities, while the low readings in February and March proved too early against the steady downtrend in the first quarter of 2001. I seek to factor in the strength of the trend when making these contrarian selections, and I also tend to use stops to get me out of signals that are not working as anticipated. This is due to the fact that when a high probability indicator like the RYDEX ratio is not working as anticipated, it tells you the market trend is likely to continue instead of reverse. Such is the case with good indicators: if they are consistently right 8 out of 10 times, the 2 times out of 10 that they are wrong will tell you something about how the market is likely to act going forward as well.

You may think that the RYDEX (Nova+OTC)/Ursa ratio looks like a coincident indicator, or that it is only mirroring the market's movements. While this can sometimes be the case, I have noticed numerous times when the sentiment among fund switchers was diverging quite noticeably from the market's performance. Perhaps the most memorable was when I told *Bar-*

ron's on September 11, 2000, that fund switchers were actually showing a new high in optimism in late August 2000, with a reading of 17.06. Yet the Nasdaq was actually down nearly 18 percent from its March 2000 peak. This was clearly bearish in my outlook. Why? Because if fund switchers are more bullish than ever before, yet the market is down, it tells you that the crowd is "buying the dip." Buying the dip can work when the rest of the crowd is worried, but it suggests more problems ahead if most investors are also buying that dip. This indicates buying power has been exhausted and there are now many more potential sellers on board as the downtrend continues.

Here are the basic rules for the buy and sell signals based on the RYDEX (Nova+OTC)/Ursa ratio, using 21-day Bollinger Bands to spot important turning points for the market.

We will buy the market if the RYDEX (Nova+OTC)/Ursa ratio has a close below the lower 21-day Bollinger Band (with −2 standard deviations), followed by a close back above it. We will hold the position for 30 days and close it at that time, or if we get a sell signal, or if we are unprofitable after five trading days. A sell signal occurs if the RYDEX (Nova+OTC)/Ursa ratio has a close above the upper 21-day Bollinger Band (with +2 standard deviations), followed by a close back below this band. We will hold the short trade for 15 days or close it if it is unprofitable after five days, or if it is reversed by a new buy signal.

This indicator has an excellent history since the RYDEX funds began trading in September 1996. Let us look at the total performance of this indicator from 1994 through 2001, while examining charts of each year's swings in the ratio (see Figures 2.2 through Figure 2.10).

I am encouraged that the RYDEX fund flows will continue to prove an excellent indicator, as this asset data is not widely available to be tracked.

Figure 2.2 Performance Summary—Nasdaq Composite versus RYDEX (Nova+OTC)/Ursa Ratio: 1994 to 2001

BollBandData2-RYstop Nasdaq Composite Index-Daily 03/18/1994 - 09/24/2001

Performance Summary: All Trades

Total net profit	$ 1474.89	Open position P/L	$ 0.00
Gross profit	$ 3619.69	Gross loss	$ -2144.80
Total # of trades	73	Percent profitable	51%
Number winning trades	37	Number losing trades	36
Largest winning trade	$ 429.29	Largest losing trade	$ -380.41
Average winning trade	$ 97.83	Average losing trade	$ -59.58
Ratio avg win/avg loss	1.64	Avg trade(win & loss)	$ 20.20
Max consec. winners	6	Max consec. losers	6
Avg # bars in winners	9	Avg # bars in losers	7
Max intraday drawdown	$ -931.45		
Profit factor	1.69	Max # contracts held	1

Chart created on TradeStation®, the flagship product of TradeStation Technologies, Inc.

Figure 2.3 Bearish Divergence in August 2000: New High in RYDEX Ratio While Nasdaq Composite is Down 18 percent

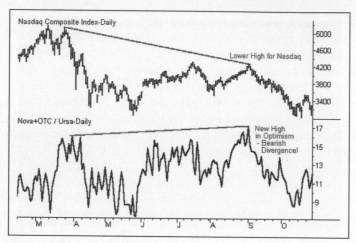

Chart created on TradeStation®, the flagship product of TradeStation Technologies, Inc.

Figure 2.4 Nasdaq Composite versus RYDEX (Nova+OTC)/Ursa Ratio: 2000

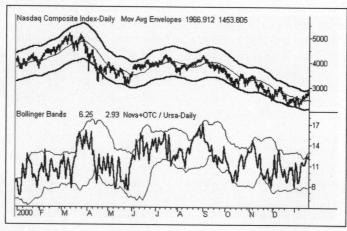

Chart created on TradeStation®, the flagship product of TradeStation Technologies, Inc.

Figure 2.5   Nasdaq Composite versus RYDEX (Nova+OTC)/Ursa Ratio: 1999

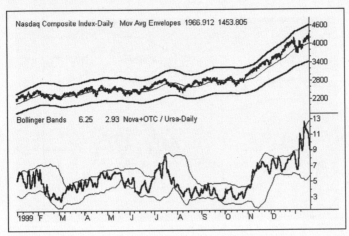

Chart created on TradeStation®, the flagship product of TradeStation Technologies, Inc.

Figure 2.6   Nasdaq Composite versus RYDEX (Nova+OTC)/Ursa Ratio: 1998

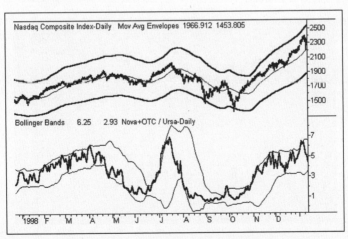

Chart created on TradeStation®, the flagship product of TradeStation Technologies, Inc.

Figure 2.7   Nasdaq Composite versus RYDEX (Nova+OTC)/Ursa Ratio: 1997

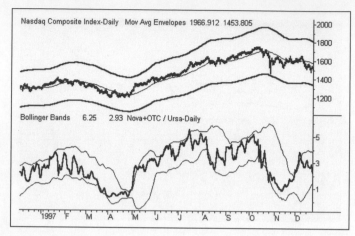

Chart created on TradeStation®, the flagship product of TradeStation Technologies, Inc.

Figure 2.8   Nasdaq Composite versus RYDEX (Nova+OTC)/Ursa Ratio: 1996

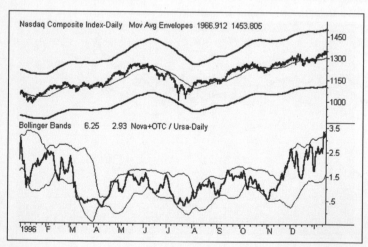

Chart created on TradeStation®, the flagship product of TradeStation Technologies, Inc.

Figure 2.9   Nasdaq Composite versus RYDEX (Nova+OTC)/Ursa
Ratio: 1995

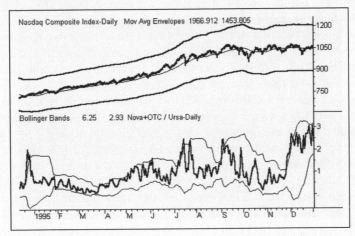

Chart created on TradeStation®, the flagship product of TradeStation Technologies, Inc.

Figure 2.10   Nasdaq Composite versus RYDEX (Nova+OTC)/Ursa
Ratio: 1994

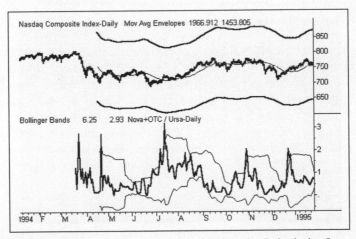

Chart created on TradeStation®, the flagship product of TradeStation Technologies, Inc.

RYDEX reports the data nightly, but it is erased when the next night's update occurs. I believe that even a good indicator can become less useful if too many investors follow it. By definition, a surge in the popularity of any method will ultimately condemn its performance to mediocrity.

I am a huge believer in the RYDEX fund flows data. Yet the fund vehicles I use to trade my RYDEX signals these days are not usually the Nova, OTC, or Ursa funds, but rather more leveraged funds that capitalize on the benefits of my market timing at major extremes in fear and greed. The leveraged funds I prefer are leveraged 2-to-1 to the Nasdaq 100, or inversely leveraged 2-to-1 versus the Nasdaq 100 (meaning a 10 percent drop should create a 20 percent gain in a bear fund with 2-to-1 leverage).

The preferred funds include leveraged funds at RYDEX and ProFunds. I have included return data from each of the fund families' web sites (see Tables 2.1 to 2.4). The two groups of leveraged funds are not particularly comparable yet, as the RYDEX group did not launch their 2-for-1 leveraged Nasdaq 100 funds until May of 2000.

Bull Funds: Leveraged 2-to-1 to the Nasdaq 100 Index

1. RYDEX Velocity 100 (RYVYX)—Inception Date: May 24, 2000
2. ProFunds UltraOTC (UOPIX)—Inception Date: December 2, 1997

Bear Funds: Leveraged 2-to-1 Inverse to the Nasdaq 100 Index

1. RYDEX Venture (RYVNX)—Inception Date: May 23, 2000
2. ProFunds UltraOTC (UOPIX)—Inception Date: June 2, 1998

The growth of a $10,000 investment over quarterly periods in the Pro-Funds tables are particularly instructive as to how all of these leveraged funds tend to function in both bull and bear markets. Notice how the bullish leveraged fund, ProFunds Ultra OTC (UOPIX) in Table 2.2, posted remarkable growth in the bull run, as the 2-for-1 leverage does not keep the fund growing at twice the Nasdaq 100 on the way up. Daily compounding causes this fund to go up over ten-fold, while the Nasdaq 100 Index itself was up just over four-fold as of March 31, 2000. This amounted to beating

Table 2.1   RYDEX Velocity 100 Performance Summary

Return Period	RYVYX	NDX
YTD (as of 09/21/01)	−83.33%	−51.87%
2nd Qtr 2001	22.13%	16.70%
1 year	−85.22%	−51.21%
Since Inception	−77.08%	−39.28%

the market on the way up by two-and-one-half times the index with this leveraged fund. Of course, the importance of proper market timing is magnified when using leverage. The subsequent plunge in the market erased all of the gains in UOPIX and caused the fund to lose a slight amount at the end of June 2001, compared to the unleveraged fund still sitting on about a 70 percent gain from its starting point at that time. These are not funds for buy and hold types, to be sure. But just as I shifted from a bullish to a neutral posture on March 10, 2000 at the peak in the Nasdaq Composite, I would want to exit bullish fund positions at such junctures as well.

Table 2.2   ProFunds UltraOTC (UOPIX) Performance Summary

$10,000 Investmant in UOPIX		
Date	UltraOTC ProFund	Nasdaq-100 Index
12/02/1997	$10,000	$10,000
12/31/1997	$8,360	$9,418
03/31/1998	$12,440	$11,602
06/30/1998	$14,560	$12,712
09/30/1998	$13,810	$12,789
12/31/1998	$23,854	$17,451
03/31/1999	$29,405	$19,896
06/30/1999	$33,366	$21,831
09/30/1999	$35,118	$22,888
12/31/1999	$79,488	$35,244
03/31/2000	$103,179	$41,802
06/30/2000	$65,581	$35,775
09/30/2000	$55,516	$33,939
12/31/2000	$20,903	$22,258
03/31/2001	$8,079	$14,954
06/30/2001	$9,911	$17,396

Table 2.3   RYDEX Velocity 100 (RYVNX) Performance Summary

Return Period	RYVYX	NDX
YTD (as of 09/21/01)	111.96%	−51.87%
2nd Qtr 2001	−41.96%	16.70%
1 year	60.71%	−51.21%
Since Inception	−6.26%	−36.34%

Table 2.4　ProFunds UltraBear OTC (USPIX) Performance Summary

$10,000 Investment in USPIX		
Date	UltraShortOTC ProFund	Nasdaq-100 Index
06/02/1998	$10,000	$10,000
06/30/1998	$10,000	$11,265
09/30/1998	$6,580	$11,334
12/31/1998	$3,252	$15,466
03/31/1999	$2,279	$17,743
06/30/1999	$1,759	$19,347
09/30/1999	$1,553	$20,283
12/31/1999	$639	$31,233
03/31/2000	$385	$37,045
06/30/2000	$391	$31,704
09/30/2000	$393	$30,077
12/31/2000	$665	$19,725
03/31/2001	$1,017	$13,252

In contrast, notice the pain in Table 2.4 that the ProFunds UltraShort OTC Fund (USPIX) endured as the market rallied in the late-1990s, losing over 95 percent of its value during the low point at the end of March 2000. But just as the Nasdaq 100 gave back its gains by a factor of three on the downside by the end of June 2001, USPIX had nearly tripled as a result. As you can see, timing is everything with these leveraged funds. You will notice that leverage is not exactly 2-to-1 over longer time periods. A common misconception is that over any given time period the total return of a leveraged long fund should correspond exactly to the total return of its index times the leverage applied to the fund on a daily basis. However, the leveraged long fund's return will not match the return of its index times the leverage factor of two applied for any period beyond one day. Why? While the two-times leveraged fund may perform properly each day, there can be "tracking error" due to market volatility. Returns are geometric for periods longer than one day, which actually benefits bull fund investors slightly more than bear fund investors over long periods of time.

In conclusion, the RYDEX fund flows offer investors a way to gauge the speculative sentiment among active fund switchers. Looking at the RYDEX daily asset data can be a valuable tool to know whether the fund crowd is relatively over-invested in the optimistic scenario, which tends to prove bearish. At the same time, the crowd's fear shows up in relatively low RYDEX bull-to-bear ratios, often near significant market bottoms.

3

THE CBOE VOLATILITY INDEX (VIX)—FEAR REIGNS AT MAJOR BOTTOMS

The CBOE Market Volatility Index (VIX) was introduced in 1993 by the Chicago Board Options Exchange (CBOE) to measure the implied volatility of the U.S. equity market. The VIX is a measure of the expected volatility of the stock market (as measured in the S&P 100 Index) going forward based on the pricing of S&P 100, or OEX, options. The index is calculated in real-time by taking a weighted average of the implied volatilities of eight OEX options (four calls and four puts) having an average time to maturity of 30 days.

At *BigTrends.com* I use the VIX index as a contrarian indicator of market sentiment. Fear and greed will often take the market to extremes, and the VIX provides an accurate measure of these extremes in investor emotions. Typically the VIX will surge on a major downside panic in the market, as option players will rush to buy puts, which pumps up the "implied volatility" that traders expect for future market movements. A VIX reading of 30.00 means that the market is expecting the volatility of the S&P 100 Index (OEX) to be roughly plus or minus 30 percent over the next year during two-thirds of the time (or one standard deviation). Yet what is typically experienced with the VIX is that major highs in the market's perceived volatility usually occur near major market bottoms. By the time market participants perceive significant risk, something has already gone wrong. Ironically, just when most investors really should not need insurance, they flock for it and pay higher insurance premiums for protection against further market declines as the VIX surges higher. In contrast, low VIX readings show that few investors perceive a major risk, and thus are not buying puts as insurance against their portfolios. That is usually the point when you want to own this insurance, as investors are too complacent right near the tops. In addition, insurance in the form of puts can be bought relatively cheaply when few other investors want protection from a market decline.

If you look back over the past several years, a VIX reading of under 20 percent, particularly one near 18 percent, suggested problems for stocks over the near term. The last time I saw this, as I pointed out in a *Barron's*

Figure 3.1   S&P 100 Index (OEX) versus CBOE Volatility Index (VIX): 1998 to 2001 Weekly

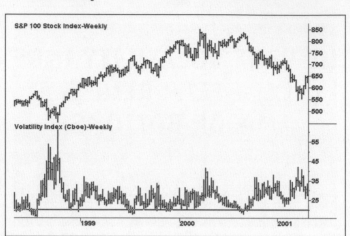

Chart created on TradeStation®, the flagship product of TradeStation Technologies, Inc.

article on September 11, 2000, was a low at 18.06 on August 28, 2000. In the prior two years, there were two readings under 18, and both signaled a market top and the beginning of a very nasty few months for the Nasdaq and the S&P. The 2000 example proved no different.

Notice how the VIX in Figure 3.1 hit the 18 level and then took a couple of weeks before the top was in. This is one characteristic about the VIX you need to understand. Tops based on low VIX readings can take several weeks to form, so you have to scale in to bearish positions and have some patience when looking for the downturn. Otherwise, you can wait until you see a lower low and lower close in the underlying market, which then usually sets off the selling pressure as the VIX starts to rise back to normal levels in the mid-20s.

A SYSTEM TO TRADE THE VIX

The secret to profiting from the VIX is to use it as a contrarian measure at extremes. As with the CBOE equity put/call ratio and the RYDEX (Nova+OTC)/Ursa ratio, the first place I start on these mean-reverting indexes is with the Bollinger Bands to help define extremes in the VIX. I use 21-day Bollinger Bands with two standard deviations to identify relative fear and greed, as reflected by high and low VIX readings. A VIX close outside of the Bollinger Bands signals an attractive buy or sell opportunity.

Buy signals occur when:

1. the VIX closes above the upper Bollinger Band, followed the next day by a close below the upper band.
2. this VIX signal must be confirmed five days later by a close in the OEX above the 10-day simple moving average.

The position is exited:

1. if it is unprofitable exactly five days after entry.
2. if it is reversed by a sell signal.

Sell signals have a slight twist, since VIX sell signals tend to be about two weeks early on average. After the VIX closes below the lower Bollinger Band, followed by a consecutive close back above the lower band confirmed by a close below the 10-day simple moving average, the sell signal is given 10 trading days thereafter. The reason for the 10-day lag effect is that sell signals on the VIX are often early, but prove to be correct later. This lag effect works well when confirmed by a technical breakdown below the moving average. The position is exited if it is either unprofitable exactly five days after entry, or if it is reversed by a buy signal.

Here is the TradeStation® EasyLanguage® code for this VIX system:

```
LONG ENTRY:

If Close > Average(Close,10) and Price1[5] < Bollinger-
Band(Close of Data2,21,2) [5] and Price[6] > Bollinger-
Band(Close of Data2,21,2)[6]

Then Buy on Close

LONG EXIT:

If BarsSinceEntry=5 and c < c[5]

Then ExitLong on Close

SHORT ENTRY:

If c < Average(c,10) and Price1[10] >
BollingerBand(Close of Data2,21,-2)[10] and Price1[11] <
BollingerBand(Close of Data2,21,-2)[11]
```

Figure 3.2   OEX versus VIX with 21-Day Bollinger Bands: January to June 2001

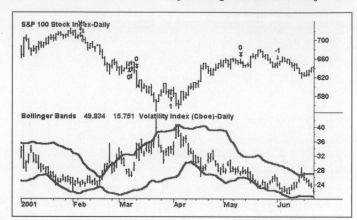

Chart created on TradeStation®, the flagship product of TradeStation Technologies, Inc.

```
Then Sell on Close

SHORT EXIT:

If BarsSinceEntry=5 and c > c[5]

Then ExitShort on Close
```

It should be noted that this is an intermediate-term trading system. Figure 3.2 shows a chart of the OEX with a recent VIX sell signal in June 2001.

Notice how the OEX tended to bottom, due to a peak in fear, on a high VIX reading over the upper 21-day Bollinger Band. Conversely, the market usually tops after an extreme in greed is reached, or after a low VIX reading under the lower band, like the one seen in the lower half of Figure 3.2. This occurred in mid-April, as optimism grew too high on the Fed's surprise rate cut. This also occurred in late July as the VIX touched down to the relatively low 20 level, after a prior bounce lulled most traders to feel too comfortable in the uptrend. I did some further research at the time and sent the following research note to my subscribers:

Low Volatility 1 Mid-July 5 T-R-O-U-B-L-E!

While low downside volatility is desirable in portfolios, I believed the low CBOE Volatility Index (VIX) readings were likely to cause problems for the market in the third quarter of 2001. In addition, the market was only days away from the middle of July, which has been a time period where intermediate-term tops have occurred in four of the last five years.

My research shows that low VIX readings (like the reading I saw in late July 2001 at 20.29) suggest excessive investor complacency, which typically occurred one to two weeks before important tops in three of the last four summers. The low VIX means that investors expect that the market will stay non-volatile, and they certainly do not expect any serious downside. As a contrarian, I have learned that the time to be worried is when few other investors are concerned. If you want to use options to protect your downside risk, this is a good time to do so because insurance premiums (in the form of put options) are relatively cheap thanks to these low volatility expectations.

Another interesting statistic is that in each of the last four years, from 1997 through 2000, volatility as measured by the VIX doubled or more in just three months, from the July low in the VIX to the October high in this volatility measure. How do volatility expectations change so drastically and so quickly? All it takes is for the downside price action to start kicking in, which raises demand for puts as protection. The final VIX spike higher usually occurs during the panic phase, when stock prices normally experience their final waterfall decline and all the "Chicken Littles" expect the worst to occur. That is when savvy contrarians acquire quality stocks for longer-term appreciation, as these points have often marked important V-bottom buying opportunities.

As a follow-up to this research note, the VIX had already more than doubled from its late July 2001 low at 20.29 to a high over 57 on September 21, 2001. It is truly amazing how complacency and greed eventually turn into fear on these high VIX readings time and time again. I believe this is because emotions will always be a big part of most investors' decisions. Thus, this cycle of fear to greed and back again will keep repeating. Those who understand these cycles are in a position to profit by turning the emotions that betray most investors into a system that can clearly benefit savvy contrarians.

Figure 3.3 shows a chart of the VIX that I predicted would have bearish implications for the market back in August of 2000. The VIX had declined to under the 20 level, and the one-day reading hit a low of 18.06 on August 28, 2000. Touches down to the 18 level had historically been a problem for stocks, but tops often occurred on a delay. This system creates a lag of five days on buy signals, and 10 days on sell signals, to seek to miss the initial choppy price action as the market is forming important tops or bottoms. This system also wants to see confirmation in the price trend, for buy signals with a close above the simple 10-day moving average, or below the 10-day moving average for sell signals in the S&P 100 Index (OEX). In this case, the VIX system stayed on a sell signal from September 6, 2000, to October 23, 2000, as the 10-day moving average on the OEX was never penetrated to the upside in conjunction with a return in the VIX below the upper 21-day Bollinger Band until October 23. The system looks to exit either on

Figure 3.3   OEX versus VIX with 21-Day Bollinger Bands: August to October 2000

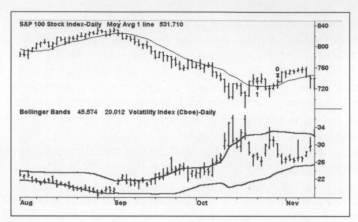

Chart created on TradeStation®, the flagship product of TradeStation Technologies, Inc.

a reversal between the buy and sell points, or if there have been more than five bars since entry and the close of today is greater than the close five days ago (which closes a short trade) or today's close is less than the close of five days ago (which closes a long trade, like it did in late October).

Since I want to eliminate unprofitable trades after five days, this system has winning percentages under 50 percent. The five-day cut-off period increases the number of small losses, but it also keeps the size of the average loss manageable. As a result, the ratio of the average winner and average loser in Figure 3.4 is very high, with the average winner being more than nine times the size of the average loser. This is the essence of any good system, as it lives up to the trading rule: let profits run, cut losses short.

Because of the longer-term uptrend in the market, most of this system's profits come from the long side. The big winners on the short side came during the recent bear market's second down-leg in September and October 2000, and again after the sell signal in August 2001. Clearly, one would expect that adding a trend filter to take signals on the right side of the broader market trend would likely improve the overall system performance.

We can test VIX signals with the broader trend by applying an additional momentum filter that screens out trades signaled against the longer-term trend, which can improve the winning percentage and confirm entries and exits. In this case, I set up the system to only follow buy parameters on higher VIX readings if the S&P 100 Index (OEX) has a Moving Average Convergence Divergence (MACD—see Chapter 4) signal that

Figure 3.4 Performance Summary—OEX versus VIX Bollinger Band System: 1990 to 2001

VIX BollBand 21 S&P 100 Stock Index-Daily 01/02/1990 - 09/24/2001

Performance Summary: All Trades

Total net profit	$ 499.56	Open position P/L	$ 0.00
Gross profit	$ 800.50	Gross loss	$ -300.94
Total # of trades	50	Percent profitable	32%
Number winning trades	16	Number losing trades	34
Largest winning trade	$ 134.68	Largest losing trade	$ -37.58
Average winning trade	$ 50.03	Average losing trade	$ -8.85
Ratio avg win/avg loss	5.65	Avg trade(win & loss)	$ 9.99
Max consec. winners	3	Max consec. losers	6
Avg # bars in winners	132	Avg # bars in losers	8
Max intraday drawdown	$ -126.06		
Profit factor	2.66	Max # contracts held	1

Chart created on TradeStation®, the flagship product of TradeStation Technologies, Inc.

Figure 3.5 Performance Summary—OEX versus VIX with Long-Term Trend Filter: 1990 to 2001

VIX BollBand 21 MACD S&P 100 Stock Index-Daily 01/02/1990 - 09/24/2001

Performance Summary: All Trades

Total net profit	$ 285.95	Open position P/L	$ 0.00
Gross profit	$ 497.54	Gross loss	$ -211.59
Total # of trades	55	Percent profitable	49%
Number winning trades	27	Number losing trades	28
Largest winning trade	$ 89.60	Largest losing trade	$ -49.94
Average winning trade	$ 18.43	Average losing trade	$ -7.56
Ratio avg win/avg loss	2.44	Avg trade(win & loss)	$ 5.20
Max consec. winners	4	Max consec. losers	4
Avg # bars in winners	19	Avg # bars in losers	6
Max intraday drawdown	$ -87.10		
Profit factor	2.35	Max # contracts held	1

Chart created on TradeStation®, the flagship product of TradeStation Technologies, Inc.

momentum is favorable. Figure 3.5 shows the results to compare with our earlier system.

Some traders say the VIX is no longer as meaningful as it used to be, because the OEX is not as active as it once was and the Nasdaq 100 Index Trust (QQQ) has become a more actively-traded index instrument. However, I still find that VIX signals, at extremes, are still effective at predicting bullish and bearish turning points in the market in both the OEX and Nasdaq markets.

CBOE VOLATILITY INDEX—BUY ON WEEKLY
SPIKES OVER 45 PERCENT

On September 17, 2001, the day that trading was re-opened after the tragedy involving terrorist attacks on the World Trade Center and the Pentagon, the CBOE Volatility Index (VIX) shot up above the 45 percent mark, signaling an extreme amount of fear from options players. Heavy demand for puts caused the VIX to surge to a higher level, which had signaled major market lows in the past. Looking back over the last decade, the VIX has only surged over the 45 percent threshold in two prior periods: the September to October 1998 period, when panic reigned due to the Long-term Capital Management hedge fund collapse, and the October 1997 period which corresponded with a bout of the Asian flu from the weak Far Eastern economies.

As you can see in Figure 3.6, the first buy signal in October 1997 came on the spike in the VIX (lower half of the chart) to the 55 level that week. Crosses above the 45 percent mark on the VIX are shown by the horizontal line at 45 on the bottom half of the chart. This gave a buy signal on the end of the week's close at 436.71 for the S&P 100 Index (OEX), signaled by the first up arrow. The market rallied for a five-week period, then came back to rest right at the levels of the buy signal. The optimal hold time on this signal historically has been around 35 weeks, which in this case gave an exit signal in early July 1998 at 559.37. This resulted in a return of 28.1 percent in the OEX over the 35-week holding period.

The second buy signal occurred in early September 1998, when the VIX spiked over the 50 mark that week. This gave a buy signal at the end of that

Figure 3.6   Nasdaq Composite versus CBOE Volatility Index: 1997 to 1999
Weekly

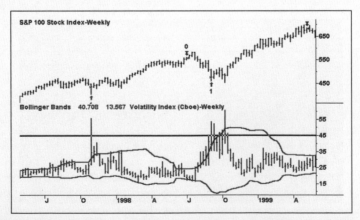

Chart created on TradeStation®, the flagship product of TradeStation Technologies, Inc.

week at 477.43, shown by the second up arrow. After a three-week bounce, the OEX came back down over the next two weeks. In fact, the OEX tested below the buy signal level during the first week of October 1998, but sharply reversed by the end of that week to close back above the buy signal level. The exit signal came in May of 1999, 35 weeks after the buy signal, at a price level of 681.74. This resulted in a gain of 42.8 percent for the 35-week holding period on the OEX.

Let us now look at the situation as of September 24, 2001, shown in Figure 3.7.

As you can see, the VIX spiked up over the 45 percent level during the week ending September 21, 2001, reaching as high as 57.31. This occurred in reaction to the tragedy involving terrorist attacks on the World Trade Center and the Pentagon. This means a new buy signal on this indicator was received at the week-ending close of 491.70. The implications are for an initial bounce, followed by an eventual retest of these lows, followed by a more significant rally to come through the spring of 2002. Projecting out based on past historical gains in the OEX in prior 35-week holding periods, the system had a 28.1 percent and 42.8 percent gain on the last two signals. This gives us a lower-end target of 629.87 based on the 28.1 percent gain and a higher end target of 702.15 based on the 42.8 percent gain, with an average target of 666.01, as shown in Figure 3.8.

While this system has only had two trades since 1990, showing how rare fear spikes in the VIX actually are over the 45 level, both trades produced strong returns over a 35-week holding period. Perhaps more importantly, the maximum drawdown on these two trades was relatively small,

Figure 3.7 Nasdaq Composite versus CBOE Volatility Index: 2000 to 2001 Weekly

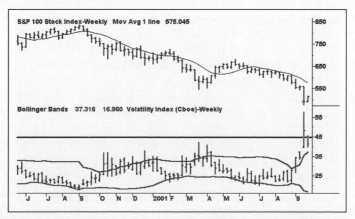

Chart created on TradeStation®, the flagship product of TradeStation Technologies, Inc.

Figure 3.8   Performance Summary—Nasdaq Composite versus CBOE Volatility
             Index over 45: 1990 to 2001 Weekly

vix > 45 S&P 100 Stock Index-Weekly 01/05/1990 - 09/28/2001			
Performance Summary: All Trades			
Total net profit	$ 326.97	Open position P/L	$ 21.34
Gross profit	$ 326.97	Gross loss	$ 0.00
Total # of trades	2	Percent profitable	100%
Number winning trades	2	Number losing trades	0
Largest winning trade	$ 204.31	Largest losing trade	$ 0.00
Average winning trade	$ 163.49	Average losing trade	$ 0.00
Ratio avg win/avg loss	100.00	Avg trade(win & loss)	$ 163.49
Max consec. winners	2	Max consec. losers	0
Avg # bars in winners	35	Avg # bars in losers	0
Max intraday drawdown	$ -22.52		
Profit factor	100.00	Max # contracts held	1

Chart created on TradeStation®, the flagship product of Tradestation Technologies, Inc.

which some might not expect since they were buying into the teeth of a panic decline, which investors always fear will turn into an outright crash. Yet the level of fear generated is what creates such good buying opportunities in the first place.

VOLATILITY ON STOCKS AS AN INDICATOR

One of the few mean-reverting systems is volatility; if volatility is up in one month, it is likely to be down the next month. One of the tools I use is the stock's historical volatility, which measures the variation of the stock's performance over a predetermined time frame. I like to use 10-unit historical volatility to look for extreme lows or highs in volatility. Let us look at examples on both daily and weekly charts.

In Figure 3.9, AOL's most reliable turning points on its 10-day historical volatility were signaled by V-shaped spikes at major extremes, as opposed to U-shaped turns. The inverted V-shaped spike to the upside in the Historical Volatility reading in April marked a significant low point for AOL shares, while the V-spike in late August marked the beginning of a much more dramatic decline. In contrast, the inverted U-shaped peaks in late June and late July were only minimal bounces within a developing downtrend, so we would not want to take those signals since they flattened out sideways after reaching their highest volatility reading. We want to see the volatility reverse right back down immediately to create the "V" pattern.

Different stocks will have unique levels at which their historical volatility will hit significant peaks and valleys. Once you define a first significant

Figure 3.9   AOL Time Warner (AOL) with 10-Day Historical Volatility: 2001

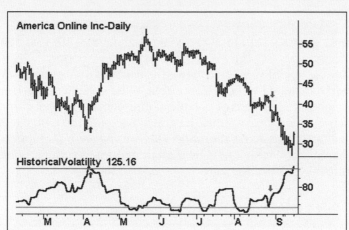

Chart created on TradeStation®, the flagship product of TradeStation Technologies, Inc.

Figure 3.10   International Business Machines (IBM) with 10-Week Historical
Volatility: Weekly 1999 to 2001

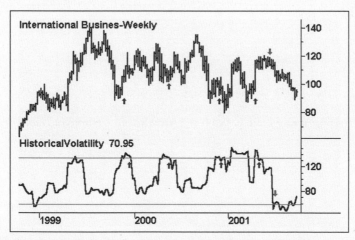

Chart created on TradeStation®, the flagship product of TradeStation Technologies, Inc.

peak and bottom level, you can draw horizontal lines on the volatility chart to look for future highs and lows. In the case of IBM in Figure 3.10, the stock had a significant low in volatility around 60 percent, while having a significant high just over 130 percent. Looking for V-shaped reversals back over 60 percent gives us new sell signals while V-shaped reversals back under 130 percent gives us buy signals.

TradeStation® Technologies System Code for 10-Unit Historical Volatility Indicator:

```
StdDev (Log (c/c[1]), 10) x Square Root (365) x 100
```

To sum up, volatility is often viewed as a dirty word by many investors, as you certainly do not want your portfolio to be volatile on the downside. However, market measures of volatility offer enormous opportunities for contrarians. Around the time that the crowd becomes too complacent after an uptrend or too panicked after a decline, we see an important change in volatility indicators, which tells us that an important turning point in the market or in a stock is appearing.

4

VOLUME INDICATORS—
CONTRARIAN OPPORTUNITIES ON
BUYING OR SELLING PANICS

The Nasdaq 100 Trust (QQQ) has become a very popular vehicle for traders since its launch in February 1999. This investment vehicle trades like a stock, with an average daily volume of over 50 million shares in the first six months of 2001. The QQQ was created to mirror the performance of the Nasdaq 100 Index (NDX), and is composed of 100 large-capitalization Nasdaq issues. Microsoft, Intel, Cisco Systems, Oracle Systems, and Sun Microsystems have been the top five largest components, making up over 30 percent of the total index value, as the index is weighted for the capitalization of the stocks in the index. Figure 4.1 is a list of the top 10 components that make up the Nasdaq 100 (as of June 30, 2001).

As you can see, much of the weighting of the QQQ's performance comes from the top 10 holdings, which account for 38.79 percent of the QQQ as shown in Figure 4.1. In addition, as of June 30, 2001, the technology sector accounted for 73.73 percent of the capitalization in the QQQ. The next largest sector was health care at 10.87 percent. The QQQ trades like a stock. The number of shares traded forms a volume number every day for every security that trades in the public markets. Since the QQQ began trading, it has become popular for use as a hedging vehicle for institutional and individual portfolios. For example, if you own Nasdaq stocks like Cisco, Microsoft, and Intel but then have a concern about the market in the short term, you do not want to sell your individual stock holdings. You want to keep your initial basis to avoid paying taxes on longer-term winners, but at the same time hedge this exposure by shorting the similar QQQ vehicle. This allows you to minimize your risk while holding on to your longer-term winning positions. In addition, you can initiate this insurance with one transaction on your entire portfolio, as opposed to hedging each individual security.

What if the level of volume was used as an indicator of market interest, and in turn looked for extreme interest in a security as a sign of a short-term peak in optimism, or extreme disinterest on a normally-active index as a sign of a potential contrarian bottom? Let us look at some examples.

Figure 4.1 Top 10 Components in the Nasdaq 100 (as of June 30, 2001)

1. Microsoft Corporation	10.97%
2. Intel Corporation	5.59%
3. Qualcomm Incorporated	4.33%
4. Cisco Systems Inc.	3.86%
5. Oracle Corporation	3.61%
6. Amgen Inc.	2.39%
7. Veritas Software Corporation	2.19%
8. Dell Computer Corporation	2.03%
9. Siebel Systems Inc.	2.01%
10. Sun Microsystems Inc.	1.81%
Total	38.79%

Figure 4.2 Nasdaq 100 Trust (QQQ) versus Daily QQQ Volume with 21-Day
Bollinger Band: December 1999 to June 2000

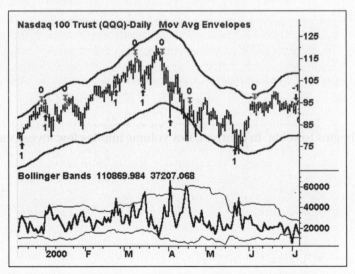

Chart created on TradeStation®, the flagship product of TradeStation Technologies, Inc.

QQQ VOLUME WITH BOLLINGER BANDS

As with prior sentiment indicators, I want to first start with Bollinger Bands
as a tool to help define extreme highs or lows in a data series. If the QQQ
daily volume is plotted on the 21-day Bollinger Band with two standard deviations, the resulting chart looks like the one in Figure 4.2.

Notice how the extremes in volume in 2000 were outstanding indicators of investor fear and greed. The surges to the upper bands indicate volume was unduly high, usually right near important market bottoms. Remember, high volume in this case creates great interest for investors who

Figure 4.3   Nasdaq 100 Trust (QQQ) versus Daily QQQ Volume with 21-Day
Bollinger Band: August 2000 to February 2001

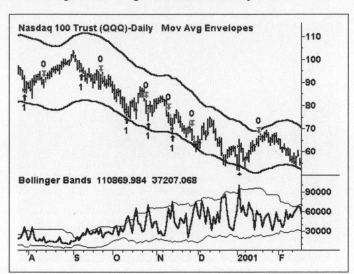

Chart created on TradeStation®, the flagship product of TradeStation Technologies, Inc.

hedge their portfolios by shorting the QQQ. This interest often gets high as panic begins to set in. In contrast, low volume implies few investors feel the need to insure their portfolios. This is reflected in a low volume reading under the lower 21-day Bollinger Band (see Figure 4.3).

Notice in Figure 4.4 that this low volume often occurs right near short-term peaks in the QQQ. Figure 4.5 shows the performance of QQQ volume spikes.

VOLUME ON S&P DEPOSITORY RECEIPTS (SPY)

Similar to the QQQ, S&P 500 Depository Receipts (SPY) trade on the American Exchange like a stock as seen in Figure 4.6. Also known as "spyders," this vehicle was actually the first major index vehicle to trade like a stock, designed to mimic the performance of the S&P 500 Index, so it makes sense that we should also investigate the SPY for its popularity as a hedging vehicle. Let us apply the same system we used previously with the QQQ volume on the SPY, and see what happens in Figure 4.6a and Figure 4.6b.

Another interesting angle is to test what would happen if we added up each day's QQQ and SPY volume combined, and then plotted our Bollinger Bands around the combined volume of both of these hedging vehicles. Figure 4.7 shows the combined QQQ and SPY volume, and Figure 4.8 shows the results of this combined volume as an indicator.

Figure 4.4   Nasdaq 100 Trust (QQQ) versus Daily QQQ Volume with 21-Day
Bollinger Band: February 2001 to August 2001

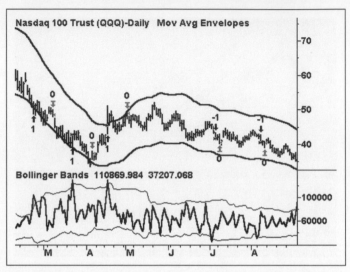

Chart created on TradeStation®, the flagship product of TradeStation Technologies, Inc.

Figure 4.5   Performance Summary—Nasdaq 100 Trust (QQQ) Volume:
1999 to 2001

BollBand Data2 SPY Nasdaq 100 Trust (QQQ)-Daily 03/10/1999 - 09/24/2001			
Performance Summary: All Trades			
Total net profit	$ 32.38	Open position P/L	$ 0.00
Gross profit	$ 63.73	Gross loss	$ -31.35
Total # of trades	24	Percent profitable	67%
Number winning trades	16	Number losing trades	8
Largest winning trade	$ 10.44	Largest losing trade	$ -9.50
Average winning trade	$ 3.98	Average losing trade	$ -3.92
Ratio avg win/avg loss	1.02	Avg trade(win & loss)	$ 1.35
Max consec. winners	3	Max consec. losers	2
Avg # bars in winners	9	Avg # bars in losers	9
Max intraday drawdown	$ -22.50		
Profit factor	2.03	Max # contracts held	1

Chart created on TradeStation®, the flagship product of TradeStation Technologies, Inc.

Figure 4.6a   S&P 500 Depository Receipts (SPY) versus SPY Volume with
21-Day Bollinger Bands

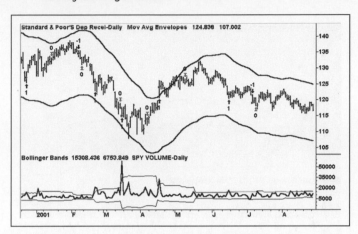

Chart created on TradeStation®, the flagship product of TradeStation Technologies, Inc.

Figure 4.6b   Performance Summary—SPY Security versus SPY Volume with
21-Day Bollinger Bands

BollBand Data2 SPY Standard & Poor'S Dep Recei-Daily 02/03/1993 - 09/24/2001			
Performance Summary: All Trades			
Total net profit	$ 67.95	Open position P/L	$ 0.00
Gross profit	$ 117.03	Gross loss	$ -49.08
Total # of trades	84	Percent profitable	71%
Number winning trades	60	Number losing trades	24
Largest winning trade	$ 11.62	Largest losing trade	$ 8.04
Average winning trade	$ 1.95	Average losing trade	$ -2.05
Ratio avg win/avg loss	0.95	Avg trade(win & loss)	$ 0.81
Max consec. winners	18	Max consec. losers	3
Avg # bars in winners	9	Avg # bars in losers	9
Max intraday drawdown	$ -18.17		
Profit factor	2.38	Max # contracts held	1

Chart created on TradeStation®, the flagship product of TradeStation Technologies, Inc.

Figure 4.7 QQQ Security versus Combined QQQ/SPY Volume with Bollinger Bands

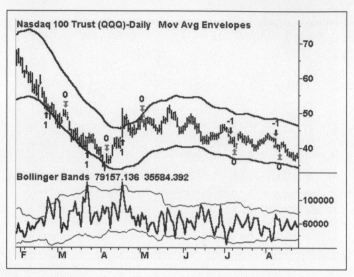

Chart created on TradeStation®, the flagship product of TradeStation Technologies, Inc.

Figure 4.8 Performance Summary—QQQ Security versus Combined QQQ/SPY Volume with 21-Day Bollinger Bands

BollBand Data2 SPY Nasdaq 100 Trust (QQQ)-Daily 03/10/1999 - 09/24/2001

Performance Summary: All Trades

Total net profit	$	15.96	Open position P/L	$ 0.00
Gross profit	$	47.54	Gross loss	$ -31.58
Total # of trades	22		Percent profitable	59%
Number winning trades	13		Number losing trades	9
Largest winning trade	$	11.25	Largest losing trade	$ -9.50
Average winning trade	$	3.66	Average losing trade	$ -3.51
Ratio avg win/avg loss	1.04		Avg trade(win & loss)	$ 0.73
Max consec. winners	3		Max consec. losers	2
Avg # bars in winners	8		Avg # bars in losers	10
Max intraday drawdown	$	-23.75		
Profit factor	1.51		Max # contracts held	1

Chart created on TradeStation®, the flagship product of TradeStation Technologies, Inc.

System Code for QQQ or SPY Volume Indicator:

```
Long Entry:
Volume of Data2 > BollingerBand(Volume of Data2,21,2)
and Volume of Data2[1] < BollingerBand(Volume of
Data,21,2)[1] or Volume of Data2[2]
Bollingerband(Volume of Data2,21,2)[2] or Volume of
Data2[3] < BollingerBand(Volume of Data2,21,2)[3]

Long Exit:
BarsSinceEntry = 10

Short Entry:
Volume of Data2[2] > BollingerBand(Volume of
Data2,21,-2)[2] and Volume of Data2[3]
BollingerBand(Volume of Data2,21,-2)[3] or Volume of
Data2[4] < BollingerBand(Volume of Data2,21,-2)[4]

Short Exit:
BarsSinceEntry = 2
```

These hedging vehicles are not only popular to trade, but their combined volume shows promise as an indicator of investor fear or complacency.

TOTAL EXCHANGE VOLUME AS A MEASURE OF SPECULATION

Let us look at total volume on the Nasdaq versus the New York Stock Exchange (NYSE) to see if that can also be a useful sign of speculation or disinterest at major turning points.

Figure 4.9 shows the weekly Nasdaq Composite (upper half of chart) compared to the ratio of Nasdaq/NYSE Volume (bottom half of the chart). To adjust for longer-term trends in volume, a ratio in both Nasdaq and NYSE weekly volume is created by dividing the 8-week volume over the 52-week volume in both cases, and then dividing the Nasdaq ratio over the NYSE ratio.

What does this indicator show? It portrays the relative interest in the Nasdaq stocks compared to NYSE stocks. Since Nasdaq is predominantly a growth-oriented index, a lack of interest in the form of a low ratio may occur near market bottoms, while a peak in interest in Nasdaq names compared to NYSE names may indicate a speculative top in the market.

As you can see from the chart, drops under 1.00 followed by an upturn historically indicate a short-term bottom. Drops down to the 0.93 level followed by upturns have often signaled intermediate-term bottoms. Peaks in

Figure 4.9   Nasdaq Volume/NYSE Volume (8 weeks over 52 weeks): 1998 to 2001

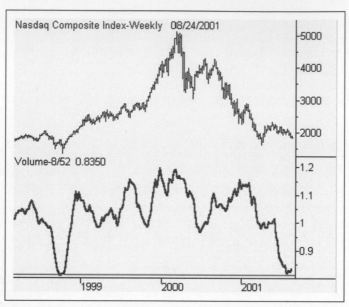

Chart created on TradeStation®, the flagship product of TradeStation Technologies, Inc.

the enthusiasm to the 1.11 level have often indicated short-term peaks, while bubbles in enthusiasm up to the 1.20 area have indicated longer-term tops (as seen in the first quarter of 2000).

Where is this volume ratio in a historical context? It is actually coming off the second lowest level on record over the last 10 years. The ratio is currently at 0.835, near the October 1998 low in Nasdaq interest at 0.82. As you can see, October 1998 was a major long-term bottom for stocks. More importantly, this indicator is now showing signs of turning up to suggest a longer-term buying opportunity is approaching. What I would like to see as confirmation is a Nasdaq Composite weekly close above the prior week's high, which would likely be the spark to ignite a significant rally in the Nasdaq and the markets as a whole.

Another interesting study is how the Nasdaq volume looks plotted against the Dow Jones Industrial Average, as shown in Figure 4.10. As you can see from the chart, the Nasdaq / Dow ratio peaked above 1.10 in late January 2001, which proved to be a relative high point in Nasdaq interest and therefore a short-term peak for stocks.

This ratio had not fallen low enough to suggest a buy point as of August 2001. Looking back since the early 1970s, the 0.90 level or lower has usually been a requirement to signal the potential for a significant market low. Currently this ratio is at 0.94.

Figure 4.10   Nasdaq Volume/Dow Jones Industrials Volume (8 weeks over
52 weeks): 1995 to 2001

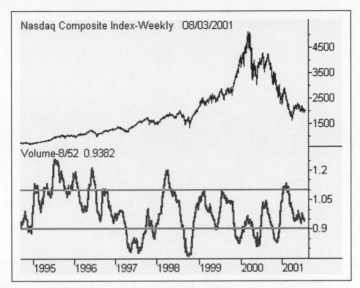

Chart created on TradeStation®, the flagship product of TradeStation Technologies, Inc.

The chart history on this indicator has marked many stellar turning
points for the markets at the extremes. Remember, while the 1.10 threshold
needs to be reached for tops and the 0.90 threshold reached for bottoms,
this is only one condition. I want to see the ratio reverse off of these extremes, as I do not want to fight the trend but rather will wait until the trend
reverses from these peaks and valleys.

As you can see in Figure 4.11 through Figure 4.14, tops over the 1.10
level can run as high as the 1.50 level before topping. This emphasizes the
importance of waiting for a turn before betting on a new trend. At the same
time, readings in the 0.90 area have historically been good buying points
considering the last 25 or more years.

Summarizing this chapter, you can see how volume plays a heavy role
in determining where the crowd is positioned. Has the crowd rushed into
stocks or have they rushed to hedge their positions? And by comparing vehicles like the QQQ and SPY, we get a clear sense of whether the crowd is
fearful on big volume spikes near the lows, or whether complacency reigns
as illustrated by low volume in front of short-term tops. We also look at the
relatively new indicator tracking total exchange volume on the Nasdaq and
NYSE, as well as on the Dow. This showed us where Nasdaq speculation
was too feverish near market peaks, while also showing where traders had
given up on the Nasdaq right near important reversals to the upside.

Figure 4.11   Nasdaq Volume/Dow Jones Industrials Volume (8 weeks over 52 weeks): 1989 to 1995

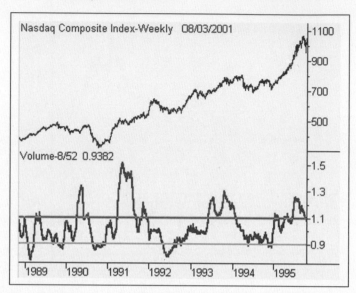

Chart created on TradeStation®, the flagship product of TradeStation Technologies, Inc.

Figure 4.12   Nasdaq Volume/Dow Jones Industrials Volume: 1983 to 1989

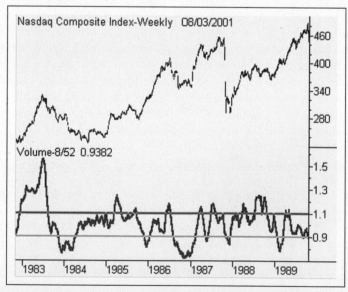

Chart created on TradeStation®, the flagship product of TradeStation Technologies, Inc.

Figure 4.13 Nasdaq Volume/Dow Jones Industrials Volume: 1977 to 1983

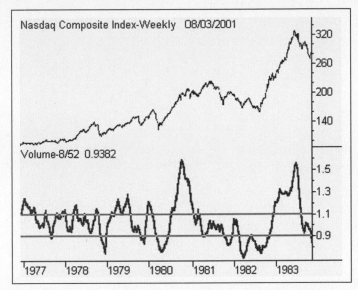

Chart created on TradeStation®, the flagship product of TradeStation Technologies, Inc.

Figure 4.14 Nasdaq Volume/Dow Jones Industrials Volume: 1974 to 1980

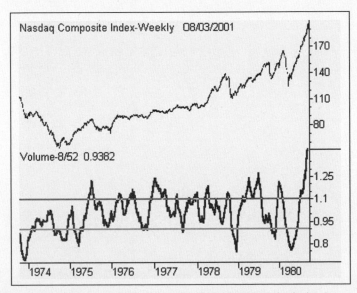

Chart created on TradeStation®, the flagship product of TradeStation Technologies, Inc.

5

SURVEYS—HOW TO USE CROWD OPINION TO YOUR ADVANTAGE AT MAJOR TURNING POINTS

One of the original tools to measure investor sentiment is the sentiment survey, in which a publication will track and report the prevailing percentage of bulls on a weekly basis, which creates an ongoing record to gauge the market trend against the prevailing mood of investors.

The granddaddy of all sentiment surveys is the Investors Intelligence (II) survey, published by Chartcraft in New Rochelle, New York. This service has been tracking investor sentiment on the stock market since 1963, and offers a weekly survey of the percentage of bulls, bears, and those expecting a correction.

Using the same system we used earlier on the RYDEX ratios, with buy signals based on a close under the lower 21-period Bollinger Band (this time on weekly data) and an exit after 50 weeks, in this case, while new sell signals occur after a cross over the upper 21-week Bollinger Band followed by a cross back below, and we hold bearish trades for seven weeks. In the bull market uptrend of the 1990s, the Investors Intelligence low bulls buy signals were particularly strong, catching many rallies, including two nice uptrends in 1996 and 1997 as shown in Figure 5.1.

In the 2000s we have seen a relatively stagnant Dow, which has not been particularly painful for buyers of this indicator. However, we have seen a relatively sideways condition develop in Figure 5.2 instead of the big rallies we saw in prior bull markets.

The overall system performance for the Investors Intelligence numbers shown in Figure 5.3 is relatively impressive, especially the 3.16 size of the average winner compared to the average loser.

Typically, bull markets are thought to begin when the percent of bullish comes from under 25 percent bulls to over 25 percent bulls in a given week. I tested this theory and found that while this indicator had seven of eight winning trades, the last trade was completed in 1989. So this notion appears to have become outdated.

Figure 5.1 Dow Jones Industrial Average versus Investors Intelligence Bulls: 1996 to 1998

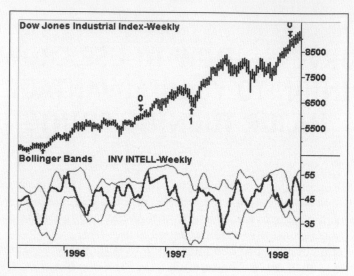

Chart created on TradeStation®, the flagship product of TradeStation Technologies, Inc.

Figure 5.2 Dow Jones Industrial Average versus Investors Intelligence Bulls: 1999 to 2001

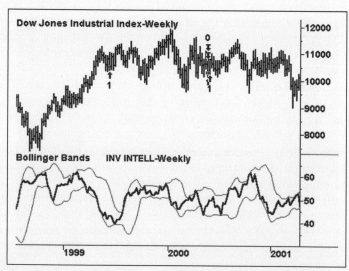

Chart created on TradeStation®, the flagship product of TradeStation Technologies, Inc.

Figure 5.3 Performance Summary of Dow Jones Industrial Average versus Investors Intelligence Bulls Crossing 21-Week Bollinger Bands: 1970 to 2001

BollBand Data2 Nova0 Dow Jones Industrial Index-Weekly 01/09/1970 - 09/21/2001			
Performance Summary: All Trades			
Total net profit	$ 5806.00	Open position P/L	$ 0.00
Gross profit	$ 7565.00	Gross loss	$ -1759.00
Total # of trades	59	Percent profitable	58%
Number winning trades	34	Number losing trades	25
Largest winning trade	$ 2380.00	Largest losing trade	$ -265.00
Average winning trade	$ 222.50	Average losing trade	$ -70.36
Ratio avg win/avg loss	3.16	Avg trade(win & loss)	$ 98.41
Max consec. winners	6	Max consec. losers	7
Avg # bars in winners	19	Avg # bars in losers	17
Max intraday drawdown	$ -1939.00		
Profit factor	4.30	Max # contracts held	1

Chart created on TradeStation®, the flagship product of TradeStation Technologies, Inc.

Figure 5.4 Performance Summary of Dow Jones Industrial Average versus Investors Intelligence Bulls Crossing Under Bears

II Bull/Bear Cross Dow Jones Industrial Index-Weekly 01/09/1970 - 09/21/2001			
Performance Summary: Long Trades			
Total net profit	$ 5026.00	Open position P/L	$ 0.00
Gross profit	$ 5656.00	Gross loss	$ -630.00
Total # of trades	25	Percent profitable	72%
Number winning trades	18	Number losing trades	7
Largest winning trade	$ 2033.00	Largest losing trade	$ -181.00
Average winning trade	$ 314.22	Average losing trade	$ -90.00
Ratio avg win/avg loss	3.49	Avg trade(win & loss)	$ 201.04
Max consec. winners	7	Max consec. losers	3
Avg # bars in winners	31	Avg # bars in losers	31
Max intraday drawdown	$ -1177.00		
Profit factor	8.98	Max # contracts held	1

Chart created on TradeStation®, the flagship product of TradeStation Technologies, Inc.

A more useful measure to track is when the bull and bear percentages cross over each other. Buy when the Percentage of Bulls crosses under the percentage of bears, and exit the bullish position when the percentage of bulls becomes greater than 2.5 times the size of the percentage of bears.

This crossover effect in Figure 5.4 appears even more successful than the Bollinger Bands in this case, perhaps because this data factors in both bearish sentiment as well as bullish sentiment in order to give a more complete picture of the prevailing consensus opinion.

PROFITING FROM EXTREMES IN FEAR AND GREED IN THE CONSENSUS SURVEY

Many traders are trend followers. As a result, trends tend to end in a glorious burst of a buying or selling climax once trend followers pile on as the trend accelerates late in the move and then reverses. After the fact, traders often say that the crowd became overly bullish, and that all the buying had been done off such buying climaxes. Can traders quantify this crowd behavior more specifically to determine when investor sentiment had grown too feverishly positioned on one side or the other? And how can a trader know if this feverish peak has finally reached an inflection point, as opposed to surging on even greater speculation?

One of the indicators I use to measure the relative extremes of fear and greed in a variety of markets is the sentiment survey Consensus Inc., based in Kansas City, Missouri. Every Thursday morning, I plot each new weekly data point against the 21-week Bollinger Bands with plus or minus 1.5 standard deviations on each side. This implies that approximately 80 percent of all activity should fall within these two bands, while unusual moves above or below the Bollinger Band imply that an unusual move is occurring (since the indicator only shows readings outside these Bollinger Bands 20 percent of the time).

When a reading outside the upper Bollinger Band occurs, followed by a consecutive reading back under the upper band (see Figure 5.5), a

Figure 5.5   Dow Jones Industrial Average versus Consensus Inc. with 21-Week Bollinger Bands

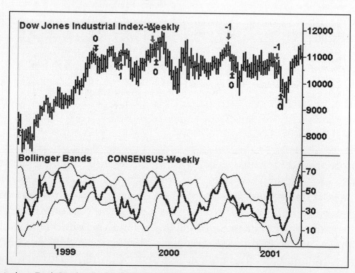

Chart created on TradeStation®, the flagship product of TradeStation Technologies, Inc.

peak in bullishness has occurred. Likewise, when a reading under the lower Bollinger Band is followed by a consecutive reading back above the lower band, a low in bullishness (equating to a peak in bearishness) has occurred.

Combining these sentiment signals within the framework of the technical trend can result in very effective buy and sell signals. If the crowd as a whole is getting optimistic in an uptrend, that activity can be considered relatively rational behavior, and it may not be wise to fight the uptrend. In contrast, an overly optimistic crowd hoping for a recovery out of an existing downtrend can be considered relatively irrational, as traders should not expect extreme optimism amid a technically weak market. Since sentiment takes time to unwind, I use a holding period of 39 weeks, or roughly 9 months, on bullish positions. Bearish positions have the short leash of two weeks to play out, as they have historically offered more risk than reward beyond this point. The buy and sell formulas are as follows:

```
Long Entry:

Close > Average(close,20) and close of Data2[1] <
BollingerBand(close,21,-2)[1] and close of Data2 >
BollingerBand(close,21,-2)

Long Exit:

BarsSinceEntry=39

Short Entry:

Close < Average(close,20) and close of Data2[1] >
BollingerBand(close,21,1.5)[1] and close of Data2 <
BollingerBand(close,21,1.5)

Short Exit:

BarsSinceEntry=2
```

Clearly, bullish signals tend to have much more staying power than bearish signals. This explains the wide difference in the holding periods between bull and bear signals. I find this to be the case with much of the sentiment-based studies that I examine. Part of this phenomenon may be due to the contrasting character of tops compared to bottoms. Tops usually take more time to develop, and thus the idea of lagging new sell signals

Figure 5.6   Performance Summary—Dow Jones Industrial Average versus Consensus Inc. with 21-Week Bollinger Bands: 1983 to 2001

```
BollBand Data2 Nova0  Dow Industrials-Weekly  07/22/1983 - 09/07/2001

                    Performance Summary:  All Trades

Total net profit        $  4843.70    Open position P/L       $    0.00
Gross profit            $  6265.73    Gross loss              $ -1422.03

Total # of trades            30       Percent profitable          57%
Number winning trades        17       Number losing trades         13

Largest winning trade   $  2295.63    Largest losing trade    $  -381.09
Average winning trade   $   368.57    Average losing trade    $  -109.39
Ratio avg win/avg loss       3.37     Avg trade(win & loss)   $   161.46

Max consec. winners           6       Max consec. losers            3
Avg # bars in winners        15       Avg # bars in losers          5

Max intraday drawdown   $ -1230.93
Profit factor                4.41     Max # contracts held          1
```

Chart created on TradeStation®, the flagship product of TradeStation Technologies, Inc.

into the future after an optimistic sentiment extreme is a subject for further study. Bottoms occur more precisely, with the panic often inspired at fear-driven extremes, and thus the buy signals tend to be more precise in their timing.

So what can we learn from longer-term sentiment-based signals in the S&P 500 (seen in Figure 5.6)? They seek to capture the bigger trend in the market, while also minimizing risk if the position is not working within five weeks. This has allowed the system to curtail drawdowns and still be around for the bigger move if the position is winning after five weeks. The synthesis of sentiment within the technical framework is particularly useful, as both methods combined appear to outperform either technicals or sentiment used by themselves.

CONSENSUS LEVELS TO CONSIDER TRULY EXTREME

I want to know where sentiment has historically hit prior extremes in bullishness or bearishness, and then I want to watch closely for a reversal to confirm my suspicions of a pending trend change. Consensus bullish sentiment on stocks of 71 or higher has historically signalled excessive optimism. Table 5.1 provides a listing of the last times we had a sentiment of 71 or above.

Such excess bullishness often leads to higher-risk markets which tend to underperform.

Table 5.1 S&P 100 Index (OEX) Performance After Consensus Readings of 71 or Higher

Date	Reading	OEX	3 Months	6 Months	3 Mo. %	6 Mo. %
4/3/98	80	538.77	563.82	480.70	4.6%	-10.8%
2/20/98	74	494.69	542.36	538.54	9.6%	8.9%
6/20/97	75	438.22	460.93	453.81	5.2%	3.6%
1/17/97	83	381.06	371.10	455.29	-2.6%	19.5%
10/4/96	77	338.47	365.81	370.75	8.1%	9.5%
7/7/95	71	265.03	275.62	295.54	4.0%	11.5%
2/15/91	71	174.90	177.17	182.39	1.3%	4.3%
8/11/89	76	159.95	157.98	156.36	-1.2%	-2.2%
5/19/89	86	150.52	161.13	157.98	7.0%	5.0%
2/17/89	78	141.20	150.52	161.13	6.6%	14.1%
8/7/87	71	158.60	122.15	119.02	-23.0%	-25.0%
8/29/86	79	118.66	114.76	136.60	-3.3%	15.1%
8/10/84	71	82.57	82.55	90.03	0.0%	9.0%
Average					1.3%	4.8%

THE AMERICAN ASSOCIATION OF INDIVIDUAL INVESTORS (AAII) SURVEY

Based in Chicago, the American Association of Individual Investors (AAII) puts out a weekly poll showing the percentage of members polled who are bullish, bearish, or neutral on the stock market over the short term. Updated every Thursday morning, the AAII poll has proved useful in determining the general market sentiment among individual investors.

The reading in Figure 5.7 is somewhat more volatile, which actually benefits users of the Bollinger Bands as a technique to pick up additional trading opportunities as the markets oscillate between fear and greed. Figure 5.8 shows the performance of AAII buy and sell signals on the Dow Jones Industrial Average.

Market Vane in Pasadena, California, also provides sentiment data on the percentage of bulls on the stock futures, as well as the other major futures markets. The company does daily surveys of traders to create a Percent Bullish reading (see Figure 5.9 and Figure 5.10). The daily service is a paid service, while the weekly data (provided for subscribers every Tuesday) is listed free each weekend in *Barron's*, as are the other sentiment polls discussed earlier.

Based on all of these individual surveys, what would happen if we average the Percentage of Bulls each week to create a composite sentiment

Figure 5.7   American Association of Individual Investors (AAII) Weekly
Percent Bullish

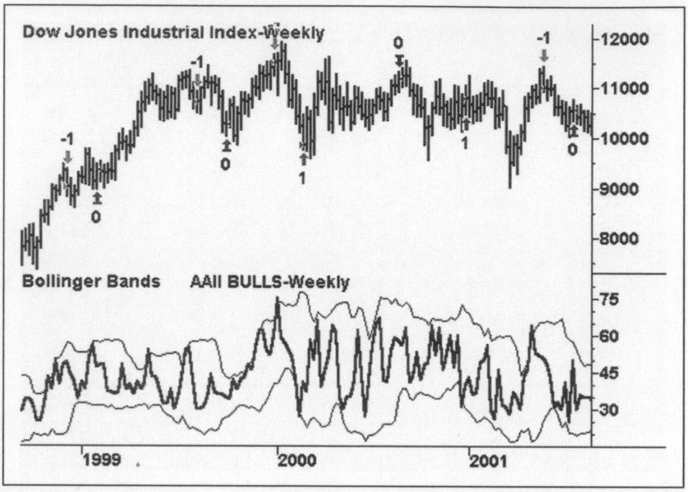

Chart created on TradeStation®, the flagship product of TradeStation Technologies, Inc.

Figure 5.8   Performance Summary—Dow Jones Industrial Average versus
American Association of Individual Investors (AAII) Weekly
Percent Bullish

BollBand Data2 NovaO Dow Jones Industrial Index-Weekly 07/24/1987 - 09/21/2001			
Performance Summary: All Trades			
Total net profit	$ 5337.00	Open position P/L	$ 0.00
Gross profit	$ 7443.00	Gross loss	$ -2106.00
Total # of trades	31	Percent profitable	71%
Number winning trades	22	Number losing trades	9
Largest winning trade	$ 1635.00	Largest losing trade	$ -505.00
Average winning trade	$ 338.32	Average losing trade	$ -234.00
Ratio avg win/avg loss	1.45	Avg trade(win & loss)	$ 172.16
Max consec. winners	5	Max consec. losers	2
Avg # bars in winners	12	Avg # bars in losers	8
Max intraday drawdown	$ -1645.00		
Profit factor	3.53	Max # contracts held	1

Chart created on TradeStation®, the flagship product of TradeStation Technologies, Inc.

indicator? This one would include the bullish percentages from each of the
four surveys we discussed—Investors Intelligence, Market Vane, Consensus, and AAII.

You can see in Figure 5.11 and Figure 5.12 that the weekly swings are
not as volatile due to averaging, but we still get a similar number of trading

Figure 5.9 Dow Jones Industrial Average versus Market Vane Weekly Percent Bullish: 1999 to 2001

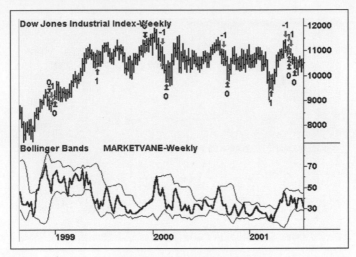

Chart created on TradeStation®, the flagship product of TradeStation Technologies, Inc.3

Figure 5.10 Performance Summary—Dow Jones Industrial Average versus Market Vane Weekly Percent Bullish: 1987 to 2001

BollBand Data2 NovaO Dow Jones Industrial Index-Weekly 07/24/1987 - 09/21/2001			
Performance Summary: All Trades			
Total net profit	$ 6135.00	Open position P/L	$ 0.00
Gross profit	$ 6960.00	Gross loss	$ -825.00
Total # of trades	26	Percent profitable	77%
Number winning trades	20	Number losing trades	6
Largest winning trade	$ 1133.00	Largest losing trade	$ -277.00
Average winning trade	$ 348.00	Average losing trade	$ -137.50
Ratio avg win/avg loss	2.53	Avg trade(win & loss)	$ 235.96
Max consec. winners	9	Max consec. losers	3
Avg # bars in winners	9	Avg # bars in losers	13
Max intraday drawdown	$ -1648.00		
Profit factor	8.44	Max # contracts held	1

Chart created on TradeStation®, the flagship product of TradeStation Technologies, Inc.

signals compared to some of the other surveys. Particularly impressive is the reduced size of the average loss, which allows the key Average Win / Average Loss statistic to zoom up to more than a 6-to-1 favorable ratio.

In summary, you can see that sentiment surveys offer us a great deal of opportunity to gauge investors' sentiment in an objective way, presented here on a weekly basis. Bullish trades produce better trades with longer

Figure 5.11 Composite Sentiment—II, Market Vane, Consensus, and AAII Weekly Percent Bullish: 1999 to 2001

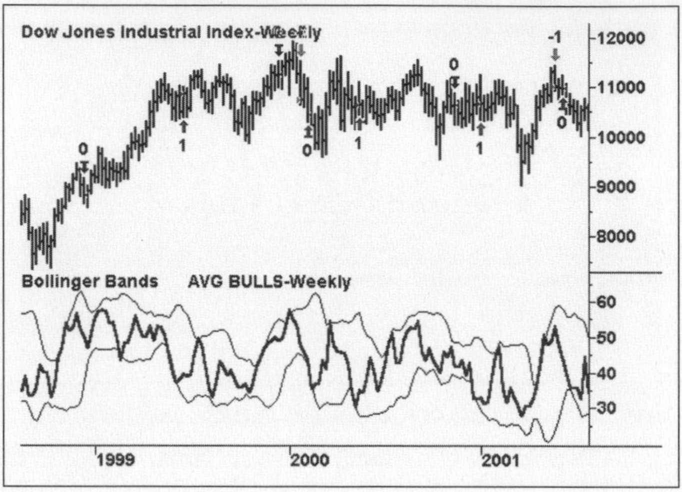

Chart created on TradeStation®, the flagship product of TradeStation Technologies, Inc.

Figure 5.12 Performance Summary—Composite Sentiment: Investors Intelligence, Market Vane, Consensus, and AAII Percent Bullish: 1987 to 2001

BollBand Data2 Nova0 Dow Jones Industrial Index-Weekly 07/24/1987 - 09/21/2001

Performance Summary: All Trades

Total net profit	$ 4347.00	Open position P/L	$ 0.00
Gross profit	$ 4742.00	Gross loss	$ -395.00
Total # of trades	23	Percent profitable	65%
Number winning trades	15	Number losing trades	8
Largest winning trade	$ 1653.00	Largest losing trade	$ -84.00
Average winning trade	$ 316.13	Average losing trade	$ -49.38
Ratio avg win/avg loss	6.40	Avg trade(win & loss)	$ 189.00
Max consec. winners	5	Max consec. losers	4
Avg # bars in winners	16	Avg # bars in losers	5
Max intraday drawdown	$ -1614.00		
Profit factor	12.01	Max # contracts held	1

Chart created on TradeStation®, the flagship product of TradeStation Technologies, Inc.

holding periods of 26 to 52 weeks, while bearish trades generally have a short rope of two weeks except for the AAII survey, where they were allowed to be held just seven weeks. Sentiment surveys give us a bigger picture sentiment tool, which nicely complements the other forms of daily sentiment analysis.

Part II

STOCK SELECTION TECHNIQUES

Now that I have covered the broader market backdrop, as defined by classic sentiment indicators, let us look at the specific stock selection strategies I use, as defined by both classic technical indicators that test well historically, plus proprietary indicators I have developed. First, let us look at the philosophy behind trends, and then explore my favorite traditional trend indicators.

TRENDS VERSUS THE EFFICIENT MARKET HYPOTHESIS

The idea of trend following is in direct opposition to what most theoreticians believe occurs via the Efficient Market Hypothesis (EMH). Let us first take a look at what these two theories believe, so you can decide which makes more sense to you:

The Nature of Trends (Contrast to Efficient Market Hypothesis)

1. Trends are feedback systems. They have longer-term memories, though more recent events affect them more than older events.
2. The further out a trader looks to forecast a trend, the less reliable that forecast becomes. At some point in the future, price action cannot be predicted with accuracy. However, shorter-term events can be predicted more often than not, based on recent trends persisting longer than expected.
3. Investors do not recognize or react to trends immediately; rather, they wait until they have been well established.
4. There is more mean reversion in daily data than monthly data—more noise on a day-to-day basis, while longer-term weekly and monthly trends have more persistence for the next bar.
5. The more pieces of information coming into a system, the higher the uncertainty of the system. Keep trend-following methods simple.

6. There are periods of stability (trading ranges) which are more random than in unstable times (trends).

Efficient Market Hypothesis (EMH)

1. In its strongest form, EMH says that all information, including insider information, is factored into current market prices.
2. All price action going forward is assumed to be random. Prices can only be influenced by new developments, since all existing developments are known and fully acted upon.
3. Trends cannot exist.

As you can already tell, I have strongly sided with the belief that trends do exist, that individuals do react at different times to news, that groupthink behavior leads to self-fulfilling prophecies within a trend, and more.

Let me note something about technical indicators. All technical indicators are derived from a few simple factors: price, time, and volume. I focus on indicators that best measure these three simple elements. I will show you the indicators that I have found to offer the best reading of the interaction between price, time, and volume, while also staying grounded and never straying too far from the simplicity that a basic bar chart can provide.

One of the other elements to factor in as a technical analyst is the impact of Multiple Time Frames. If you are only looking at an intraday chart, you are missing what the bigger trend is doing on the daily chart. If you think you have the daily chart covered, what does the weekly and monthly time frame look like? I like to start out with monthly charts and work my way down to weekly, daily, and finally intraday. What I find is that monthly and weekly time frames will tend to show the proper trend direction, while daily, and especially intraday, charts are better used as counter-trend measures. Why would this make sense? Well, if a pullback to a monthly uptrend line is a buy signal, how is that going to look on an intraday chart? It will look like a sell signal as the stock is declining in the short term. I am not saying you should not trade these short-term moves down, but I am saying that you had better be careful, as you are fighting the longer-term uptrend. Have you ever had a short-term trade that you thought looked perfect, entered it, then watched in horror as it reversed in the exact opposite direction. When I did this, I would look back at the higher time frames and realize that I was putting on trades going against the longer-term trend. As a result, I now seek to get these time frames lined up for the highest confidence trades. If the long-term charts are in uptrends, I will often wait for a short-term sell to be reversed by a buy signal, to get all my time frames aligned. This gives me the greatest probability of being correct, in this case by attracting buyers across all different time frames.

6

MY FAVORITE CLASSIC TREND INDICATORS

Over the bull and bear market extremes of the past few years, I have found that my proprietary combination of unique fundamental, technical, and sentiment indicators are among the most reliable predictors of market action. However, it is important to note that I also make use of numerous standard technical indicators and measures to identify only the most promising trends.

MOVING AVERAGES

Bottom line: One of the most important charting tools to gauge a recent price trend in a stock.

Definition: Simple Moving Averages (SMAs) trace the average share price of a stock over a given time period, weighting price action over each trading session equally. For example, a 10-day SMA is the average of the last 10 days' closing prices for a security. It is called a "moving" average because the average will change as the stock price changes. Exponential moving averages (EMAs) provide an additional analytic dimension by being weighted more heavily toward the most recent price action within any specified time frame. Extensive analysis has shown that EMA lines, particularly in shorter time increments, tend to adjust more quickly than SMAs as support, as well as resistance. In contrast, a sustained breakout above an EMA over two to three trading days, generally speaking, is considered a short-term buy signal. It is important to note, however, that a strong jump or drop in share prices will usually be followed by a movement back to the EMA uptrend line. In such a case, you are better off looking for buying opportunities as stocks revert back to key EMA levels. In other words, you do not want to simply chase a "breakout" stock when there may be opportunities to buy at more favorable levels. A break of the EMA trend line, conversely, could well mean it is time to exit or lock in profits.

Figure 6.1   Comparison of 20-Day Moving Averages: Simple versus Exponential for Human Genome Sciences (HGSI)

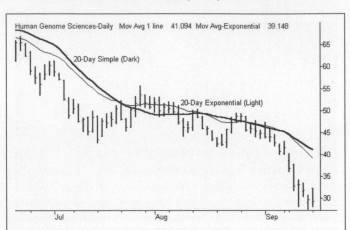

Chart created on TradeStation®, the flagship product of TradeStation Technologies, Inc.

Example: As you can see in Figure 6.1, exponential moving averages will tend to be more sensitive to more recent price changes, since exponential averages weight recent price action more while underweighting older price moves. The simple average weights all days evenly.

People ask me whether I like simple or exponential moving averages better. I use both, but I find that on longer-term charts I like the simple moving averages, while on shorter-term charts I will often gravitate towards exponential moving averages, which are more responsive to shorter-term changes in the trend.

We have configured portfolios across different time frames (daily, weekly, and monthly), but then the technical action and sentiment reaction of the crowd will determine the length of time a trend can remain intact.

Though trading swings have become compressed into shorter time periods, I have found the noise levels on intraday charts have gone up dramatically in the last three years. As a result, I generally seek to avoid making trading decisions based on intraday activity alone. A lot of battles are fought during the day, but the war is won at the close. Therefore, I prefer a daily chart to an intraday chart, and similarly will focus on weekly and monthly charts before I look at daily charts. As a general rule, the trend in the longer time frame will generally win over the shorter time frame. At the same time, the best set-ups occur when the longer and shorter time frames are in synch.

For example, in 1999, when Qualcomm (QCOM) broke down below its 50-day simple moving average, many investors received an exit signal, and it created some short-term downside in the stock during that week. But if

Figure 6.2 Qualcomm (QCOM) Daily with 50-Day Simple Moving Average

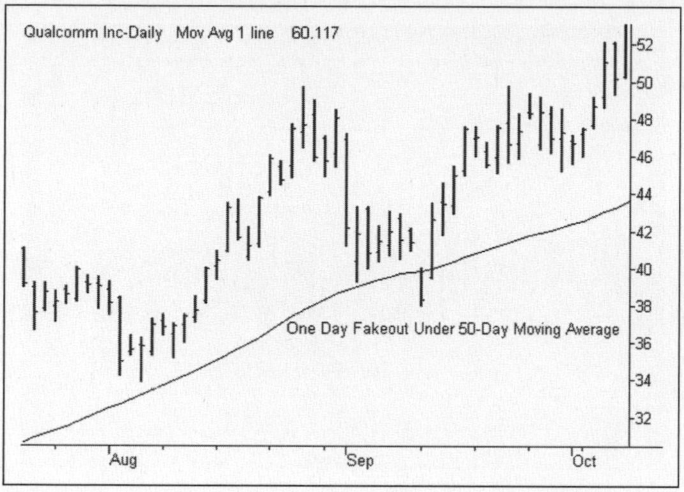

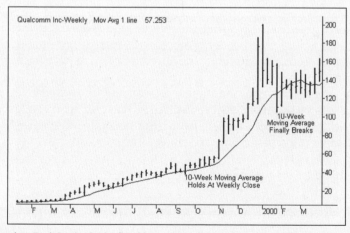

Chart created on TradeStation®, the flagship product of TradeStation Technologies, Inc.

Figure 6.3 Qualcomm (QCOM) Weekly with 10-Week Simple Moving Average

Chart created on TradeStation®, the flagship product of TradeStation Technologies, Inc.

you followed the weekly chart with a 10-week simple moving average—similar to a 50-day SMA—you would have waited until the close at the end of the week and you would have avoided losing your Qualcomm stock because, by the end of that week, it had reversed and closed well back above the 10-week average (see Figure 6.2 and Figure 6.3). The stock then went on to rise another 300 percent over the next six months.

Figure 6.4   Microsoft (MSFT) Weekly with 50-Week Exponential Moving Average

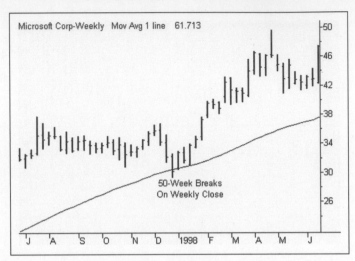

Chart created on TradeStation®, the flagship product of TradeStation Technologies, Inc.

Some people tell me they do not have the stomach for riding out this intrabar volatility, as they are uncomfortable waiting all week if the position is going sharply against them during the middle of the week. If that is the case, then you may want to consider a more conservative investment than the growth stock arena. By extending the time frame to a weekly basis, the daily noise from your investment decisions is blocked out, saving you from costly fakeouts. The market will oftentimes test you and try to shake you out of a good position on these pullbacks. The stocks that hold up on a closing basis are usually the ones that can help carry your portfolio to new heights.

The same principle applies to a longer-term investor, who should consider a monthly chart over a weekly chart. Let us look at the example of Microsoft in Figure 6.4 and Figure 6.5.

MOVING AVERAGE CONVERGENCE DIVERGENCE (MACD)

Bottom line: A shorthand indicator which detects trending price action as reflected in the relative performance of two exponential moving averages.

Definition: MACD represents the interaction of two exponential moving averages, which weight recent price action more heavily. Market technicians often view convergence and divergence as buy or sell signals, depending on a number of factors. More information on MACD will appear in Chapter 8.

Example: Nvidia (NVDA) sees new buy signals as the "fast" (darker) line crosses over the slow (lighter shaded) line in Figure 6.6, while seeing sell signals when the fast line crosses under the slow line.

Figure 6.5 Microsoft (MSFT) Monthly with 10-Month Exponential Moving Average

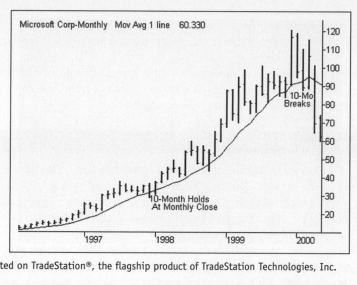

Chart created on TradeStation®, the flagship product of TradeStation Technologies, Inc.

Figure 6.6 Nvidia (NVDA) with Moving Average Convergence Divergence (MACD)

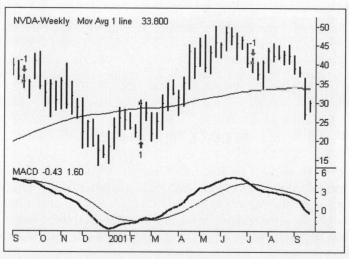

Chart created on TradeStation®, the flagship product of TradeStation Technologies, Inc.

SUPPORT AND RESISTANCE

Bottom line: Key levels where stocks are likely to build (or lose) momentum. Just about any stock chart will show significant price levels known as resistance and support.

Definition: Support is the level a stock typically will not fall below. Resistance is the level beyond which a stock cannot seem to surmount. Support is "the floor" and resistance "the ceiling."

Some simple rules:

The longer a support or resistance level has held, the more likely it is to be maintained. This means, for example, buying a stock at a major resistance level probably will not pay off soon. The same goes for support levels. You may wait forever to buy a stock if you are looking for prices below key levels of support.

The wider the gap between support and resistance, the stronger these lines are. Support and resistance levels in a narrow band, by contrast, are not likely to hold for long.

Active trading (high volume) within a support/resistance band should also indicate the strength of the price range between these levels.

Example: Support and resistance can best be seen on a stock in a clear trading range. In fact, resistance defines the upper end of the range and support defines the lower end. In the case of Amgen (AMGN) in Figure 6.7, the stock trades down near 51, just over 50, and tends to hold as support. Rallies up to the 75 area meet with heavy selling, which offers resistance each time the stock tests the 75 level.

AVERAGE TRUE RANGE

Bottom line: Developed by Welles Wilder, the Average True Range (ATR) helps measure the volatility of a security. Wilder believed that high ATR values often appeared near market bottoms after a final capitulation sell-off. He also noted that low ATR values occurred after prolonged sideways consolidations. When I look at the ATR, I look for the reversal of these peaks and valleys in a stock's ATR to signify that an important move is coming. Two closes in a row in the opposite direction is usually enough to signal that the peak or valley is in place in the short term.

Like ADX, which will be discussed later, this indicator is not a directional predictor, but rather it shows when to expect a stock to make a significant move.

Figure 6.7　Amgen (AMGN)—Support at 51, Resistance At 75

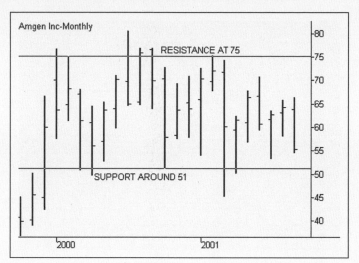

Chart created on TradeStation®, the flagship product of TradeStation Technologies, Inc.

Definition: The True Range is calculated to be the highest value among the following three variables:

1. The distance from today's high to today's low.
2. The distance from yesterday's close to today's high.
3. The distance from yesterday's close to today's low.

The Average True Range is calculated as a moving average of the True Range bars (generally 14 units though 9 bars is another alternative I also study).

Example. Figure 6.8 is a good example of high volatility as prices peak and consolidate after nice run-ups (points "H") and low volatility as prices consolidate prior to breaking out (points "L").

WILDER'S AVERAGE DIRECTIONAL MOVEMENT INDEX (ADX)

Bottom line: Welles Wilder also developed the concept of Directional Movement as a technique to find securities starting meaningful trends.

Definition: The starting points for analysis are the +DI (positive Directional Movement) and −DI (negative Directional Movement) lines. Traditionally, analysts look for a crossover of the two lines to signal a reversal in trend. Wilder used the "Extreme Point" rule to look for confirmation.

Figure 6.8 Example of Average True Range—Autozone (AZO)

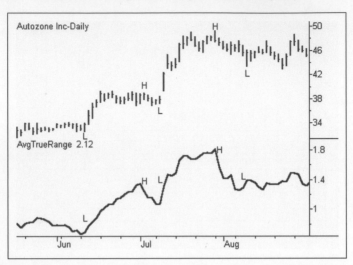

If +DI crosses above −DI, then Wilder looked for confirmation when the price subsequently moved above the high of the day of the bullish crossover (or below the low from the day of a negative crossover).

The Average Directional Movement Index (ADX) is then constructed to show whether a trend is in effect by smoothing the difference between the +DI and −DI lines. The typical measurement period is 14 bars, though I will also look at 9 bars on historically trending securities for a quicker response time. The Average Directional Movement Index acts as a filter, as it should be uptrending to confirm that a trend is in place if a signal is to be taken. A flat or downtrending ADX suggests the DM crossover signal should be disregarded.

Figure 6.9 shows an example of the traditional ADX interpretation.

The bullish crossovers of +DM over −DM are shown with up arrows, while the bearish crossovers of −DM over +DM are shown with down arrows. As you can see it eventually caught a nice move on the upside in KKD in early April 2001. However, before that signal the stock experienced many whipsaw trades. What I found in trying to trade the Directional Movement system under traditional interpretation is that I still experienced too many whipsaw trades. As a result, I noticed a pattern that worked more consistently for me, especially as an options trader.

What I look for is ADX coming off a low level, preferably under 20, and then not only turning up, but also crossing above the lower DM line to suggest a forceful trend is developing. The key here is that ADX is a mean reverting indicator at the extremes. If you buy a stock whose ADX is already over 50, that says the trend has already been in force for quite a while and

Figure 6.9   ADX Reading on Krispy Kreme Doughnuts (KKD) Daily 2001

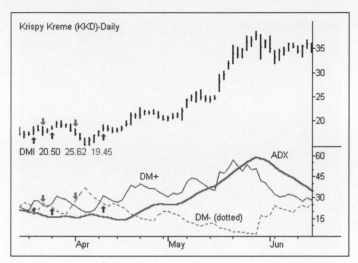

Chart created on TradeStation®, the flagship product of TradeStation Technologies, Inc.

could be at extra risk of reversing. As a result, I prefer to catch the ADX when it is just crossing over the lower DM line after having been under the 20 level. In a new bullish trend, ADX should cross over the −DM line for a new buy signal, while as a bearish trend starts, ADX should cross over the +DM line.

In addition, I am much more quick to close out positions than wait for a new crossover. What I notice in the best trends is that the ADX line will continue to trend higher, and should not roll over to the downside. If it goes flat, the position should be held. This is the most strict approach, which I primarily use for options trading, as I want to get the maximum trend over minimum time with my options purchases.

Let us look at Figure 6.10, a new chart of Krispy Kreme (KKD), based on this criteria.

Calculating ADX

1. The first Directional Indicators (+DI and −DI) are calculated by sum-ming the positive and negative Directional Movements and dividing that by the True Range over a period of time (default 14 days):

+DM (Positive Directional Movement) = High Price (today) − High Price (yesterday)

−DM (Negative Directional Movement) = Low Price (today) − Low Price (yesterday)

Figure 6.10   Krispy Kreme (KKD) with Exits on Peaking ADX

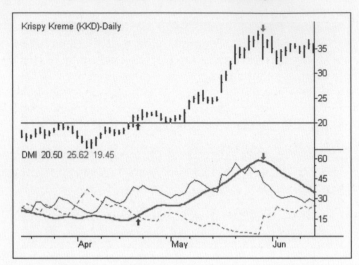

Chart created on TradeStation®, the flagship product of TradeStation Technologies, Inc.

Days for which today's high or low do not exceed yesterday's are ignored.

2. True Range is determined by the largest absolute value of:
   a. Today's high − today's low.
   b. Today's high − yesterday's close.
   c. Today's low − yesterday's close.

3. The 1DI measures upward movement and the 2DI measures downward movement:

   +DI (Positive Directional Index) = sum[+DM(# of days)/True Range (# of days)]*100

   −DI (Negative Directional Index) 5 sum[2DM(# of days)/True Range (# of days)]*100

4. Subsequent DMs, True Range, and DIs are calculated using a smoothing method once the first 1DI and 2DI have been obtained:

   +DM(today) = +DM(previous point) − (+DM(previous point/cycle length) + (+DM(today))

   −DM(today) = −DM(previous point) − (−DM(previous point/cycle length) + (−DM(today))

   True Range (today) = True Range(previous point) − (True Range(previous point)/cycle length + (True Range(today))

+DI(today) = (1DM(today)/True Range(today))*100

−DI(today) = (2DM(today)/True Range(today))*100

5. The DX is the Directional Movement Index. It is calculated by dividing the absolute value of the difference of DIs by the sum of DIs; the result is normalized by multiplying by 100. The higher the DX, the more Directional Movement; the lower the DX, the less Directional Movement. Whether the price movement is up or down is irrelevant—the DX solely measures the degree to which the movement is up or down:

DX = (1(+DI) − (−DI)1/(+DI) + (−DI))*100

6. The ADX (Average Directional Movement Index) is a moving average of N bars of the DX:

Today's ADX = ((Previous ADX*(# of days − 1)) + Today's DX)/N days

EFFICIENCY RATIO

Bottom line: Perry Kaufman's book, *Smarter Trading*, shows an interesting way to measure the trend or range of a stock. This indicator formed the start of my search for a method to find clearly trending stocks, which further developed into my Acceleration Bands and Momentum Divergence indicators.

Definition: Kaufman notes that if a security was perfectly trending (for example, moving up one point per day when the range from low to high was also one point per day), that over 20 days the security would have moved a total of 20 points, while the summation of its total range over the 20 days would also be 20 points. This uptrend would be totally efficient, with no wasted price movement. Thus, the Efficiency Ratio is the net points moved from the beginning to the end of a period, divided over the total range the stock has moved over that period. In the case above, 20 points moved over a total range of 20 points amounts to an Efficiency Ratio of 1.0, the highest possible reading. In contrast, a move totally 10 points up followed by 10 points down would leave a net move of 0 points, divided over the total points moved of 20, which would lead to an Efficiency Ratio of 0.0. Another way to think of this is that if you were able to take 10 points profit on the move up and 10 points profit by shorting the move down, you would be operating with total efficiency relative to what the stock gave you for opportunity. If you sit still and the stock goes nowhere, your potential efficiency at catching the 10 points up and the 10 points down is zero.

Kaufman preferred to take the absolute value of the net directional trend in the numerator, which is shown in Figure 6.11.

Figure 6.11   Kaufman's Efficiency Ratio on Krispy Kreme (KKD) Daily 2001

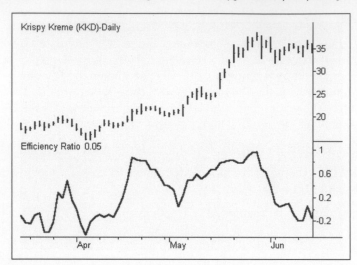

Chart created on TradeStation®, the flagship product of TradeStation Technologies, Inc.

CANDLESTICK CHARTS

Bottom line: Candlestick charts give you a large amount of information at a quick visual glance, particularly whether the stock closed higher or lower than it opened, as well as the range outside the difference between the open and the close.

Definition: A bullish candlestick will show its close higher than its open, which throughout this book will show up as a white or "hollow" body on the candle for that day. A black or "filled" body will show a close under that day's open, which reveals a decline in the price of the stock.

Example: Figure 6.12 of eBay (EBAY) shows upside progress where the white hollow bars occur, while the dark bars indicate declines for the week. Occasionally the white or black bodies may not exist if the close was exactly equal to the open, as shown for the week ending July 20. Numerous candlestick patterns have been defined. See Steve Nison's books listed in the bibliography for more details on candlestick patterns.

"ELEPHANT-TRUNK" SIGNALS

Bottom line: The Elephant-Trunk (ET) formation is based on a stock that has had a nice run-up in value and then reverses direction to move the other way, in order to eliminate the excesses inherently built up during a strong appreciation phase.

Figure 6.12   eBay (EBAY) Weekly Chart with Candlesticks: 2001

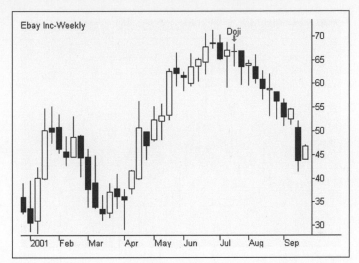

Chart created on TradeStation®, the flagship product of TradeStation Technologies, Inc.

Definition: The parameters for the setup (which is most often a short rather than a long) are an extension in price, followed by an open at the high of the bar (preferably at the prior day's close), and a subsequent trade below the low of the high day (the prior bar), preferably a close below this low.

Example: This setup is best illustrated in Figure 6.13. Gentiva Health Services (GTIV) shows a move off its 50-day exponential moving average (EMA − 18.50) up to the 23.50 mark, or a gain of just over 25 percent. Following this four-day buying surge, the stock opened the fifth day at the prior close and never traded above it. Trading in GTIV was weak throughout the session until the low of the high day was taken out, and the close would come right at that key level. However, the ET formation was already in place, so the stock had nowhere to go but lower. This particular setup was an impressive performer in that the entire up move was retraced, plus an additional 5.4 percent before the system exited the trade on the fifth day.

Entry came at the close of the ET sell day just above 22, while exit came in at 17.50, for a gain of 20 percent in five days. You now understand why I tend to reference the formation on a regular basis to my daily subscribers, as it can be a very powerful profit driver. By the same token, if the conditions are not just right, the ET formation has a habit of "reversing the reversal." Reversing a reversal can also be a powerful phenomenon. Generally, when you see a setup like GTIV, the odds are well in your favor on the short side. If, however, you have a stock that is in a strong but steady uptrend, not too extended above its key EMAs, then you may just get a two to three-day pullback to the first EMA (generally the 10-day EMA) before the stock then

Figure 6.13   Gentiva Health Services (GTIV) with "Elephant-Trunk" Sell Signal

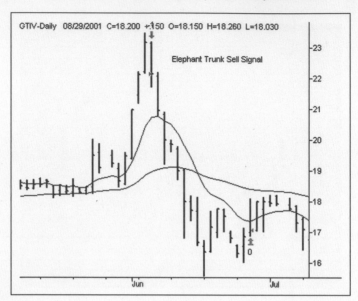

GTIV-Daily 08/29/2001 C=18.200 +.150 O=18.150 H=18.260 L=18.030

Elephant Trunk Sell Signal

Chart created on TradeStation®, the flagship product of TradeStation Technologies, Inc.

explodes higher. Therefore, depending on the circumstances, if the trade does not follow through quickly in two to three sessions, while holding above a key EMA, you should probably exit the setup. That said, the ET sell signal can be a very profitable and reliable signal for the aggressive trader, given the right market dynamics, as shown by the GTIV chart.

Figure 6.14 through Figure 6.16 show additional Elephant-Trunk examples.

THOUGHTS ON SYSTEMS TESTING

A good system will only be as effective as its fit with the personality and preferences of the individual trader. Some traders need to trade at a higher winning percentage system even if it is less profitable than a system with big home runs mixed with more frequent smaller losses, because such traders psychologically cannot handle a string of consecutive small losses. There is nothing wrong with that. You just need to go into a systematized trading approach understanding the characteristics of a system (mainly winning percentage, size of average win/loss, and drawdown percentage) in order to create the highest probability of success in finding a good fit. You

Figure 6.14 Abgenics (ABGX) with "Elephant-Trunk" Sell Signal

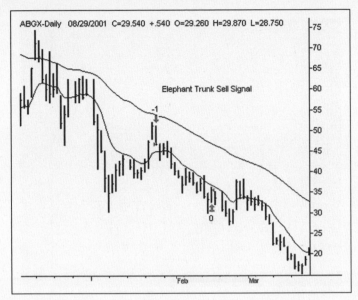

Chart created on TradeStation®, the flagship product of TradeStation Technologies, Inc.

Figure 6.15 Ciena (CIEN) with "Elephant-Trunk" Sell Signal

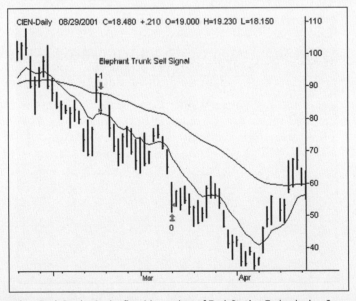

Chart created on TradeStation®, the flagship product of TradeStation Technologies, Inc.

87

Figure 6.16   Juniper Networks (JNPR) with "Elephant-Trunk" Sell Signal

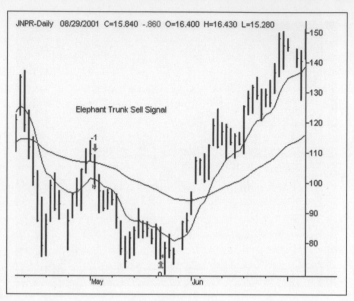

Chart created on TradeStation®, the flagship product of TradeStation Technologies, Inc.

also should factor into your testing plans that systems often need different parameters for longs versus shorts as well as for entries versus exits.

TESTING TRADING SYSTEMS: WHICH PERFORMANCE STATISTICS MATTER MOST?

Many traders think that having a high Percentage Profitable is the main thing to target. But that is not the only factor that affects total profitability. The other primary factor is the Ratio of Average Win/Average Loss. If you have a 90 percent winning percentage, but your one loser out of 10 trades is 10 times your average winner, you are not going to do well. Similarly, I have seen numerous systems with low winning percentages do well, because they keep their losses small and let their winners ride, forming a very large Ratio of Average Win/Average Loss. For example, with a winning percentage of 30 percent, if the size of the Average Win is five times greater than the size of the Average Loss, this system will do well.

A way to evaluate systems is to create a baseline for comparison. Bernie Schaeffer's book, *The Option Advisor*, details an excellent way to benchmark your system's performance. Start with a sample random system, say flipping a coin. If you have a 50-50 chance of calling heads, and you win the same amount as you lose on any particular flip, then your Percent Profitable is 50 percent and your Ratio of Average Win/Average Loss is 1.00. So if you multiply these two factors together, you get a random Profitability Factor of 0.50 (.50 winning percentage $\times$ 1.00 Average Win/Average Loss). I like systems that can at least double the random baseline, giving me a Profitability Factor of 1.00 or higher. This makes sure I have accounted for the impact of commissions and slippage (the cost of buying at the offering price or selling at the bid price).

Let us evaluate several systems' Performance Summaries in this context. For example, say we have four stocks:

	Percentage Profitable		Ratio Avg. Win/ Avg. Loss		Profitability Factor
Stock A:	.60	×	0.50	=	0.30
Stock B:	.55	×	2.00	=	1.10
Stock C:	.90	×	1.50	=	1.35
Stock D:	.30	×	8.50	=	2.55

In the above table we see that only Stock A offers worse results than our random coin-flip benchmark Profitability Factor of 0.50. All other systems do more than twice as well as the random benchmark, with Stock D doing five times as well as the random model. Even though Stock D had the lowest percentage of profitable trades, its profitability overall was superior because it cut losses quickly while letting winners ride, resulting in winners which were 8.50 times greater in size than the losers, on average.

This gives you a good overview of the traditional trend-oriented indicators I consider to be among my favorites at spotting trends. The next chapter will move us forward to examine my favorite trend-driven techniques, starting with my unique Acceleration Bands indicator and then moving on to Moving Average Envelopes.

7

ACCELERATION BANDS AND MOVING AVERAGE ENVELOPES— SPOTTING THE POINTS WHEN A STOCK CAN GO PARABOLIC

The principle of Acceleration is one of the most critical lessons that active traders must learn. Stock traders need to get the best bang for their buck. They desire to rotate capital to the best performing stocks quickly and then rotate out of those stocks when the acceleration period ends. The goal is to keep moving capital into the best-performing stocks. Options buyers especially need to be in the best trending stocks, as the time lost while holding an option can best be overcome by stocks that move sharply in the anticipated direction. As a trader, I want to achieve maximum movement in the stock over the least amount of time possible.

I started my trading career focused on trendlines as a way to buy stocks at important support points and sell stocks at resistance points. As my trading progressed, I noticed that the biggest winners were the stocks that broke out and never provided another chance to buy them back at support. I have learned that the best profits come from the "parabolic" stock moves. These are the stocks that do not give you easy chances to get into them— what some might call "runaway" situations. Some call these stocks "bubbles" after they have made their major move, but we prefer to get into these stocks earlier, when the bubble is just starting to rapidly inflate, and then have a strategy to exit before the bubble is truly popped.

Based on years of researching and monitoring the profiles of these stocks, I noticed that these runaway stocks have several factors in common:

1. They are usually in growth industries, like technology, communications, biotechnology, and health care.
2. Earnings are usually growing at very fast rates, typically 25 percent or more, and many times at 100 percent or more.
3. Some amount of media debate exists about the company's future prospects. The best scenario is to find a stock that is getting attention

91

for being "overvalued." I often find that Acceleration Stocks often get overvalued until the crowd recognizes the stock as a clear winner.

4. Usually there is a breakout to a new high over the prior 50-bar high— these breakouts have the most longevity in my experience. Most investors like to buy stocks near their 52-week low and hope it returns to the 52-week high. Historically, the studies I have done show that over 80 percent of the leaders for the next 12 months were typically within 15 percent of their highs when their upside breakouts began.

After studying many different indicators to find where this "breakout point" appeared to reside in most stocks, I developed my Acceleration Bands indicator.

Here is my Acceleration Bands formula, written in TradeStation's EasyLanguage code:

```
UpperBand = Average((high x (1+2 x ((((high -
low)/((high + low)/2)) x 1000) x .001))) , 20)

MidPoint = Average (close , 20)

LowerBand = Average ((low x (1 - 2 x ((((high -
low)/((high + low) / 2)) x 1000) x .001))) , 20)
```

Basically I am taking the net directional movement each day (high − low) and dividing it over the average price of the stock (high + low divided by 2) to get a percentage of directional movement for the stock. When the stock is non-trending, these bands will contract, while the bands will tend to expand when the stock is trending.

1. Usually I am looking at the last 20 bars on the Acceleration Bands. On a daily chart, this incorporates roughly the last month's trading activity, while on a weekly chart this covers 4-1/2 months, and on a monthly chart just over 1-1/2 years of price action.

2. The upper and lower Acceleration Bands are plotted equidistant from the simple 20-period simple moving average (the middle line between the bands in Figure 7.1 and Figure 7.2). A daily chart shows a 20-day moving average, and a weekly chart plots a 20-week moving average.

3. Acceleration Bands adjust for a stock's volatility. The more volatile the stock's price action over the last 20 periods, the wider the bands will be around the moving average.

4. Once I see two consecutive closes above the upper Acceleration Band, I get a buy signal. On trending stocks, this will often lead to a major

Figure 7.1 CMGI Daily Chart with Acceleration Bands

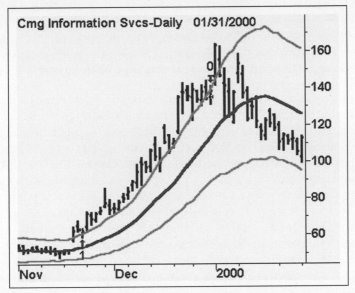

Figure 7.2 S1 Corp. (SONE) Weekly Chart with Acceleration Bands

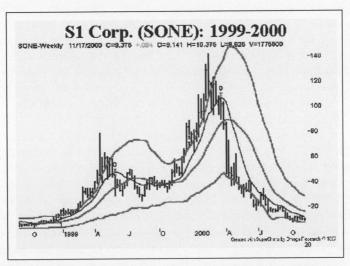

upside Acceleration move; on choppy trading range stocks, this will often be a headfake. I use historical data which I share with subscribers to show which stocks have performed the best (and the worst) based on several entry and exit rules.

5. One close back into the Acceleration Band signals a traditional exit of the trade, as the Acceleration period is now likely to end.

Here are examples of how Acceleration Bands work. First, let us look at the daily chart of CMGI from late 1999 and early 2000 shown in Figure 7.1. An Acceleration Buy signal was given on the second straight close above the upper Acceleration Band on November 18, 1999 at 63.03, with the entry coming at the next morning's open at 63.25. As you can see, this upper Acceleration Band acted as an impressive support on a closing basis, with the stock holding on a closing basis on several key tests, with the stock finally closing under the upper Acceleration Band on December 30, 2000 at 134.41. Therefore, the system's exit signal came on the next morning's opening at 135.25. However, in this case, I used a covered call strategy to lock in profits on this position. At the same time I was able to delay my realized gain of over 100 percent for a few weeks until the next tax year, thus allowing these gains to compound for an extra 12 months before paying the tax man.

Next, let us look at the weekly chart of S1 Corp. (SONE) shown in Figure 7.2, which was among the first to pioneer Internet banking. Not many traders had heard of this stock when I started trading it in 1999, but my Acceleration Bands system showed it had a very strong upside potential with limited risk.

The first Acceleration Buy signal in 1999 occurred on February 19th, with the stock trading at 24.19. The entry the following Monday morning was at 26.38, and the stock managed to surge as high as 79.25. News of a 2-for-1 stock split, which proved to be the short-term top in the shares, was released on April 14th. The official system exit came on the close below the upper Acceleration Band on May 7th at 47.25 (though I had already recommended that subscribers scale out of options positions earlier for a gain of over 100 percent based on my money management rules).

The next Acceleration Buy signal for SONE officially came on December 17, 1999 at a price of 84.00. Due to my concerns about the market in late 1999, I used my market timing to wait and buy the next retest of the upper Acceleration Band, which I thought would prove to be as important a support for SONE as it had been in past Acceleration uptrends. As a result, I recommended that traders place limit orders to buy the stock at 70 or better in early January 2000, which were filled on January 5th. Note that the stock did go below the upper Acceleration Band during the week I purchased it, trading as low as 65. But the stock managed to close out the week around 75, back over the upper band. I call this a "Bend But Don't Break Signal." When the bears take their shot at the stock during the week, getting it under the upper Acceleration Band, then the bulls regain control by the close at the end of the week by finishing the stock back over the upper Acceleration Band, the trend has bent briefly but did not break. This often leads to further acceleration to the upside, as the bears must now run to cover short positions after the failed effort to break the stock.

As I said before, the close is the point on the chart where I determine whether to hold the position or exit. Therefore, on a weekly chart I want to wait until the close at the end of the week, usually on Friday. This takes more patience during the week than most traders are accustomed to, but it often results in being able to stay with the best trades longer than the rest of the crowd. SONE went on to run as high as 142.25, peaking based on a major brokerage firm's new coverage of the stock with a strong buy, with the official exit signal coming on the weekly close below the upper band on February 25th at 99.13. Again, based on my money management exits, my recommended options position managed to gain an average of over 200 percent over the course of less than one month.

On the downside, breaks back under the upper Acceleration Band can often prove to be great shorting points, especially on stocks coming off big prior up moves. In SONE's case, as the Internet bubble burst in March 2000, notice how SONE shares declined sharply as the market's focus turned from market share leaders (often at big losses) to profitability (which hurt the perception of many of these Internet stocks). Thus, Acceleration Bands allow you to trade stocks which many claim to be in bubbles, yet still get you out of these stocks with excellent gains in many cases before the bubble truly bursts.

USING NEWS AS AN EXIT POINT

I often use news that is not earnings-related as a contrarian indicator. One interesting indicator is to watch stocks which are added to the S&P 500 Index. There have been a number of cases of bad timing. Yahoo (YHOO) was added on December 7, 1999, and surged 24 percent that day. However, it hit an all-time high 18 days later and then fell over 85 percent since, as shown in Figure 7.3. Look at another former high flier, JDS Uniphase (JDSU), in Figure 7.4. It went straight down from there, losing over 90 percent after it was added to the S&P 500 Index on July 26, 2000.

A question I am asked a lot is whether value stocks will continue to lead growth stocks going forward. In my work, the distinction is very blurry, as I am looking for stocks that are accelerating, regardless of the growth or value moniker the stock is known for. Take a look at the stock in Figure 7.5, H&R Block (HRB), the tax preparer. Is HRB a growth or a value stock? I do not know about the label, but clearly since the stock broke out above my weekly Acceleration Bands in March 2001, the stock has been an awesome

Figure 7.3   Yahoo (YHOO) added to S&P 500 December 7, 1999

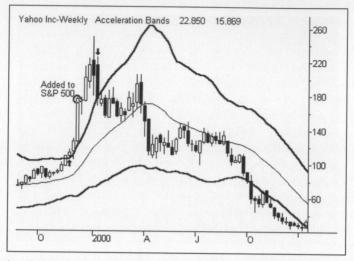

Chart created on TradeStation®, the flagship product of TradeStation Technologies, Inc.

Figure 7.4   JDS Uniphase (JDSU) added to S&P 500 July 26, 2000

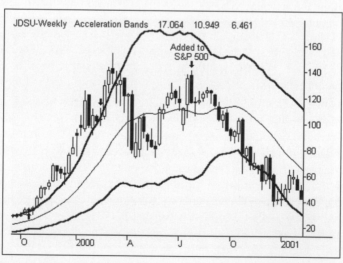

Chart created on TradeStation®, the flagship product of TradeStation Technologies, Inc.

Figure 7.5   H&R Block (HRB): Acceleration Buy March 2001

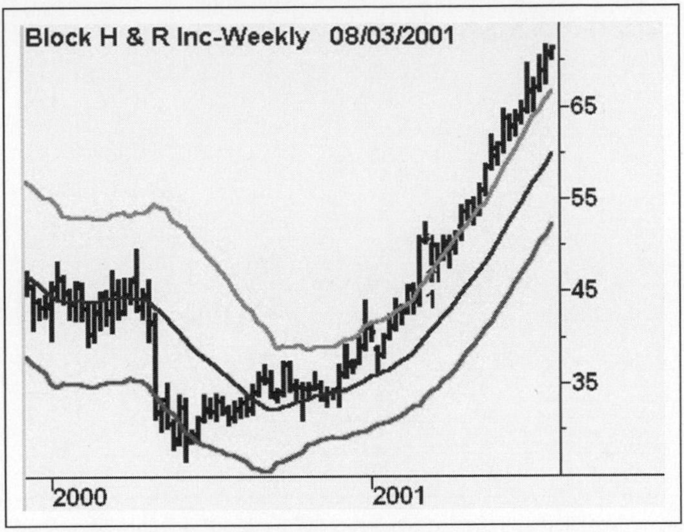

Chart created on TradeStation®, the flagship product of TradeStation Technologies, Inc.

relative performer. And relative outperformance is the secret of this game called investing. My expectation is that the former growth stocks will continue to underperform into October, as few if any of them have favorable Acceleration profiles. I want to be in the stocks showing the next Big Trend potential, and indicators like Acceleration Bands keep you looking forward for future leaders, not backwards at the past leaders. In case you thought the bear market of 2001 could not have possibly seen upside accelerations like we saw in prior years, think again. Figure 7.5 through Figure 7.7 show just a few of the year's big winners.

ACCELERATION BANDS FOR BROADER MARKET TIMING

I like to follow the major market averages using Acceleration Bands, though the major indexes actually tend to act quite differently around the Acceleration Bands in my experience. My favorite trending index is the Russell 2000 Index (RUT), which has spotted outstanding moves using Acceleration Bands (see Figure 7.8 through Figure 7.10).

Another interesting broad market vehicle that has had excellent trending characteristics is the Nasdaq 100 Trust (QQQ) (see Figure 7.11).

In addition, the longer-term monthly charts on broad averages like the Nasdaq Composite and the S&P 500 Index have signaled important breakouts to the upside and the downside (see Figure 7.12 and Figure 7.13).

Figure 7.6 Movie Gallery (MOVI): Acceleration Buy March 2001

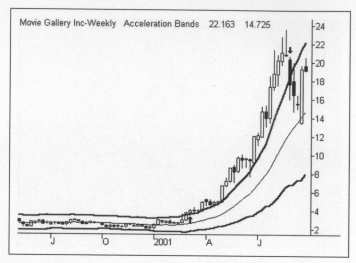

Chart created on TradeStation®, the flagship product of TradeStation Technologies, Inc.

Figure 7.7 Flir Systems (FLIR): Acceleration Buy March 2001

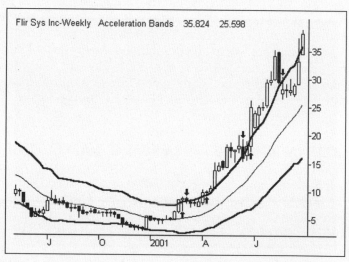

Chart created on TradeStation®, the flagship product of TradeStation Technologies, Inc.

Figure 7.8 Daily Chart of Russell 2000 with Acceleration Bands: March to
September 2001

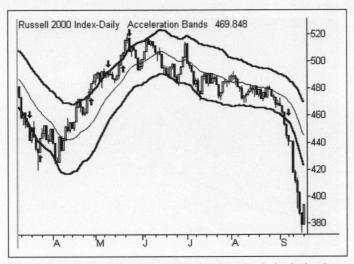

Chart created on TradeStation®, the flagship product of TradeStation Technologies, Inc.

Figure 7.9 Weekly Chart of Russell 2000 with Acceleration Bands: July 1998
to April 2000

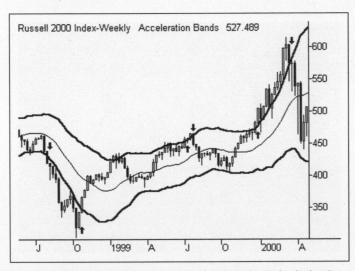

Chart created on TradeStation®, the flagship product of TradeStation Technologies, Inc.

Figure 7.10 Monthly Chart of Russell 2000 with Acceleration Bands: 1993 to 2001

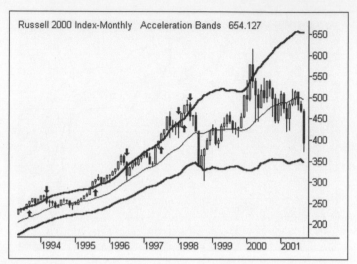

Chart created on TradeStation®, the flagship product of TradeStation Technologies, Inc.

Figure 7.11 Weekly Chart of Nasdaq 100 Trust (QQQ) with Acceleration Bands: 1999 to 2001

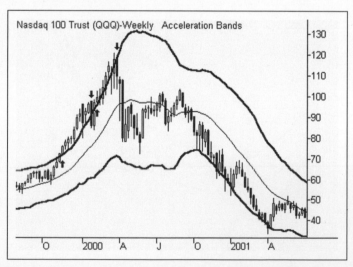

Chart created on TradeStation®, the flagship product of TradeStation Technologies, Inc.

Figure 7.12 Monthly Chart of the Nasdaq Composite with Acceleration Bands: 1990 to 2001

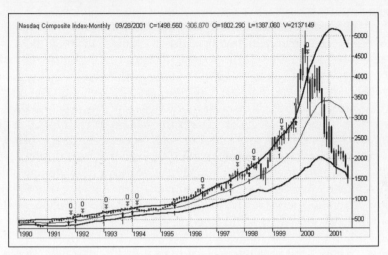

Chart created on TradeStation®, the flagship product of TradeStation Technologies, Inc.

Figure 7.13 Monthly Chart of S&P 500 with Acceleration Bands: 1995 to 2001

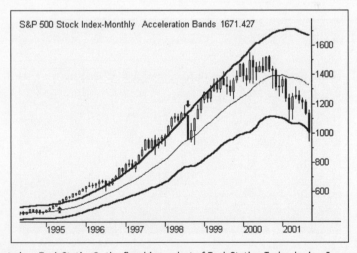

Chart created on TradeStation®, the flagship product of TradeStation Technologies, Inc.

MOVING AVERAGE ENVELOPES—HOW NEW TRENDS BEGIN

Heading into Cisco System's earnings report after the close on August 7, 2001, it was instructive to look at an intermediate-term chart of CSCO's price trend to get an understanding of the stock's technical outlook.

In this weekly chart in Figure 7.14, I plotted a candlestick trend (where light candles indicate a close above the open, while dark candles indicate a weekly close below the open). On the chart I plotted a 20-week simple moving average (the thin line) and around this trendline I plotted a Moving Average Envelope (the upper and lower thick bands). The typical setting I use for Nasdaq stocks is plus and minus 15 percent above and below the 20-period moving average. As an example, if a stock's moving average is at 100, the upper envelope would be at 115 and the lower envelope would be at 85. A Moving Average Envelope is similar to my Acceleration Bands indicator, in that a stock's true breakout occurs with two consecutive closes outside of the envelope, while trading activity between these two envelopes exhibits trading range characteristics.

Notice how CSCO has moved best once it had two straight closes outside its envelopes. This occurred on the upside in late 1999 through March of 2000, while on the downside the second straight close under the lower envelope occurred in December 2000 through May 2001. (The system buys

Figure 7.14   Cisco Systems (CSCO) Weekly Chart with Moving Average Envelope

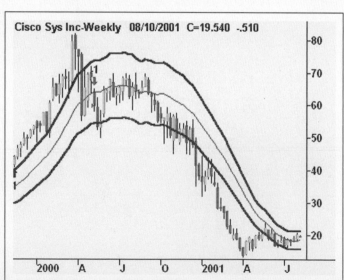

and sells are based on my *Momentum Divergence* indicator, which has historically been very accurate for CSCO.)

Where is the stock now? The stock came close to testing its upper envelope from underneath last week, suggesting CSCO was close to the upper end of its trading range. The envelopes have flattened out, telling us that the intermediate-term downtrend is now moving into a basing pattern. But with the upper band at 21.11 and the lower band at 15.60, I expected to see CSCO trade in-between this range until it saw two consecutive closes outside either of these envelopes. The stock subsequently went on to fail at the upper band near 20 and cruise down to the lower band and below as the market sold off in September 2001.

Headed into Applied Material's (AMAT) earnings report after the close on August 14, 2001 (see Figure 7.15), it is worth a look at an intermediate-term chart of AMAT's price trend to get an understanding of the stock's technical outlook.

Notice how AMAT has moved best once it had two straight closes outside its envelopes. This occurred on the upside in late 1999 through March of 2000, while on the downside the second straight close under the lower envelope occurred in July 2000 and saw a bounce back to the 20-week average as resistance before plummeting further in the second half of 2000.

Figure 7.15   Applied Materials (AMAT) Weekly Chart with Moving Average Envelopes and Acceleration Bands

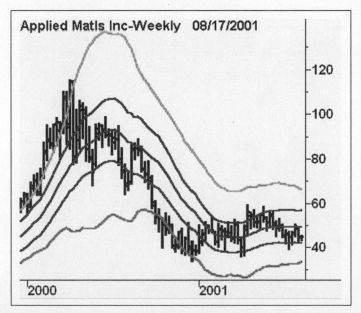

Where did AMAT go? The stock tested its lower envelope from underneath last week, suggesting AMAT is close to the lower end of its trading range. The envelopes had flattened out, telling me that the prior downtrend was now moving into a basing pattern. But with the upper band at 56.82 and the lower band at 42.00, I expected to see AMAT trade in-between this range until the stock saw two consecutive closes outside either of these envelopes. This suggested AMAT has more upside potential than downside risk if the stock stays in a trading range, with a violation of the 42 level the only thing that would call this scenario into question. As it turned out, the 42 level did break, and that was the point where the stock really accelerated to the downside, making a quick run to 35 in only two weeks in September 2001.

Market Timing with Moving Average Envelopes

Heading into the Fed meeting Tuesday, August 21, 2001, it was instructive to look at an intermediate-term chart of the Nasdaq 100 Index Trust (QQQ) and its weekly price trend to get an understanding of the technical outlook for the Nasdaq.

In Figure 7.16, I again plot a 20-week simple moving average (the middle line) and around this trendline I plot the Moving Average Envelope (the

Figure 7.16 Nasdaq 100 Index Trust (QQQ) Weekly Chart with Moving Average Envelope and Acceleration Bands

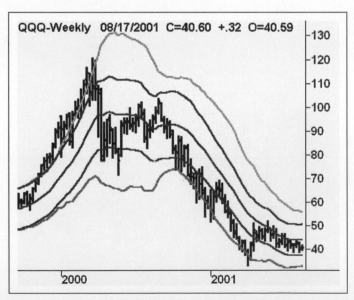

Chart created on TradeStation®, the flagship product of TradeStation Technologies, Inc.

upper and lower bands). Notice how QQQ moved best once it had two straight closes outside its envelopes. This occurred on the upside in late 1999 through March of 2000, while on the downside the second straight close under the lower envelope occurred in July 2000 and saw a bounce back to the 20-week average as resistance before plummeting further in the second half of 2000.

Where were the QQQs in August 2001? The QQQ was in an intermediate-term trading range between its Moving Average Envelopes. The QQQ was closer to the lower envelope, suggesting the market was close to the lower end of the trading range for the Nasdaq. The envelopes flattened out, telling me that the prior downtrend was now moving into a basing pattern. But with the upper band at 50.83 and the lower band at 37.42, I expected to see QQQ trade in-between this range until it saw two consecutive closes above or below either of these envelopes. I noted that a violation of the 37 level would be the only thing that would call this scenario into question. QQQ shares did end up violating the 37 level, and quickly plummeted to the next major support near 30 over the next six weeks.

Longer-Term Timing with Moving Average Envelopes

Let us also look at how the Nasdaq Composite can be timed on a longer-term basis with Moving Average Envelopes. Look at Figure 7.17 through Figure 7.19 to see if you can guess the pattern I was seeing in the Envelopes on these monthly charts of the Nasdaq Composite.

Figure 7.17   Nasdaq Composite Monthly with Moving Average Envelopes: 1973

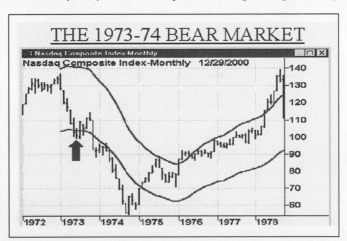

Chart created on TradeStation®, the flagship product of TradeStation Technologies, Inc.

Figure 7.18   Nasdaq Composite Monthly with Moving Average Envelopes: 1987

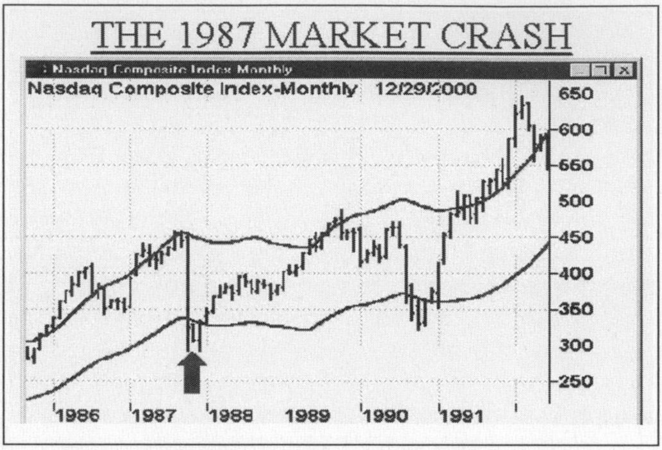

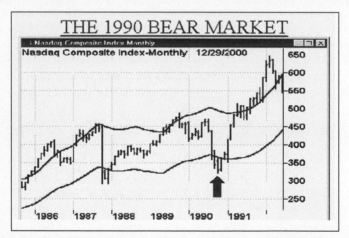

Chart created on TradeStation®, the flagship product of TradeStation Technologies, Inc.

Figure 7.19   Nasdaq Composite Monthly with Moving Average Envelopes: 1990

Chart created on TradeStation®, the flagship product of TradeStation Technologies, Inc.

In each of these cases, the second straight monthly close under the monthly Moving Average Envelope (again, plotted 15 percent below the 20-month simple moving average) had been the closing low for at least a short-term bounce in 1973, and more important market bottoms at the 1987 and 1990 monthly closing lows. So when the Nasdaq recorded a second monthly close in a row under this lower Envelope at the end of December 2000 at 2,470, it suggested to me that the market could see a nice trading rally over

Figure 7.20   Nasdaq Composite Monthly with Moving Average Envelopes: 2000 to 2001

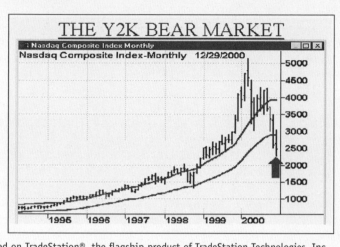

Chart created on TradeStation®, the flagship product of TradeStation Technologies, Inc.

the subsequent four months to the end of April. Why did I think four months initially? Even in the 1973 rally before the more significant decline, the market bounced to its highest high four months later. The first rally leg in late 1987 and early 1988 was basically completed in four months, while 1990 to 1991's first rally leg lasted six months. Even if this bear market in 2000 was to persist in 2001, I did not figure it would happen until after April of 2001 (see Figure 7.20).

So what actually transpired? The market did see a first monster rally effort in January 2001, with the Nasdaq Composite charging as high as 2,892 in the first month, just under the lower band at 2,900. But then conditions changed for the worse. In February the market took a nasty dive, and finished that month at 2,151.83, breaking the low close pattern that had held previously. This is when the pattern that usually worked changed. Subsequently in the next six weeks, the Nasdaq broke to as low as 1,619 and then bounced. But the April bounce did not come close to recovering above the lower Envelope, instead only retesting the prior break point at the 2,150 area but not retaking it on two straight closes. Going forward, the market will need to see two closes over 2,150 to regain confidence, plus eventually retake the lower Envelope, currently at 2,600 and declining, before having a longer-term chance at stabilizing.

TradeStation® EasyLanguage® Code for Moving Average Envelopes:

1. I use a 20-unit simple moving average, with 15 percent plus or minus, for the charts I show.

```
Inputs: HPrice(High), LPrice(Low), Length(20),
PrcntAbv(15), PrcntBlw(15), Displace(0);
Variables: UpperEnvelope(0), LowerEnvelope(0);

UpperEnvelope = AverageFC(HPrice, Length) * (100 +
PrcntAbv) / 100;
LowerEnvelope = AverageFC(LPrice, Length) * (100 -
PrcntBlw) / 100;

If Displace >= 0 OR CurrentBar > AbsValue(Displace) Then
Begin
    Plot1[Displace](UpperEnvelope, "PrcntAbove");
    Plot2[Displace](LowerEnvelope, "PrcntBelow");
```

2. Function Formula for "AverageFC".

```
Inputs: Price(NumericSeries), Length(NumericSimple);
Variables: Sum(0), Counter(0);

If CurrentBar = 1 Then Begin
    Sum = 0;
    For counter = 0 To Length - 1     Begin
        Sum = Sum + Price[counter];
    End;
End
Else
    Sum = Sum + Price - Price[Length];

If Length > 0 Then
    AverageFC = Sum / Length
Else
    AverageFC = 0;

{Force Series Function}
If False Then
    value1 = AverageFC[1];
```

In summary, both Acceleration Bands and Moving Average Envelopes give you the tools to determine specific price levels where a stock is breaking outside of these bands. This allows you to find the best trending stocks outside of these bands, instead of getting distracted by relative nonmovers that are stuck in-between these envelopes.

8

MOMENTUM DIVERGENCES—WHEN TO TAKE OR AVOID STOCK PRICE BREAKOUTS

The concept of "divergence" has always intrigued me, since the idea that an indicator could be forecasting a coming trend reversal has already been reinforced by my sentiment indicators, which tend to lead price action. In the same way, my years of studying divergence theories found many cases where divergence simply resulted in trouble by betting on a trend reversal too quickly. Divergence provides the greatest opportunity of any technically-based indicator to offer you the most potential from a coming trend move, but it also has the greatest potential to get you in against a trend and get stuck riding that trend in the opposite direction.

Before we get to momentum divergences, let us first explain a popular momentum indicator. I first started to notice many divergences from price action in the popular Moving Average Convergence Divergence (MACD), which is one of the best indicators for spotting important turning points in market momentum. Developed by Gerald Appel of Signalert Corporation, MACD shows when momentum is starting to weaken and roll over at the end of uptrends, while showing where bottoms are likely to occur when MACD starts to turn up.

MACD is made up of several components: a short-term (also known as "fast" since it will adjust to more recent price action more quickly) Exponential Moving Average (EMA), a longer ("slow") Exponential Moving Average, and an exponential moving average of a defined number of recent MACD readings, plus a measurement known as the "MACD Histogram" which measures the daily difference between the slow and fast EMAs (if the fast EMA is above the slow EMA, the Histogram will be positive).

The most common settings are 12 periods for the fast EMA, 26 periods for the slow EMA, and 9 periods for the average of the last nine days of the 12 to 26 EMA differential.

Figure 8.1 shows a MACD example. The top half of the chart shows Microsoft's (MSFT) daily price action, with a 12-day exponential moving average plotted in black, along with a 26-day exponential moving average

Figure 8.1   Microsoft (MSFT) with Daily MACD: February to June 2001

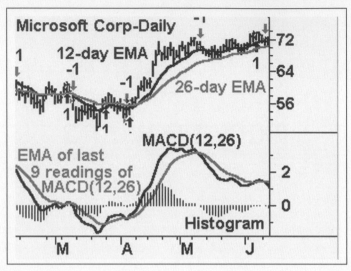

Chart created on TradeStation®, the flagship product of TradeStation Technologies, Inc.

plotted in gray. The bottom half of the chart shows the MACD indicator. The black line is the daily plot of the difference between the 12-day and 26-day moving averages in the upper part of the chart, plotted as a line. The gray line in the bottom half of the chart is the exponential moving average (EMA) of the last nine days of readings on the black line. The Histogram plots the difference between the lower black and gray lines, against an axis of zero. This means that when the lower black line is above the lower gray line, the Histogram of this difference will be positive, or above zero. In contrast, when the daily MACD (12,26) differential (black line) is less than the average of the last nine days' differential (gray line), the Histogram is then negative, or less than zero.

Traditionally, buy signals occur on a crossover of the Histogram from under zero to positive (meaning the lower black line crosses above the lower gray line). These show up as black arrows pointing upward to buy MSFT on the upper half of the chart. In contrast, sell signals occur when the daily MACD (12,26) differential (gray line in lower chart) crosses below the last nine-day average (the lower gray line). This shows up in the upper half of the chart as gray downward arrows, showing sell points in Microsoft.

At the same time, an observation of the charts brings up other ideas one could look for to still further improve performance of the traditional MACD system. There are many new ideas one could test, including putting time stops on positions (as with most systems, the best trades tend to be right very quickly like the MSFT buy on April 5th at 56.75—if a position is not

Figure 8.2 Microsoft (MSFT) Daily Chart with Bullish and Bearish MACD Divergences

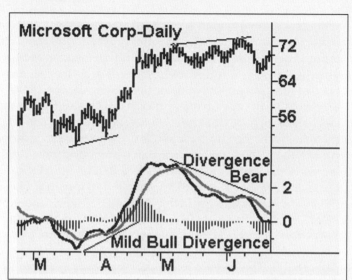

Chart created on TradeStation®, the flagship product of TradeStation Technologies, Inc.

profitable in three to five trading days, it often makes sense to close non-performers quickly and move on to other opportunities). Another angle on this is waiting for three sessions and then putting on trades if they are winners. This will serve to leave some money on the table on winners but still get on board good trades, while improving your winning percentage and minimizing your drawdown risk on those trades that are bad signals from the start, like the March 7th and March 26th buy signals. But perhaps the most effective indicator I have found to complement MACD analysis is to look for divergences between the price action and the MACD chart.

MOMENTUM DIVERGENCES

Momentum tends to precede a price high. We look for divergences or confirmation of the price move by tracking a momentum indicator like MACD and then comparing it to the price action. The traditional way a technical analyst looks for divergences is to draw trendlines from significant low points or significant high points on the price chart, and then comparing the slope of those trendlines to the slope of the corresponding momentum indicator between those same points in time.

In Figure 8.2, you will notice two trendlines in the case of Microsoft's (MSFT) daily price action: one slightly upsloped dotted line, connecting the

March and April lows, and one line that connects the highs in May and June. When I draw corresponding trendlines on the MACD itself (the light straight lines in the bottom half of the chart), I notice divergences start to develop. A bullish divergence shapes up in early April, since the MACD trendline is more dramatically upsloped off the secondary low in the stock than the stock trendline is at that time. This suggests underlying momentum is picking up dramatically, even if the stock price still appears lackluster. This highlights one of the key benefits of divergence analysis: it is clearly a leading indicator, which will pick up impending major market moves in a surprisingly high percentage of situations. At the same time, it can sometimes be too early, so a divergence trader must know where to place stops.

You can see the bearish divergence that occurs as drawn by the lines ending in June. In the upper chart of the price action, MSFT's stock price makes a new high in early June near 75, compared to the prior high in early May near 72.50. Despite this new high, the corresponding momentum as measured by MACD shows a significantly lower high, resulting in a downtrending momentum line. As a result, this breakout in the stock price is not supported by momentum, causing a bearish divergence which suggests the stock is likely to fall. This occurs as the stock breaks back under 72 and heads to the 66 level over the next week.

One of the challenges of the MACD indicator is that it plots MACD levels relative to the stock's price. This means that, all things being equal, a higher-priced stock will have a higher MACD reading than a lower-priced stock, even if they have the same pattern. Yet as an analyst, I consistently want to compare apples to apples, and for the exact same pattern, I consistently want the same reading of the strength or weakness inherent in that pattern, across all stocks.

As a result, I created the Momentum Divergence indicator, which normalizes momentum readings across all stocks between 0 and 100 (with 0 showing the weakest momentum and 100 showing the strongest momentum). The Momentum line is shown in gray in the lower two indicators. The strength of the Price is also plotted in from 0 to 100. The lowest indicator plotted is an intermediate-term divergence time frame of 40 bars, while the divergence above that is a shorter-term divergence of 15 bars.

What you can see from the chart in Figure 8.3 is the following:

1. Momentum is clearly strengthening in late March in MSFT. In the intermediate-term MACD-Divergence (at the very bottom of the chart), the blue Momentum line turns up in the third week of March from the zero line. While the price action has not caught up yet, it should soon, as momentum is a leading indicator. The break above the 30th percentile line in both readings (the lower horizontal line in each of the Momentum Divergence charts) is the trigger to suggest that momentum is confirmed to the upside.

Figure 8.3 Microsoft (MSFT) Daily Chart with Momentum Divergences

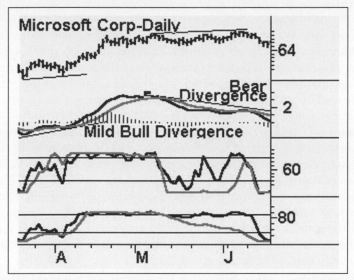

Chart created on TradeStation®, the flagship product of TradeStation Technologies, Inc.

2. Similarly, momentum is weakening after the first week of May in MSFT—both the short-term and, more importantly, the intermediate-term momentum lines are breaking down. The break under the 90th percentile line in both readings (the upper horizontal line in each plot of the Momentum Divergence indicator) signifies a downturn in momentum, and price action should soon weaken.

   In this case, MSFT flattens out more than declining. However, this information is still useful to know in that the stock's upside potential is limited versus an increased probability of short-term downside risk or sideways price action. How? An owner of MSFT shares could use this indicator to determine that it is an excellent time to sell Covered Calls (discussed in Chapter 11). This would allow the MSFT shareholder to collect additional income, although the stock was going nowhere until momentum turned back up.

3. The intermediate-term filter helps avoid short-term whipsaws from the shorter-term indicator—the short-term momentum line will jump under 90 percent or above 30 percent more quickly, while the intermediate-term indicator's turns above 30 percent or below 90 percent screen out some of the short-term momentum indicator's false signals. I am a big fan of using multiple time frames to help smooth out noise, and that certainly proves to be the case here.

Moving back to my initial divergence concept, when the Momentum line has turned up but the Price trend falls underneath the momentum line, this creates a Bullish Divergence. You can see this in early April for MSFT, especially in the short-term Momentum Divergence indicator and mildly in the intermediate-term indicator, as the gray Momentum line is moving higher but the Price line falls off quickly in early April, creating the noticeable Bullish Divergence.

In contrast, when the Momentum line moves down but the Price line moves higher above the Momentum line, then a Bearish Divergence forms. This occurs in mid-May and persists for several weeks before the stock finally sees a serious sell-off. That is where the Momentum Divergence indicator can really help traders versus traditional divergence analysis. Usually a trader who has traded using divergences may get in too early, before the Price finally starts to roll over to catch up with the divergence. In this case, once the intermediate-term Divergence line crossed under the 30 percent threshold, and the Price line in black went from above 90 percent to back under 90 percent, it showed that the price action could now quickly catch up on the downside. That is what happened, as over the next week MSFT shares nearly saw a 10 percent correction.

TradeStation® Easy Language® Code for Momentum Divergence Indicator:

```
(with setting = 15 bars; 40 bars is intermediate-term
setting)

Input:FastMA(12),SlowMA(26),MacdMA(9),Input2(15),BuyZone
(30),SellZone(90);

Value1=IFF(Highest(MACD(Close,FastMA,SlowMA),Input2) -
Lowest(MACD(Close,FastMA,SlowMA),Input2)<>0,Highest
(MACD(Close,FastMA,
SlowMA),Input2) - Lowest(MACD(Close,FastMA,SlowMA),In-
put2),50);

Value2=IFF(Highest(close,Input2) - Lowest(close,In-
put2)<>0,Highest(close,Input2) - Lowest(close,In-
put2),50);

Plot1(100*(close-Lowest(close,Input2))/Value2,"Close%");

Plot2(100*(MACD(Close,FastMA,SlowMA) -
Lowest(MACD(Close,FastMA,SlowMA),Input2))/Value1,"MACD%");

Plot3(BuyZone, "BuyZone");

Plot4(SellZone, "SellZone");
```

INTRADAY CHART PATTERNS USING MOMENTUM DIVERGENCES

Siebel Systems (SEBL) gave a Bearish Momentum Divergence signal below its intraday Acceleration Bands on the 15-minute chart on September 17, 2001. In Figure 8.4, notice how SEBL broke down under 18.00 just after the MACD made a lower high. This was picked up in the MACD-Divergence indicator over both the 15- and 40-period time frames, as the price reversal on the last 15-minute bar sent the Price component of the MACD-Divergence broke to the 0th percentile in both cases (the darker line on the third and fourth charts). This suggested that price would now carry the weakening Momentum line via a downside move. This move was considered complete when SEBL shares closed back above the lower Acceleration Band at the end of the trading day on September 19, 2001.

When Siebel Systems (SEBL) broke under its lower Acceleration Band on the 15-minute chart, combined with the Bearish Momentum Divergence signal, this was a particularly potent combination for a fierce downtrend over the next two sessions, as seen in Figure 8.4 and Figure 8.5.

As you can see, volatile but trending stocks like SEBL offer excellent opportunities to capture gains on the upside and the downside. So while tech stocks did a round trip to the moon and then crashed back to earth, the Momentum Divergence indicator allowed you to capture healthy profits on both sides of the market. What I like best is the relatively low drawdowns

Figure 8.4   Siebel Systems (SEBL) 15-Minute Charts with Bearish Momentum Divergence: September 2001

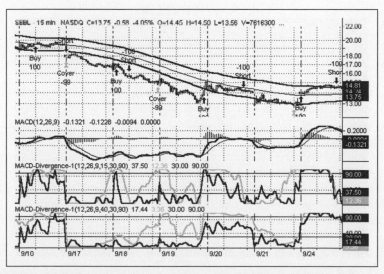

Chart created on TradeStation®, the flagship product of TradeStation Technologies, Inc.

Figure 8.5   Performance Summary—Siebel Systems (SEBL) 15-Minute
Momentum Divergence

TradeStation Strategy Performance Report - MACD-Divergence-4 SEBL-15 min (11/6/00·

Performance Summary: All Trades

Total Net Profit	$19,549.68	Open position P/L	$92.00
Gross Profit	$37,837.86	Gross Loss	($18,288.18)
Total # of trades	207	Percent profitable	52.66%
Number winning trades	109	Number losing trades	98
Largest winning trade	$2,019.37	Largest losing trade	($807.00)
Average winning trade	$347.14	Average losing trade	($186.61)
Ratio avg win/avg loss	1.86	Avg trade (win & loss)	$94.44
Max consec. Winners	5	Max consec. losers	5
Avg # bars in winners	37	Avg # bars in losers	16
Max intraday drawdown	($1,889.00)		
Profit Factor	2.07	Max # contracts held	100

Chart created on TradeStation®, the flagship product of TradeStation Technologies, Inc.

in this system. You can see that SEBL made nine times the total profit of its maximum intraday drawdown. Those are exciting numbers for short-term traders to find big trends in both bull and bear phases.

COMBINING MOMENTUM DIVERGENCE WITH MOVING AVERAGE ENVELOPES

Some really powerful combinations start to develop when these individual indicators are merged into one framework. What happens when I merge the idea of Momentum Divergence, where both momentum and price strength move above 90 percent, with the requirement that the stock closes above its upper Moving Average Envelope? The fireworks really get started then. Let us look at some examples in Figure 8.6 through Figure 8.25.

As you can see, the Momentum Divergence concept has great potential to either confirm a move as a breakout or as a fakeout. Knowing the difference is the critical factor that separates trend analysts from the rest of the herd that simply follows price action by looking for these important confirmation signals. Adding the Moving Average Envelope as an additional filter in combination with Momentum Divergence screens out additional noise, allowing you to focus your energy and your capital on those stocks with the greatest potential for truly massive trends.

Figure 8.6 Iomega (IOM) Weekly 1995 to 1996

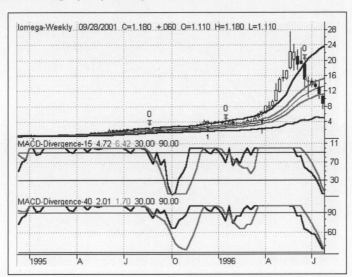

Chart created on TradeStation®, the flagship product of TradeStation Technologies, Inc.

Figure 8.7 Performance Summary—Iomega (IOM) Weekly 1992 to 1996

MACD-DivergTrendBul2 Iomega-Weekly 01/03/1992 - 12/27/1996			
Performance Summary: All Trades			
Total net profit	$ 37.03	Open position P/L	$ 0.00
Gross profit	$ 51.91	Gross loss	$ -14.88
Total # of trades	6	Percent profitable	50%
Number winning trades	3	Number losing trades	3
Largest winning trade	$ 43.28	Largest losing trade	$ -11.88
Average winning trade	$ 17.30	Average losing trade	$ -4.96
Ratio avg win/avg loss	3.49	Avg trade(win & loss)	$ 6.17
Max consec. winners	2	Max consec. losers	1
Avg # bars in winners	19	Avg # bars in losers	3
Max intraday drawdown	$ -12.83		
Profit factor	3.49	Max # contracts held	1

Chart created on TradeStation®, the flagship product of TradeStation Technologies, Inc.

Iomega (IOM) was a controversial stock in 1995 and 1996, as the portable disk drive maker attracted many shortsellers who believed the stock was overpriced. The combination of bullish momentum divergence and an upside breakout above the weekly moving average envelopes said the trend was up in the first seven months of 1995 and the second quarter of 1996.

Figure 8.8 America Online Weekly 1998 to 2000

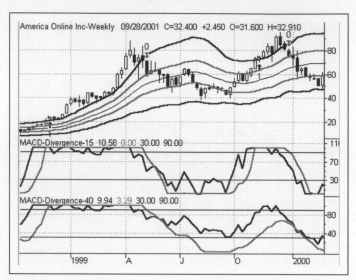

Chart created on TradeStation®, the flagship product of TradeStation Technologies, Inc.

Figure 8.9 Performance Summary—America Online Weekly 1992 to 2001

MACD-DivergTrendBul2 America Online Inc-Weekly 03/20/1992 - 12/07/2001

Performance Summary: All Trades

Total net profit	$ 39.48	Open position P/L	$ 0.00
Gross profit	$ 42.64	Gross loss	$ -3.16
Total # of trades	15	Percent profitable	67%
Number winning trades	10	Number losing trades	5
Largest winning trade	$ 35.37	Largest losing trade	$ -1.95
Average winning trade	$ 4.26	Average losing trade	$ -0.63
Ratio avg win/avg loss	6.75	Avg trade(win & loss)	$ 2.63
Max consec. winners	4	Max consec. losers	2
Avg # bars in winners	14	Avg # bars in losers	2
Max intraday drawdown	$ -4.02		
Profit factor	13.50	Max # contracts held	1

Chart created on TradeStation®, the flagship product of TradeStation Technologies, Inc.

America Online (AOL) gave a bullish momentum divergence and moving average envelope buy signal in November 1998 for more than a 100 percent gain through May 1999. A similar upside breakout in November 1999 started well but was then closed for a slight gain before AOL and fellow Internet stocks went into a deeper correction in 2000.

Figure 8.10 Microsoft Monthly 1990 to 2001

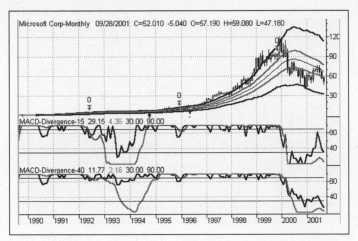

Chart created on TradeStation®, the flagship product of TradeStation Technologies, Inc.

Figure 8.11 Performance Summary—Microsoft Monthly 1986 to 2001

MACD-DivergTrendBul2 Microsoft Corp-Monthly 03/31/1986 - 09/28/2001			
Performance Summary: All Trades			
Total net profit	$ 82.48	Open position P/L	$ 0.00
Gross profit	$ 82.48	Gross loss	$ 0.00
Total # of trades	3	Percent profitable	100%
Number winning trades	3	Number losing trades	0
Largest winning trade	$ 76.22	Largest losing trade	$ 0.00
Average winning trade	$ 27.49	Average losing trade	$ 0.00
Ratio avg win/avg loss	100.00	Avg trade(win & loss)	$ 27.49
Max consec. winners	3	Max consec. losers	0
Avg # bars in winners	29	Avg # bars in losers	0
Max intraday drawdown	$ -1.41		
Profit factor	100.00	Max # contracts held	1

Chart created on TradeStation®, the flagship product of TradeStation Technologies, Inc.

Microsoft (MSFT) gave 3 bullish buy signals on the monthly chart in the last fifteen years, based on the bullish momentum divergence and moving average envelope filters. Most impressive was the early-1996 buy and subsequent October 1999 exit, which spared MSFT stock owners the carnage of 2000.

Figure 8.12   Dell Monthly 1995 to 2001

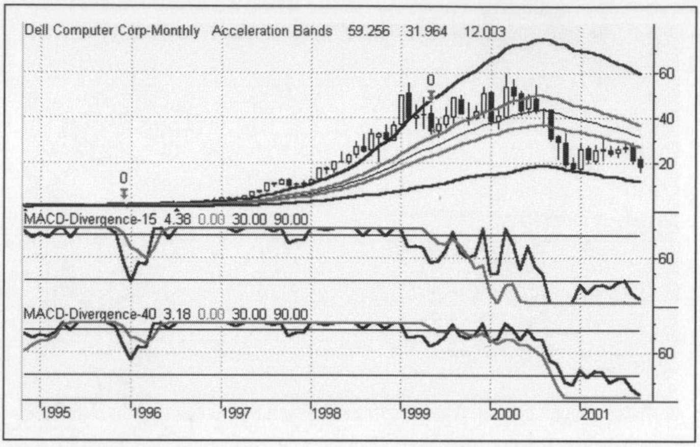

Chart created on TradeStation®, the flagship product of TradeStation Technologies, Inc.

Figure 8.13   Performance Summary—Dell Monthly 1988 to 2001

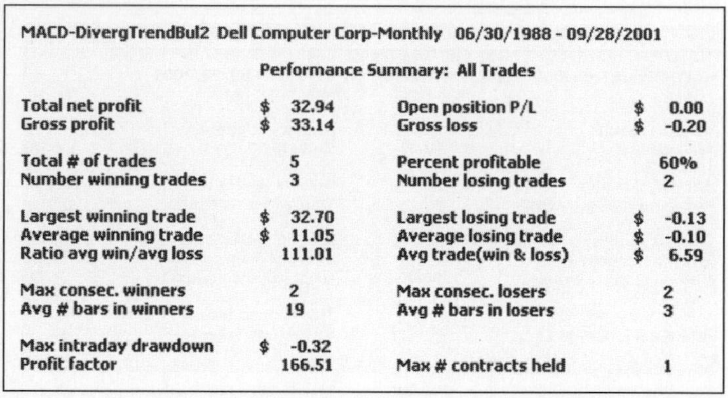

MACD-DivergTrendBul2 Dell Computer Corp-Monthly 06/30/1988 - 09/28/2001

Performance Summary: All Trades

Total net profit	$ 32.94	Open position P/L	$ 0.00
Gross profit	$ 33.14	Gross loss	$ -0.20
Total # of trades	5	Percent profitable	60%
Number winning trades	3	Number losing trades	2
Largest winning trade	$ 32.70	Largest losing trade	$ -0.13
Average winning trade	$ 11.05	Average losing trade	$ -0.10
Ratio avg win/avg loss	111.01	Avg trade(win & loss)	$ 6.59
Max consec. winners	2	Max consec. losers	2
Avg # bars in winners	19	Avg # bars in losers	3
Max intraday drawdown	$ -0.32		
Profit factor	166.51	Max # contracts held	1

Chart created on TradeStation®, the flagship product of TradeStation Technologies, Inc.

Leading computer maker Dell computer (DELL) gave a monthly buy signal in the middle of 1996 with Dell shares under 5. The stock went on to soar seven-fold through the May 1999 exit. Interestingly, while some upside was missed over the next year, the subsequent decline 15 points under the signal's exit point saved DELL followers from giving back too much of their profits.

Figure 8.14   Yahoo Weekly 1998 to 2000

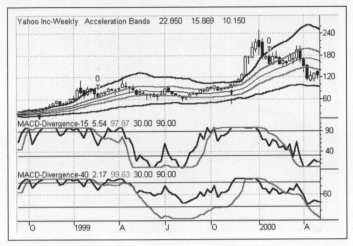

Chart created on TradeStation®, the flagship product of TradeStation Technologies, Inc.

Figure 8.15   Performance Summary—Yahoo Weekly 1996 to 2000

MACD-DivergTrendBul2 Yahoo Inc-Weekly 04/12/1996 - 09/28/2001			
Performance Summary: All Trades			
Total net profit	$ 98.14	Open position P/L	$ 0.00
Gross profit	$ 100.74	Gross loss	$ -2.60
Total # of trades	6	Percent profitable	67%
Number winning trades	4	Number losing trades	2
Largest winning trade	$ 58.28	Largest losing trade	$ -2.05
Average winning trade	$ 25.19	Average losing trade	$ -1.30
Ratio avg win/avg loss	19.34	Avg trade(win & loss)	$ 16.36
Max consec. winners	2	Max consec. losers	1
Avg # bars in winners	13	Avg # bars in losers	6
Max intraday drawdown	$ -3.07		
Profit factor	38.69	Max # contracts held	1

Chart created on TradeStation®, the flagship product of TradeStation Technologies, Inc.

Yahoo (YHOO) gave two impressive weekly buy signals while Internet stocks were still heating up. YHOO tripled on a momentum divergence and moving average envelope buy from October 1998 through February 1999. YHOO shares rose over 150 percent on a November 1999 buy signal at their peak in January 2000 while the actual exit still captures a gain over 60 percent.

Figure 8.16　Qualcomm Weekly 1999 to 2000

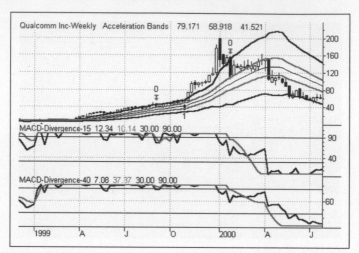

Chart created on TradeStation®, the flagship product of TradeStation Technologies, Inc.

Figure 8.17　Performance Summary—Qualcomm Weekly 1996 to 2001

MACD-DivergTrendBul2 Qualcomm Inc-Weekly 10/04/1996 - 09/28/2001			
Performance Summary: All Trades			
Total net profit	$ 86.08	Open position P/L	$ 0.00
Gross profit	$ 89.49	Gross loss	$ -3.41
Total # of trades	5	Percent profitable	60%
Number winning trades	3	Number losing trades	2
Largest winning trade	$ 54.88	Largest losing trade	$ -2.39
Average winning trade	$ 29.83	Average losing trade	$ -1.70
Ratio avg win/avg loss	17.51	Avg trade(win & loss)	$ 17.22
Max consec. winners	3	Max consec. losers	2
Avg # bars in winners	19	Avg # bars in losers	4
Max intraday drawdown	$ -16.81		
Profit factor	26.27	Max # contracts held	1

Chart created on TradeStation®, the flagship product of TradeStation Technologies, Inc.

Qualcomm (QCOM) and its CDMA technology to become the standard for cell phones, was the big story of 1999. We received two buy signals on QCOM in 1999, with a January buy signal exited in August for an eight-fold gain, while an October buy signal resulted in a double to the end of January 2000.

Figure 8.18   CMGI Weekly 1999 to 2000

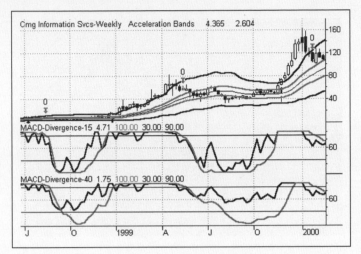

Chart created on TradeStation®, the flagship product of TradeStation Technologies, Inc.

Figure 8.19   Performance Summary—CMGI Weekly 1999 to 2001

MACD-DivergTrendBul2 Cmg Information Svcs-Weekly 03/04/1994 - 09/28/2001			
Performance Summary: All Trades			
Total net profit	$ 78.01	Open position P/L	$ 0.00
Gross profit	$ 78.33	Gross loss	$ -0.32
Total # of trades	10	Percent profitable	70%
Number winning trades	7	Number losing trades	3
Largest winning trade	$ 42.16	Largest losing trade	$ -0.20
Average winning trade	$ 11.19	Average losing trade	$ -0.11
Ratio avg win/avg loss	104.58	Avg trade(win & loss)	$ 7.80
Max consec. winners	5	Max consec. losers	2
Avg # bars in winners	12	Avg # bars in losers	5
Max intraday drawdown	$ -2.11		
Profit factor	244.03	Max # contracts held	1

Chart created on TradeStation®, the flagship product of TradeStation Technologies, Inc.

CMGI was a popular Internet stock, as the company planned to cash in on many Internet investments as the Internet took off. The buy signal of December 1998 resulted in more than a five-fold gain by May 1999. A December 1999 buy signal more than doubled before the stock was exited in late January 2000 for a 40 percent gain.

Figure 8.20   S1 Corp. Weekly 1999 to 2000

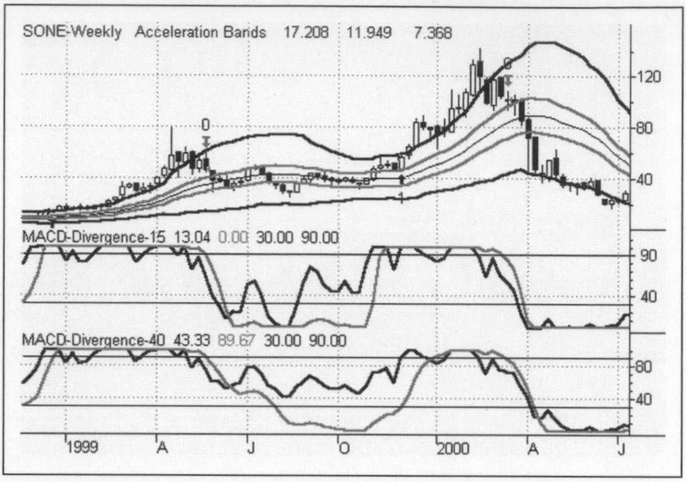

Chart created on TradeStation®, the flagship product of TradeStation Technologies, Inc.

Figure 8.21   Performance Summary—S1 Corp. Weekly 1996 to 2001

MACD-DivergTrendBul2 SONE-Weekly 05/24/1996 - 09/28/2001

Performance Summary: All Trades

Total net profit	$	75.81	Open position P/L	$ 0.00
Gross profit	$	77.69	Gross loss	$ -1.88
Total # of trades		5	Percent profitable	40%
Number winning trades		2	Number losing trades	3
Largest winning trade	$	45.25	Largest losing trade	$ -0.88
Average winning trade	$	38.84	Average losing trade	$ -0.63
Ratio avg win/avg loss		62.15	Avg trade(win & loss)	$ 15.16
Max consec. winners		2	Max consec. losers	3
Avg # bars in winners		19	Avg # bars in losers	5
Max intraday drawdown	$	-2.13		
Profit factor		41.43	Max # contracts held	1

Chart created on TradeStation®, the flagship product of TradeStation Technologies, Inc.

S1 Corp. (SONE), an early leader in Internet banking, gave two impressive buy signals during the Internet gold rush. In December 1998 the stock rose five-fold through its May 1999 exit. On its next run, a November 1999 bullish signal resulted in a double in SONE shares through its March 2000 exit.

Figure 8.22 Qualcomm Daily 2001

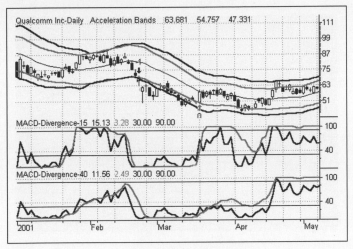

Chart created on TradeStation®, the flagship product of TradeStation Technologies, Inc.

Figure 8.23 Performance Summary—Qualcomm Daily 1996 to 2001

MACD-DivergTrendBear Qualcomm Inc-Daily 10/02/1996 - 09/24/2001			
Performance Summary: All Trades			
Total net profit	$ -18.73	Open position P/L	$ 0.00
Gross profit	$ 11.00	Gross loss	$ -29.73
Total # of trades	7	Percent profitable	43%
Number winning trades	3	Number losing trades	4
Largest winning trade	$ 8.75	Largest losing trade	$ -17.44
Average winning trade	$ 3.67	Average losing trade	$ -7.43
Ratio avg win/avg loss	0.49	Avg trade(win & loss)	$ -2.68
Max consec. winners	2	Max consec. losers	3
Avg # bars in winners	11	Avg # bars in losers	7
Max intraday drawdown	$ -38.16		
Profit factor	0.37	Max # contracts held	1

Chart created on TradeStation®, the flagship product of TradeStation Technologies, Inc.

Bearish signals in the combined momentum divergence and moving average envelopes can also be effective. Qualcomm (QCOM) gave a bearish sell signal in late February 2000 at 65 and the stock ran down under 50 in 12 trading days before giving the official exit at 57.

Figure 8.24   S1 Corp. Daily 2000

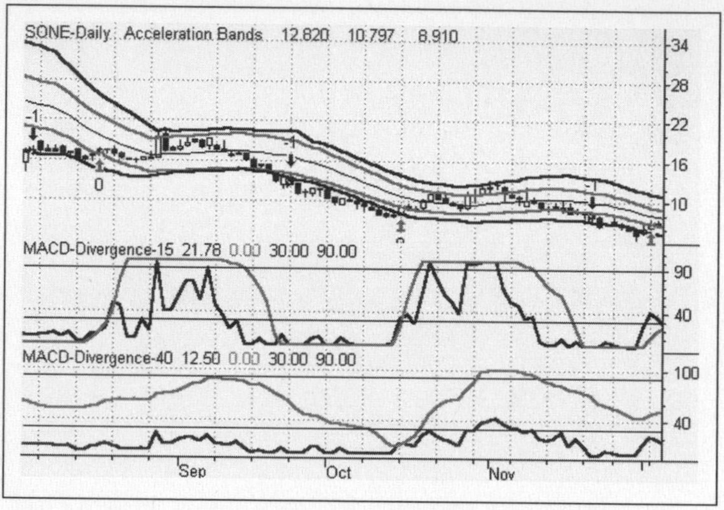

Chart created on TradeStation®, the flagship product of TradeStation Technologies, Inc.

Figure 8.25   Performance Summary—S1 Corp. Daily 1996 to 2001

MACD-DivergTrendBear SONE-Daily 05/23/1996 - 09/24/2001

Performance Summary: All Trades

Total net profit	$ 39.28	Open position P/L	$ 0.00
Gross profit	$ 52.47	Gross loss	$ -13.19
Total # of trades	15	Percent profitable	40%
Number winning trades	6	Number losing trades	9
Largest winning trade	$ 36.88	Largest losing trade	$ -5.56
Average winning trade	$ 8.74	Average losing trade	$ -1.47
Ratio avg win/avg loss	5.97	Avg trade(win & loss)	$ 2.62
Max consec. winners	3	Max consec. losers	6
Avg # bars in winners	16	Avg # bars in losers	6
Max intraday drawdown	$ -7.31		
Profit factor	3.98	Max # contracts held	1

Chart created on TradeStation®, the flagship product of TradeStation Technologies, Inc.

S1 Corp. (SONE) also gave a nice short-term bearish signal in September 2000. The stock's breakdown under the lower moving average envelope combined with the bearish momentum divergence as information resulted in a steady downtrend in SONE shares from 13 to 9 in 15 trading days.

In conclusion, momentum divergence signals can be effective as a confirmation to other indicators, which are signalling technical breakouts. In particular, the combination of momentum divergence analysis with moving average envelopes offers excellent reward-to-risk ratios across a variety of time horizons. We will now examine another technical indicator to keep you focused on the best performing stocks, using relative strength.

9

RELATIVE STRENGTH—YOUR KEY TO MAXIMIZING THE BANG FOR YOUR BUCK

If someone offered you the ability to make 20 percent per year on your money, would you take it? When I ask this question, most hands usually go up, as investors know the challenge of getting 20 percent on their money consistently over time. However, I personally consider the answer to be very dependent on what my other investment alternatives are. If another investment is producing 30 percent annualized, then the answer on the 20 percent per year scenario is clearly "No." The 10 percentage points you would leave on the table if you held the lesser-performing asset is known as the opportunity cost that was lost. Most traders and investors tend to get stuck thinking about a stock they have purchased in absolute terms: Is the stock up or down from where I bought it? I encourage you to shift your frame of reference from an absolute form to a more relative form: Is the stock outperforming most of the other stocks where I could put my money instead?

An indicator you can use to gauge the stock's level of outperformance or underperformance is Relative Strength. I track the Relative Strength of a stock versus a broad market index (usually the Nasdaq Composite or the S&P 500 Index). You can also track the Relative Strength of any two investment vehicles, including a sector against the broader market, one sector versus another sector, a stock against its relevant sector, and a comparison of the relative performance between any two stocks, either in the same sector or in different industry groups. As you can see, Relative Strength gives you many possibilities to explore to find the best-performing assets.

The Relative Strength (RS) indicator (not to be confused with the Relative Strength Index, which is an oscillator that looks for overbought and oversold stocks) generates a relative performance line, which tends to be very volatile. As a result, I prefer to smooth the RS line with moving averages. I use the 5, 10, 20, and 50-day simple moving average of the RS line, and then look for crossovers of these trendlines to give new buy or sell signals. Let us look at the ways you can use the RS indicator to find top performers about to move into major uptrends or downtrends.

Figure 9.1   Weekly Chart Qualcomm (QCOM): 1996 to 1998

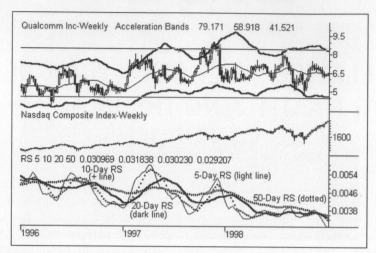

Chart created on TradeStation®, the flagship product of TradeStation Technologies, Inc.

Let us start with a review of past RS patterns on the big winners from the 1990s. Qualcomm (QCOM) was not a big winner until 1999. If you look back at the prior several years for QCOM, the stock was in a trading range while the Nasdaq was going up from 1996 through 1998. As a result, QCOM's RS trend was actually downtrending, since flat performance versus a rising market signals an underperformer, as we see in Figure 9.1.

The RS performance lines are plotted on the bottom of Figure 9.1. The 5-period simple moving average is shown as the light line, which is the most volatile of these smoothed lines. The 10-unit line is shown with pluses (+), the 20-period line is shown as the dark solid line, and the 50-unit line is plotted as a dotted line. Overall, you can see the stock's relative performance was headed in a slow but steady downtrend compared to the Nasdaq Composite between 1996 and 1998. QCOM was trading in a range between 4.50 and just under 9 over these three years. Let us say that you were able to buy QCOM at 4.5 and sell it at 9, making 100 percent per year over each of these three years. Now compare those best-case gains to the impact when you see the stock breakout to the upside in Figure 9.2.

In Figure 9.2 the RS indicator effectively signals the new outperformance cycle for QCOM in early 1999. The ideal conditions occur when the faster moving averages are above their slower counterparts, signaling a significant upturn in relative performance. In this case we want to see the 5-week RS line above the 10-week RS line, which is above the 20-week RS line, and the 20-week RS line should also be above the 50-week RS line. In this example the 20-week RS line is last to move in line, and when it does

Figure 9.2 Weekly Chart Qualcomm (QCOM): February to April 1999

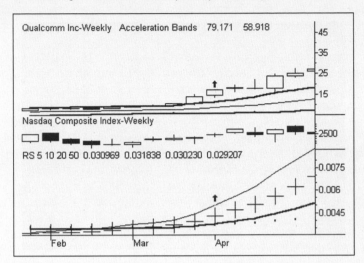

Chart created on TradeStation®, the flagship product of TradeStation Technologies, Inc.

by crossing above the 50-week RS line, QCOM receives a new RS buy signal. For QCOM shares, this occurred on the week ending April 2, 1999, when the stock closed at 17.125. The week before, the stock had also given an Acceleration Band buy signal on its second straight close above the upper 20-week Acceleration Band. Many traders would tend to say that QCOM nearly doubling in one month would be "overbought" and thus ripe to be sold. But this is a major mistake when you are looking at new breakouts in relative performance. You actually want to see as much strength as possible to signal the first thrust to the upside. A useful analogy is a rocket taking off into space. Most of the energy is required to get the rocket off the ground. Once the rocket moves far enough above the planet to no longer feel the effects of gravity, the rocket boosters are no longer needed, and the rocket continues higher relatively effortlessly. Stocks that breakout to the upside, once they move into new high ground or get a big buying surge to clear out potential sellers, can build upside momentum for prolonged periods.

One of the great ironies of investing is that stocks that appear overvalued at high prices, which most people assume to be risky investments, are actually the type of stocks which continue to perform well despite conventional expectations. If you expect to find Big Trends and ride them for serious gains, you need to get rid of the psychology of "overbought" and "oversold" indicators. That way you stay on board the leaders that are overbought while not getting stuck with the oversold dogs. Breakouts to new highs are good; new 52-week lows that attract many bottom-fishers are actually bad. As I alluded to earlier in this book, technical price action often signals pending news from a company. Your goal should be to act before the news occurs, and sell some or all of your position to those buyers who flock in once the news actually hits the wires.

My biggest challenge psychologically on these breakout trends was feeling like I had already missed the move. But as you are seeing in this chapter, the initial burst that a stock sees on an initial breakout are often the precursor of future gains. Bill O'Neil of Investors Business Daily talks about not buying a stock more than 5 percent above the top of its prior base (5 percent above its prior set of highs) as a way to make sure the breakout is not too extended. As you can see here, when you are expecting true leading stocks to really move by double, triple, or more on your initial purchase, you do not want to get left behind on these high RS breakouts like QCOM.

Figure 9.3 shows the effect of QCOM's breakout to the upside, which results in a significant upside trend. The breakdown point in this case is signaled by the first cross of a fast RS line under a slower RS line. In this case, when the 5-week RS line crosses under the 10-week RS line on the week ending February 11, 2000, at a price of 132.000, the stock's outperformance cycle is considered ended and the position should be closed. This does not mean that the stock will necessarily underperform the market now. This just means that our defined edge is now no longer present. Interestingly, while the RS method was a little slower to enter compared to the Acceleration Bands, the

Figure 9.3   Weekly Chart Qualcomm (QCOM): 1999 to 2000

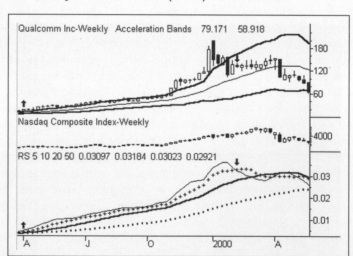

Chart created on TradeStation®, the flagship product of TradeStation Technologies, Inc.

slower exit (by two weeks in this case) compared to the Acceleration Band exit near 110 garners an extra 22 points on the way out for the RS method.

I am always looking for the heroes in the tough markets, seeking out stocks which are refusing to buckle despite tough market conditions. I use the RS line during market pullbacks as a sign of accumulation. Even a stock that is flat in a declining market will be attractive to me, since when the market starts to recover, the resilient stocks seem to rally first and often rally the sharpest. Coming out of the "Asian Contagion" drop in late 1997, Yahoo (YHOO) was a stock which had acted very strongly. The Internet was still in its early stages of growth, though at the time there were a lot of doubters due mostly to valuation arguments, suggesting the stock was too richly priced. I do not listen to what the talking heads are saying on these stock market leaders—I listen to what the market is telling me via the RS line and other objective indicators. For YHOO the RS line gave a very nice longer-term buy signal as we moved into 1998, when YHOO shares saw the 5-week RS line cross over the 10-week RS line, in conjunction with the 20-week RS line over the 50-week RS line on March 13, 1998, with the stock closing at 10.422 (see Figure 9.4). The 5-week RS line came close to breaking the 10-week RS line a couple of times, in June 1998 and September 1998, but it still managed to hold above at the end of each week's close. I have circled the Nasdaq's performance during the July to October 1998 period, as the Nasdaq went through a nasty decline on the heels of the Long-Term Capital Management hedge fund crisis. Yet

Figure 9.4 Weekly Chart Yahoo (YHOO): 1998 to 1999

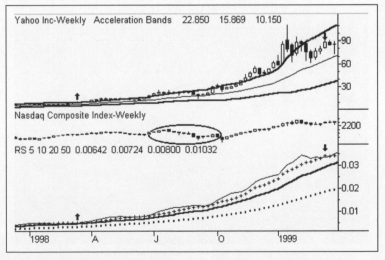

Chart created on TradeStation®, the flagship product of TradeStation Technologies, Inc.

YHOO's RS lines never broke down during this period! This positioned the stock to be a huge leader to the upside on the next upleg for the broader market, and YHOO's uptrend sped up greatly in the subsequent period from late 1998 through early 1999. The exit signal was finally given on March 12, 1999 at a price of 88.00, making a move of over eight-fold in just one year's time.

A recent example of a stock that bucked the downtrend in technology and came out smoking when the market finally had a bounce was eBay (EBAY) in the spring of 2001, shown in Figure 9.5. EBAY had been in a negative RS cycle during 2000, as the stock corrected from its upper weekly Acceleration Band near 120 all the way back to its lower weekly Acceleration Band under 40 by the beginning of 2001, the same pattern that occurred in a variety of technology shares. Yet EBAY started to firm up as the first quarter of 2001 came to a close. Interestingly, EBAY actually started to make a higher low in late March even as the Nasdaq Composite was making a lower low. That was the first sign that EBAY was starting to buck the general market decline. The stock gave the official RS buy signal on April 6th at a price of 35.50, as the 20-week RS line was again last to catch up in crossing the 50-week RS line to issue the "all aboard" signal. Notice the difference between EBAY and past examples like QCOM and YHOO. EBAY was hovering just under its 20-week moving average, while other breakout signals were occurring outside the upper Acceleration Bands. So this could not be expected to be the runaway mover that we had seen in past bull markets. Yet even as the Nasdaq churned in the second quarter of 2000, EBAY steadily trended higher, reach-

Figure 9.5   Weekly Chart eBay (EBAY): 2000 to 2001

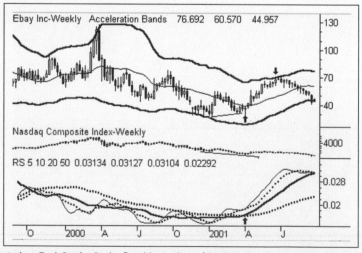

ing a double the week of June 29th and, more importantly, tagging the upper Acceleration Band the week of June 22nd. This Acceleration Band often acts as resistance from underneath until the stock has two straight closes above this upper band. And for those who just wanted to follow the official 5-week RS line crossing under the 10-week RS line, this gave its exit signal on August 17th at a price of 59.00, still well over a 50 percent gain. Given the flat-to-bearish trend of the broader market, the RS line again spotted an unusual anomaly that led to a steady uptrend in EBAY shares.

In a similar way to looking for stocks which refuse to buckle in tough markets, I also like to find stocks that are not participating near the end of up moves, as those stocks often get hammered the hardest when the market more clearly tops and heads lower. An example was CMGI in March 2001, when the stock made a lower high even as the Nasdaq was blasting to a higher high over 5,000 in early March. For a former market leader like CMGI, the failure to join in the party was an ominous warning to me, and I unloaded all of my former long positions in the stock that month. The official sell signal occurred June 23, 2001 at 47.625, and it certainly was a successful one. As you can see in Figure 9.6, the alert to look for stocks not participating with the market can be a great early warning indicator to head for the exits. The thinking here is "If a stock can't rally when times are good, what will happen when times get bad?" That is how smart investors think, and this indicator gives you the caution flag when a stock starts to misbehave.

Figure 9.6   Weekly Chart CMGI: 2000 to 2001

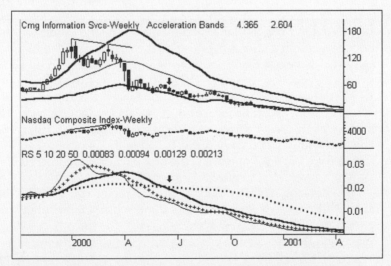

Chart created on TradeStation®, the flagship product of TradeStation Technologies, Inc.

FUNDAMENTAL ANALYSIS: FILTERS AND OTHER CONSIDERATIONS

The main fundamental indicators I watch are sales and earnings trends. If a company is beating (or missing) analyst forecasts, it will tend to do so longer than expected over time, as analysts are slow to catch up to many company's accelerating (or decelerating) business prospects.

However, you have to be careful on measures like price/earnings ratios. I have found over time that the p/e ratio would have cost me many of my favorite situations, which I call Acceleration Plays. A recent example was Nvidia (NVDA). I recommended buying the stock at 80.51, and some subscribers complained the stock was too expensive. Yet in less than three weeks the stock was sold at my target of 99.75 for a quick gain of more than 20 percent, and my conservative options on Nvidia went up more than 40 percent. This is due to the fact that the trend tends to rule in the short term, and that is why I give technical considerations more weight in my models.

Earnings *reactions* are the key. Let us look back at past quarterly earnings periods, and evaluate the reaction after the period was over. If a stock has good earnings above expectations, and the stock drops on the day, what does that mean for the future? If a stock cannot rally on good news, it may have some trouble ahead of it.

Analysts cut their ratings when a stock reaches its price objective. This often creates short-term buying opportunities in nicely uptrending stocks. Think about it. If an analyst is only lowering his or her rating because of a price move in the stock, does it imply that any fundamentals have changed? No. That is why early declines on these type of downgrades are often bought up quickly, as smart investors generally expect the stock to have at least one more good run as the fundamentals carry the stock up on the short-term momentum it still possesses.

Another fundamental factor I like to buy into is when an uptrending stock reports a secondary offering. These stocks usually drop for one-to-two days when this news is announced, as the fear that earnings per share will be diluted by the extra shares is now available. Yet in most cases these sell-offs prove to be an overreaction and thus a buying opportunity. Similarly, when an acquiring company drops based on fears of dilution or paying too much for a buyout, sometimes the stock will get hammered over.

What about news? Unless the news relates to earnings or sales, I tend to lighten positions on news, not add to them. I tend to go with the direction of the trend if there is no news. Something is likely happening behind the scenes, but most traders just have not heard the news yet. Once the news comes out, then you might consider taking partial or total profits on a trending position. Think of this another way: when stocks report news they often fail to maintain early gains. Who do you think is selling? Likely it is the smart money looking to capitalize on the opportunity of a number of willing buyers for the stock. A famous maxim for bigger investors is "Sell when you can, not when you have to." This means that when there is a high demand for shares that the smart money owns, they will start selling out of positions, especially if news appears to be running the stock up.

As a technical analyst, I have always believed that price action gives you a leading clue of a stock's future direction much sooner than if you actually waited to buy once good news is released, or sell on the bad news. In fact, the well-known trading motto, "Buy on the rumor, sell on the news," is based on this principle: you want to be in before the news hits, and once the news is released and the unsuspecting average investor is ready to buy, you gladly offer your shares for sale at a tidy profit. Most positive news items usually correlate to short-term peaks in a stock (with the primary exception being earnings-related news).

Yet I also like to use news in a way that most would not expect. When I see what most consider to be bad news (for example, a company reports an earnings miss, or a weaker-than-expected economic number is released), yet the stock actually reverses early losses and finishes higher for the session, that is a VERY bullish combination. I do not worry so much about the news itself, but rather the stock's *reaction* to the news. A positive reaction to bad news tells you that the majority of investors had already expected that bad news, or perhaps expected something even worse. Whatever the reason, more buying was likely to occur in that stock over time. Investors start to think: If the stock cannot go down on bad news, I have limited risk. In addition, think about what could happen if the stock has good news.

Is there a general price pattern a stock takes when a split is announced? Most traders believe that you should trade stocks that are about to split, buying them one-to-two weeks before the split, then selling the day of the split. This pattern certainly worked well in the bull market between 1995 and 1999, while it worked badly during the bear market of 2000 and 2001. On a longer-term note, stock splits often mark intermediate-term peaks for stocks, as buying enthusiasm often peaks around stock splits.

One other strong fundamental situation I like to look for in weak markets is when companies are considered strong enough to have an initial public offering (IPO) despite an awful market environment. For example, when eBay (EBAY) went public in September 1998, it could not have come to the market at a worse time. The Long-Term Capital Management hedge fund crisis had crippled the markets at the time, and very few new IPOs were coming out in that awful market environment. So when Wall Street underwriters had the confidence to bring EBAY public in spite of the environment, it told investors that this was one of the strong companies to watch

Figure 9.7   eBay (EBAY) Weekly Chart: 1998 to 1999

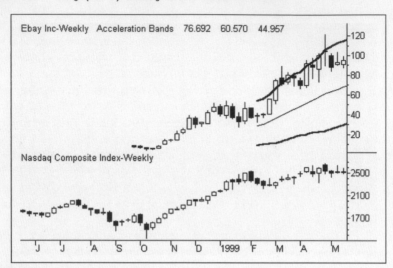

Chart created on TradeStation®, the flagship product of TradeStation Technologies, Inc.

when the market improved. And EBAY certainly roared after the market bottomed in October 1998 (see Figure 9.7), rising from a split-adjusted $5 per share to a high of $127.50 over the next 18 months.

Now you understand the techniques of relative strength and other growth-oriented fundamental factors to use as filters with the other prevailing technical and sentiment indicators previously discussed. Next, we will move forward from stocks to options, to discuss the power of trends for options buyers, and various options strategies to profit from different market environments.

Part III

OPTIONS

While most options strategy texts will present readers with many complex and at times interesting strategies, I am a big believer in keeping it simple to maximize your focus and increase your odds of success. In the next two chapters, I will share with you the key options principles and simple strategies you need to know to leverage your returns over time while also managing your risk.

Chapter 10 will give you an understanding of how the options pricing model works. More importantly, you will learn about a major flaw in the traditional options prizing model that gives you an opportunity to gain a major advantage once you understand this flaw in the model.

Chapter 11 gives you simple and effective options techniques to profit from major trends in the underlying stock or index. My experience with directional trading of the big trends is that you get the best bang for you buck as an options buyer. I'll share with you the options techniques I use to ride winning trades while managing an option's risk.

10

BIG TRENDS—YOUR EDGE VERSUS THE OPTIONS PRICING MODEL

Why do trends exist? From years of experience I have learned that the underperformers will tend to stay underperformers for a longer time than most expect, due to the fact that investors stuck in these stocks will tend to sell at every bounce. In addition, you can get a tax loss to use against future capital gains if you sell losers. The simple answer is to sell your losers as quickly as possible and try to get new winners on board instead. The impact of trends is more pronounced for options traders due to the effect of leverage.

One of the traps many investors fall into is to look at a past trend and to assume it will again resume at some point in the future. The higher a stock rallied, the more investors seemed to want to buy it at "bargain" prices on the way down. Look at technology stocks in 1999 to 2001. Most of the major tech stocks corrected over 50 percent, and in many cases over 90 percent. Yet volume actually surged even more on some stocks as they were trading lower, even as they moved under $1.00 per share. An example is Exodus Communications (EXDS), shown in Figure 10.1. As the stock moved under $2 and then under $1, the stock was regularly on the most actives list for the Nasdaq. Speculators apparently thought that the company was a good value and bet on a recovery. Instead, the stock kept dropping, falling under 20 cents per share as of this writing.

For a longer-term example, look at what happened to the "Nifty Fifty" stocks that peaked in the early 1970s. Polaroid (PRD) surged over 1,000 percent from the start of the 1962 bull market to its peak in May 1972. By September 1974, PRD crashed at just over 90 percent from its high. The stock then went into a 25-year trading range, rallying back toward its old highs in 25 years but again crashing lower after that (see Figure 10.2 and Figure 10.3). Investors buying these alleged bargains might have to wait decades for a recovery to old highs. I doubt whether they indeed have that much patience, but regardless, the opportunity cost on your capital is too great to ever consider cluttering your portfolio with such bottom-fishing.

Figure 10.1 Exodus Communications Monthly Chart 1999 to 2001 with Weekly Volume

Chart created on TradeStation®, the flagship product of TradeStation Technologies, Inc.

Figure 10.2 Polaroid Long-Term Trading Range: Monthly 1972 to 1984

Chart created on TradeStation®, the flagship product of TradeStation Technologies, Inc.

Figure 10.3 Polaroid Long-Term Trading Range: Monthly 1989 to 2001

Chart created on TradeStation®, the flagship product of TradeStation Technologies, Inc.

WHY MORE INVESTORS ARE TURNING TO OPTIONS FOR BULL *AND* BEAR MARKET PROFITS

Options trading volume nearly doubled in 2000–2001 with growth accelerating through the bull and bear market extremes of the past several years.

Here is why you should consider using options to expand your growth strategy:

1. *Leveraged Profits*

Percentage gains on options contracts often outpace those of underlying securities by 5 to 10 times or more. Potential for individual trading gains of 50 to 200 percent or more makes strategic options trading a powerful growth engine for your portfolio.

2. *Limited Initial Investment*

Buying options contracts (each of which "controls" 100 shares of the corresponding stock) typically involves only a fraction of the cost of buying the underlying stock or index.

3. *Bull and Bear Market Profits*

Savvy options traders use strategies to generate profits on both uptrending and downtrending stocks alike. Call options contracts allow you to profit on expectations of a stock moving higher, while options puts allow you to profit on a downtrending issue. Options traders have always been faced with the additional work of not only correctly predicting the underlying security's price, but then also choosing the appropriate option strategy.

THE KEY DIFFERENCE BETWEEN STOCK AND OPTIONS TRADING

In order to make money in options on an ongoing basis, a trader needs to understand the major difference between stock and options trading. The biggest difference is the impact of *time* on stock and options positions. With stocks, time is your ally, as the stocks of quality companies tend to rise over longer periods of time. However, with options buying, time is your enemy, as each day that passes without any significant change leads to a decline in the value of the time premium, which declines more rapidly as the option approaches expiration (see Figure 10.4).

The important factor that options traders should assess from the TradeStation® Performance Summaries I have discussed throughout this book to account for the impact of time is the "Average # bars" of the system's winning or losing trades. It is most useful to look at the holding period for long trades and short trades separately, as the character of advances is often quite different from the nature of declines. Given the accelerated impact of time decay the closer the options are to expiration, the options buyer should look to buy more time before expiration than will be needed, having at least one month before expiration to spare when the position must be closed out. This allows the options buyer to avoid the especially painful time decay which occurs in the final month before expiration. However, the options seller seeks to benefit from the time decay

Figure 10.4   Time Decay of an Option

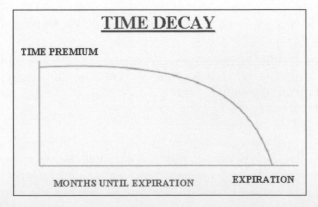

which occurs most rapidly in the final month, so the expiration month chosen for sellers should be aligned to reach expiration in conjunction with the time that the expected holding period is reached.

Most options analysts will tell you to focus on the volatility assumption within the options pricing model, as that is the only factor the standard options model assumes to be unknown. The more volatile the stock is assumed to be, the more expensive the options become in the options pricing model. The stock price is assumed to be basically unchanged, except for a carrying cost equivalent to the short-term interest rate. This assumption is due to the Efficient Market Theory notion that stock prices incorporate all available information and cannot be predicted into the future. We believe trends occur and can be predicted, and thus this options pricing model assumption creates an opportunity for options traders. Our approach is to focus first on the expected movement in the underlying stock's price, as we find the average off-the-floor options trader gets a much bigger impact from a given percentage gain in the stock than from the same percentage change in the volatility assumption. Let us look at the example of XYZ December 60 call options with approximately 10 weeks until expiration in Figure 10.5.

As you can see, the 25 percent gain in the stock price amounts to a 403 percent gain in the options price, while the 25 percent jump in volatility leads to a 30 percent gain in the options price. If these events are equally probable, you have about a 13-to-1 edge in focusing on the stock price change relative to the volatility change. Looked at another way, the 25 percent change in volatility would have to occur 13 times for every one time the

Figure 10.5   Impact of 25 Percent Rise in Volatility versus 25 Percent Rise in Stock Price

---

A Flaw in the Options Pricing Model

- Which is more important in the Options Model?
  - A 25% Rise in Price or a 25% Rise in Volatility?
    - Assume: XYZ shares at 60, Volatility starts at 30.00%, Expiration in 64 days, Strike price is 60

- <u>**25% Volatility Rise (30% to 36%) in 32 days**</u>
  - XYZ Dec. 60 call 3.00 => 3.90 ... a **30% gain**

- <u>**25% Stock Price Rise (60.00 to 75.00) in 32 days**</u>
  - XYZ Dec. 60 call 3.00 => 15.10 ... a **403% gain**

- <u>**Trend impact is 13 X greater than Volatility**</u>

stock price changed by 25 percent, if there were to be no edge in focusing on expected stock price over volatility. Individual options traders will find much more value in focusing on expected stock prices. Clearly the bigger the expected trend, the bigger your edge versus the standard options pricing assumptions.

Note that there are adjustments you can make for your comfort level as well. Many times traders will be too optimistic in the scenarios they input. A way to moderate this is by employing one of the following two tactics. Traders wanting to employ more conservative tactics can either buy one strike further in-the-money, or buy the next expiration month further than they think they will need. Options traders, or any traders or investors, will always be faced with being wrong no matter what they do: if the position is a winner, they should have bought twice as much, or if the position loses, they should have never bought it. The point is that we can always second-guess ourselves, but we will be better positioned over many trades taking a more conservative approach to mitigate those situations which could knock us out of the game entirely, as opposed to worrying that we left some profits on the table by choosing a less-leveraged option (see Figure 10.6).

Regarding how I choose my price and time targets on an option, I have found that there is no "Holy Grail" answer. But the answer that has served me best over time is the one that reduces my Greed Factor. Once I do my analysis, I tend to want to be more conservative that my analysis suggests. Why? I find that by not being greedy on the front end of a trade, I have less risk of a short-term adverse move causing me to be fearful once in the trade. Options are leveraged instruments, so you are already magnifying the impact of stock swings many times over when you trade options. If you have not mastered fear or greed when trading stocks, how will you expect to

Figure 10.6   Determining Which Option to Buy

Determining Which Option to Buy

- **Be more Conservative than you think you should based on your market view**

  We all have a tendency to exaggerate our upside targets as traders, and downplay or avoid thinking about the downside risk

  – Buy 1 more month of time than you think you need
  – Or Buy 1 strike in from what you think you need

master it on an options vehicle that swings five or more times more violently? I believe that is why my options indicators are such a great contrarian tool: they pick up more easily on the fear and greed that underlies the price swings within the options market.

My general rules for strike price and expiration selection are simple:

OPTIONS TRADING RULES—KISS (KEEP IT SIMPLE STUPID) PRINCIPLE

1. Find the big trends first, then worry about option selection.
2. Spot Increasing Velocity within Trends (resulting in a huge edge for option buyers) The Acceleration Bands are my favorite indicator to get a huge edge on the options markets.
3. Buy one more month of time than I think I need.
4. Buy one strike price in from what I think I need.

"Fat Tails"

The standard options pricing models tend to underprice options during Big Trends. Markets tend to have fatter tails than the normal distribution suggests (more big moves at the "low probability" ends of the curve). Let us first examine the underpinning of the options pricing model via the standard distribution curve. Normal distribution curves can be described in two ways: by the peak of the curve (equating to the current price of the stock, as this is the point where Efficient Markets Theory assumes the stock will finish where it is currently, on average), or by their standard deviation which shows how quickly the curve spreads out. The higher the standard deviation, the quicker the curve will expand. The standard deviation shows the probabilities that a random event will occur. Statistics show us the percentage chance that an outcome within a certain range can occur.

The following approximations represent a good rule of thumb:

1. One standard deviation (plus or minus from the mean) accounts for 68.3 percent of all potential outcomes.
2. Two standard deviations (plus or minus from the mean) accounts for 95.4 percent of all potential outcomes.
3. Three standard deviations (plus or minus from the mean) accounts for 99.7 percent of all possible outcomes.

So when we say a move is expected to occur with plus or minus two standard deviations' degree of confidence, this means the move should occur 19 times out of 20, while the move will not occur as expected 1 out of 20 times.

Let us tie this back in with a specific range for a stock based on the standard distribution theory. Typically, a stock is said to move plus or minus one standard deviation by a certain percentage over one year. This percentage number becomes the volatility input in the standard options pricing models. For example, if Microsoft is trading at $60 and has a volatility of 50 percent, this would mean a one standard deviation price change over a year's time would be 30 points ($.50 \times 60$). One year from now, Microsoft is expected to trade between $30 and $90 (60 +/− 30) about two-thirds of the time, between $0 and $120 (60 +/− [2 × 30]) 19 times out of 20, and between $0 and $150 (60 +/− [3 × 30]) 369 times out of 370.

So where is the catch for options traders? The big assumption is that stock prices move in a random fashion, which would make the odds of ever getting a two standard deviation move only 1 in 20 and a three standard deviation move only 1 in 370. But what would happen if price changes were trending, where past gains provided a feedback mechanism for future price gains to occur, leading to more events at the two and three standard deviation mark than could be predicted by the model? This is the circumstance I regularly see occurring in these models, which means that trends are occurring with greater frequency than what is predicted by the standard distribution models upon which options are priced. This creates an opportunity for options buyers to buy relatively undervalued options on stocks that generate these big trends. In contrast, note that option sellers are at a relative disadvantage on these big moves, as they are effectively selling options too cheaply when the stock makes a big move. In contrast, the lognormal distribution model will tend to slightly overestimate the smaller moves close to the current price, thus making options traded for smaller moves moderately overpriced. This can benefit options sellers if a stock is expected not to trend and instead can be expected to have a relatively narrow range (see Figure 10.7).

Many investors tend to use absolute past reference points for a stock as a means to gauge the potential "value" the stock may possess. This is very dangerous in the world of trends. Markets will look high as they make new 52-week highs, but often that is just the beginning of a strong move in a stock. In contrast, markets look low when the stock has already had a big decline from its 52-week high, as investors buy in anticipation that the 52-week high could again be reached. Let us look at an example in Figure 10.8.

Forgive me if you think I am a master of the obvious, but look at Figure 10.8 and answer one question: "Is there a difference in XYZ stock at a price of 50 in 1999 versus XYZ stock at a price of 50 in 2000?" The answer is obviously "Yes," since in 1999 XYZ was headed from 50 to 150, while in 2000 XYZ was headed from 50 to 5. Yet traditional options pricing models like the Black-Scholes model assume that, all other factors being equal (time until expiration, strike price, and volatility are the other primary factors), there

Figure 10.7 Lognormal Distribution versus Trending "Fat Tail" Distribution

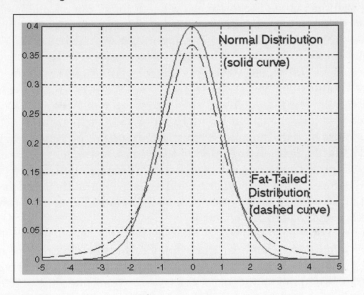

Figure 10.8 XYZ Stock at 50 in 1999 and at 50 in 2000—Is There a Difference? Weekly 1999 to 2001

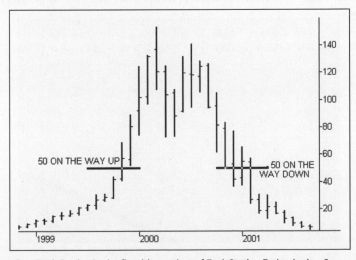

Chart created on TradeStation®, the flagship product of TradeStation Technologies, Inc.

is no difference in these two clearly different trends. These options models assume that the market is completely efficient for all intents and purposes, and that one cannot predict these trends, so future price direction must be considered random. I believe this is a major flaw which creates opportunities for options buyers who can spot significant price trends.

Another factor to consider in how options are priced is to look at the effect of volatility changes in an uptrend versus a downtrend. Downtrends will tend to increase volatility as they progress, much like in Chapter 3 when we saw how the CBOE Volatility Index (VIX) spikes up as declines become more severe. In contrast, steady uptrends often reduce a stock's volatility. The implications are profound. Options can remain cheap relative to a stock's powerful trend higher, allowing you to wait until a stock proves its trend before having to put your capital at risk, while at the same time not generating the fear of missing out in such situations. Figure 10.9 can help you further understand this concept.

Let us say we have two stocks moving the same distance from the beginning to the end of a period of time. Stock A (the light-colored line in Figure 10.9) moves in a volatile fashion on its way to the target, while Stock B (the dark-colored line in Figure 10.9) moves up the same slow percentage in every period on its way to the same target. Would you rather buy calls on Stock A or Stock B in this circumstance? They are both getting the same trend impact from the beginning to the end of our assessment, so the main factor that must be considered is the volatility. Since most options texts focus so heavily on volatility, most traders assume that they want to own options on the more volatile Stock A. Yet think about this: We know Stock A is much more volatile than Stock B. If Stock A had twice the volatility as

Figure 10.9 Which Stock Would You Rather Own Calls On?

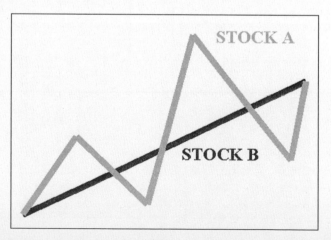

Stock B, how much more would Stock A's options cost compared to Stock B? With all other factors the same, Stock A's options would cost roughly twice as much as Stock B's options. Yet remember that we are getting the same directional move in both cases. Essentially you are getting twice the bang for your buck in Stock B's call options compared to Stock A. As an aside, what would be the volatility of Stock B if it moved up at the same constant percentage rate every day with no fluctuation? Volatility would be zero. Based on the options pricing model's focus on volatility, a zero volatility input would lead to a value of zero in the at-the-money and out-of-the-money options. Imagine an option you could buy in unlimited quantities for no cost, with an infinite return on your money if the option went in-the-money! While this perfect scenario is a pipe dream, the next best thing is finding stocks in nice steady trends where volatility is low but the degree of trend is high. That is how you really maximize your upside potential when buying options.

Perhaps the most dramatic story of how options traders went wrong by assuming no trends could persist in the options pricing model comes from the creators of the Black-Scholes options pricing model. This incredible story's history is well chronicled in Roger Lowenstein's book, *When Genius Failed: The Rise & Fall of Long-Term Capital Management*. The developers of the options pricing model used to price standardized options contracts won a Nobel Prize in economics for their work in 1997, and then parlayed that success into positions at one of the largest hedge funds at the time, Long-Term Capital Management (LTCM). They traded based on quantitative models designed by Robert Merton and Myron Scholes, two of the three individuals who created the options pricing model. Their quaint models took years of historical data about how various markets interrelate and created what were believed to be no-lose arbitrage plays to capitalize on pricing disparities between different investments which were thought to trade in a predictable relationship to each other. Most of LTCM's bets had been variations on the same theme, looking for a "reversion to the mean" between liquid Treasury bonds and more complex investments that possessed a premium yield due to a lack of liquidity or broader credit risk that the securities could go into default. As the Russian ruble crisis hit in August of 1998, the expected reversion to the mean via tighter anticipated spreads instead became a greater trend toward widening spreads. In one day, August 21, 1998, the LTCM portfolio lost $550 million. Yet the leader of the fund, John Meriwether, sought additional capital investments from outside investors to try to shore up the fund and ride out this crisis, believing in the merit of the fund's positions. However, as losses intensified, it became clear that the fund was in deep financial trouble. On September 2, 1998, Meriwether sent a letter to LTCM's investors saying that the fund had lost $2.5 billion, or 52 percent of its value that year, and amazingly $2.1 billion of the losses occurred in just the month of August. This began a process in which the Federal Reserve eventually had to step in, for fear of aftershocks to many counterparties, in an effort to shore up confidence in the financial system's structural integrity.

The principle of "mean reversion" is a trading technique that many options traders focus on, but I believe Long-Term Capital Management shows how even the smartest investors can be humbled with this dangerous mentality. Traders of volatility like to bet on the reversion of volatility, where high volatility should drop and low volatility should increase back to historical norms. While this may occur a majority of the time, the few times that it does not occur can be fatal to an options trader's portfolio. For example, if you think volatility is too high and you sell options to profit from an anticipated implosion in volatility, and the price trend continues to make a move not expected by the reversion theory, you can find yourself deep under water.

Table 10.1 shows a simple way to calculate an option's Reward-to-Risk ratio. The rule of thumb I like to use if I am expecting a quick move in an option is shown in Table 10.1. This shows the available call options for XYZ shares, currently trading at 95 with six weeks before expiration. What would happen to the January 95 call, 100 call, and 105 call if you saw a very quick five point move to the upside? Could you quickly figure out how much each option would gain? With any options montage like this table, you can. Let us take the January 95 call for starters. It is currently at 5.00. If XYZ shares make a very quick five point move from 95 to 100, the value of the 95 call when the stock is at 100 will equate with the value of the 90 call when the stock was back at 95. So the 95 call would move from 5.00 to 8.38 on a quick five-point move up in XYZ shares. This assumes a nearly instantaneous move, with other factors like the volatility priced into the options un-

Table 10.1 Options Pricing Made Easy

		Reward	Risk	Ratio
01 Jan 90	8.38			
01 Jan 95	5.00	68%	43%	1.59
01 Jan 100	2.88	74%	46%	1.62
01 Jan 105	1.56	84%	52%	1.63
01 Jan 110	0.75			

changed. The more time goes by, the more erosion you will see in this easy estimate of potential value. Likewise, the January 100 call would move from 2.88 to 5.00, and the January 105 call would jump from 1.56 to 2.88. As a result, I calculate the Reward in a column to the right, with the 105 call having the best reward on a five-point rally in XYZ shares. So does that mean the 105 call is the right option to buy? Not necessarily. We must also factor in what happens to the calls if the stock moves against us. Using the same rationale we used previously on the upside, a five-point instant decline in XYZ shares will make the January 95 call's previous value of 5.00 now worth 2.88. When XYZ is at 95, the January 100 call is 2.88. Moving down instantly by five points, the January 95 call can now be expected to also be worth 2.88. I do the same exercise with the other options, and come up with a downside risk estimate for each option. Trading is all about how much reward you can get relative to your risk. In this example in Table 10.1, the Reward-to-Risk ratio is a tie between the January 100 call and the January 105 call. While most traders might think to buy the cheaper 105 call option in a tie, I would recommend buying the relatively safer 100 call. Why? Remember that we are assuming we get an instant move. What happens if time starts getting away from us? The 105 call is in relatively more danger of melting faster due to time decay than is the 100 call. So this shows you a framework for making quick assessments on the fly if you need to. This does not mean that you cannot use options software to model all types of scenarios. I am a believer in options software to do this, especially with more complex options positions. It is just a plus to know how you can do some quick figuring in your head, too.

This chapter examined the impact that focusing on trends can have for you as an options trader, as opposed to the conventional focus on volatility as the main unknown factor in the options pricing model. We will now move on to specific options strategies that can be used to capture significant trends in the underlying stock in our next chapter.

11

OPTIONS STRATEGIES FOR DIFFERENT MARKET CONDITIONS

I am a big believer in the KISS principle (Keep It Simple Stupid) when it comes to options strategies. I often find that the more complicated a strategy, the less money I make. As a directional trader, most of the hedging or selling of additional legs of a position tends to minimize my potential gain too much in most cases. We will look at the primary strategies I use in options trading. But first let us review the important terms you need to know to trade options:

Call Option: A call is a contract between a buyer and a seller, in which the buyer has the right, but not the obligation, to purchase a stock or cash index at a predetermined price.

Put Option: A put is a contract between a buyer and a seller, in which the buyer has the right, but not the obligation, to sell a stock or cash index at a predetermined price.

Expiration Date: The date after which the option no longer exists.

Underlying: The stock, or cash index, to be delivered in the event the option is exercised.

Strike Price (Exercise Price): The price in the contract at which the underlying will be bought or sold.

Premium: The total price of the option = intrinsic value + time premium.

Intrinsic Value: Calls = underlying − strike price. Puts = strike price − underlying. If negative, then there is no intrinsic value.

Time Premium: The additional value of the option due to the volatility of the underlying security and the time remaining until expiration. Premium − intrinsic value.

Volatility: A measure of the underlying security's price swings.

Implied Volatility: The volatility of the underlying stock that is factored in by the option's current market price.

Exercise: To demand the right granted under the terms of the contract to buy or sell the underlying security.

Assign: To force the seller of an option to fulfill his obligation to deliver the stock.

In-The-Money (ITM): When the stock price is greater than the strike price for a call, or when the stock price is less than the strike price for puts.

At-The-Money (ATM): When the stock price, or underlying price, is equal to the strike price.

Out-Of-The-Money (OTM): When the stock price is less than the strike price for calls, or the stock price is greater than the strike price for puts.

Naked Option: An option sold (written) without an underlying position.

Covered Option: An option sold (written) against an existing underlying stock.

STRATEGY #1: BUY 100-STRIKE CALL FOR 8.00 (STOCK AT 100)

Benefit if: Stock closes over 108 at expiration. The position would be a 100 percent gain at a price of 116, and a 200 percent gain at a price of 124.

Breakeven if: Stock closes at 108 at expiration.

Lose if: Stock closes below 108 at expiration. This position would be a 100 percent loss if the stock closes at 100 or lower at expiration.

Discussion: I always try to think like a stock owner when I purchase options, because that is what an options buyer does in leasing the ownership of the stock for a limited period of time. By leasing, you control a higher-priced asset for a fraction of the cost over a defined time period. The key to success is to be able to own the leveraged vehicle only for the periods of above-average performance, and then cash out of it and wait for another opportunity later.

Table 11.1 shows us an example. ABC shares are trading at $100; it would cost you $10,000 to buy 100 shares. If you buy the stock, you have a dollar risk of up to $10,000. Whether you have the cash available or not, in today's volatile markets, you may not want all of these dollars at risk, but you still may want a vehicle to participate in the upside you see for ABC shares.

Therefore, you would want to investigate ABC options as an alternative investment. If you bought ABC call options instead of ABC shares, it would

Table 11.1 ABC Shares Rise from $100 to $120

	Buy Price	Sell Price	Profit (Loss)	% Gain (Loss)
Vehicle	$100	$120	$20	20%
100 shares of stock	$10,000	$12,000	$2,000	20%
A 100-strike call	$800	$2,000	$1,200	150%

Table 11.2 ABC Shares Drop from $100 to $80

	Buy Price	Sell Price	Profit (Loss)	% Gain (Loss)
Vehicle	$100	$80	($20)	−20%
100 shares of stock	$10,000	$8,000	($2,000)	−20%
A 100-strike call	$800	$0	($800)	−100%

cost $800 for the right to control 100 shares of ABC for each call purchased, which is good for the next two months. The strike price at $100 means you have a right to buy ABC shares at a price of $100, which becomes more valuable as the stock price rises. If the stock fails to move above $100 by the time the options expire in two months, $800 is the most you could lose. If the stock rises to $120 at expiration, the options will be trading around $20 (current price: $120 − strike price: $100). This would make your $800 purchase now worth $2,000, which would be a 150 percent return on your investment. In comparison, a move to 120 for the ABC stock owner would result in a $2,000 gain on a $10,000 investment, or a 20 percent return on capital.

In contrast, let us examine the situation if ABC shares drop to 80 as shown in Table 11.2.

While no one likes the thought of losing all of an investment, as is the case with the ABC 100-strike calls in this example, you also need to consider your total dollars lost when you think about options as a stock substitute. While you lost $800 in your call option, the rest of that money was safe in a cash-like security. So you have lost $800 on a total $10,000 portfolio, for a loss of 8 percent. In contrast, the stock's drop from 100 to 75 more adversely impacts the shareholder, as his 100 shares bought at $100 are now worth just $7,500. This results in a loss of 25 percent on the portfolio in this case, more than three times the loss incurred by the option holder.

The main risk to the options buyer is where the stock is relatively nontrending and fails to move dramatically over the course of the holding period. If the stock stays flat at 100 the option will slowly lose value as the option gets closer to its expiration. A close at 100 or below at expiration is the worst case scenario for the options buyer here, as a loss of 100 percent occurs for the options buyer while the stockholder has stayed at breakeven in this scenario. The key for the options holders to avoid such scenarios is to use price stops and time stops on their positions to make sure that they have an exit plan in case the stock is not moving as initially expected.

STRATEGY #2: BUY PROTECTIVE PUTS AT 8.00 (STOCK AT 100)

You can hedge your portfolio against declines by purchasing put options. With puts, you buy the right, not the obligation, to sell your shares to someone else at a specified price. This is similar to buying insurance on your home in case of a disaster, only in this case you are protecting stocks that you own from a disaster. Your insurance premium in this case is a function of both the time period that you want protection and the odds of a disaster occurring (as measured by the stock's volatility). An increased amount of time that the insurance is valid and heightened volatility of the underlying stock will both raise the cost of the put option.

Benefit if: Stock closes under 92 at expiration.

Breakeven if: Stock closes at 92 at expiration.

Lose if: Stock closes above 92 at expiration. This position would be a 100 percent loss if the stock closes over 100 at expiration (see Table 11.3).

Discussion: Regarding this insurance, how do you choose at which strike price to hedge your stock position? The choice of strike prices is similar to the choice of deductibles on normal insurance. The higher the deductible you have to pay, the less expensive the insurance.

In options terms, if the stock is at 100 and you decide to take the first 10 points down as your deductible by buying a 90-strike put for $100, this option is cheaper than protecting yourself right away from the 100-strike price of $800. The choice depends on how bearish you are. If you are really

Table 11.3   ABC Shares Fall from $100 to $80

	Buy Price	Sell Price	Profit (Loss)	% Gain (Loss)
Vehicle	$100	$80	($20)	−20%
100 shares of stock	$10,000	$8,000	($2,000)	−20%
Stock with 100 put	$10,800	$10,000	($800)	−7%

concerned about a market drop, you could buy in-the-money puts (say $110-strike puts for $1,500 per 100 shares covered), which would benefit more closely point-for-point on the downside. The negative here, besides the higher premium cost, is that you risk losing more of this premium if the underlying stock keeps going up.

If you are moderately concerned (i.e., you think there is a 50-50 chance of a drop or rise), at-the-money puts are usually the best option. They are not as expensive, and they will serve to cushion about half of any QQQ drop.

If you think it is a long shot that the stock declines, but still fear a big gap down scenario, then you should buy out-of-the-money puts. You should look to buy 5 to 10 percent out of the money if you think it is unlikely the stock shoots down but that, if it does, a decline could be sharp. This would cushion about 25 to 33 percent of your loss on the stock position.

STRATEGY #3: SELL COVERED CALL AT 8.00 (STOCK AT 100)

Benefit if: Stock closes between 92 and 108 at expiration.

Breakeven if: Stock closes at 108 at expiration.

Lose if: Stock closes under 92 at expiration, or if stock closes above 108 at expiration (opportunity loss compared to owning stock outright).

Discussion: You can create an income generator for your portfolio by selling or "writing" a call option against shares that you own. This is known as covered call writing (see Table 11.4). For instance, if you own 100 shares of Coca-Cola (KO) and you are concerned the stock or the market as a whole is at risk of a decline, you could write one KO call option. If someone was not available to buy the call, the options market makers would purchase this from you. You are giving up the stock's appreciation over 100, but are collecting $800 per 100 shares on each contract that you sell. You win on this strategy relative to holding the stock outright if the stock does not go above 108 (the price you bought the stock—100 + the premium you received of eight points).

How I Prefer to Use Covered Calls

When you write covered calls as an entry strategy, and you own the stock and sell out-of-the-money calls against it, the problem is that you tend to capture only a fraction of the upside potential if the stock roars ahead. Clearly when a trader buys a stock, he or she expects it to perform relatively well—otherwise, why would a trader buy the stock?

Table 11.4 ABC Shares versus Covered Call

	Buy Price	Sell Price	Profit (Loss)	% Gain (Loss)
Vehicle (Down)	$100	$80	($20)	−20%
100 shares of stock	$10,000	$8,000	($2,000)	−20%
Stock & Covered Call	$9,200	$8,800	($800)	−9%
Vehicle (Flat)	$100	$100	$0	0%
100 shares of stock	$10,000	$10,000	$0	0%
Stock & Covered Call	$9,200	$10,000	$800	9%
Vehicle (Up)	$100	$120	$20	20%
100 shares of stock	$10,000	$12,000	$2,000	20%
Stock & Covered Call	$9,200	$10,000	$800	9%

A Strategy to Convert Short-Term Gains into Long-Term Gains, or Delay Recognition until the Next Year

Here is how I like to use covered calls:

In trending markets, you want to buy options, while a trading-range market is better for selling options. In a trading range, stocks move relatively little, and the evaporation of time benefits the seller of options.

I will occasionally sell call options against stock that I own for tax purposes, when I have grown concerned about a stock but want to hold it until the next year to delay my taxable gain. This call writing strategy would also apply if I am getting nervous about a stock I own and am nearing the one-year holding period anniversary to convert a stock position to "long-term" status. For example, with CMGI in late 1999, I purchased the stock in mid-October under 51, and the stock gave an Acceleration Bands (see Chapter 6) breakout signal to the upside in November 1999. CMGI shares closed below the upper Acceleration Band in late December 1999, yet I did not want to sell it until January 2000. Why? Because then I could delay paying out taxes on my capital gain for a full 12 months, until April 2001 instead of April 2000. As a result, when the stock gave me my exit signal on December 28, 1999, instead of selling the stock at that time, when it was trading at 139, I decided to sell the January 145 call (adjusted for a 2-for-1 split), and collected a net premium of 13 points for this 3-1/2 week option. Considering that this premium was already over 20 percent of my initial purchase price, if the stock flattened out I could generate an impressive annualized return of 240 percent. My concern was that the stock could start

Figure 11.1   Covered Call Exit Strategy—CMGI: 1999 to 2000

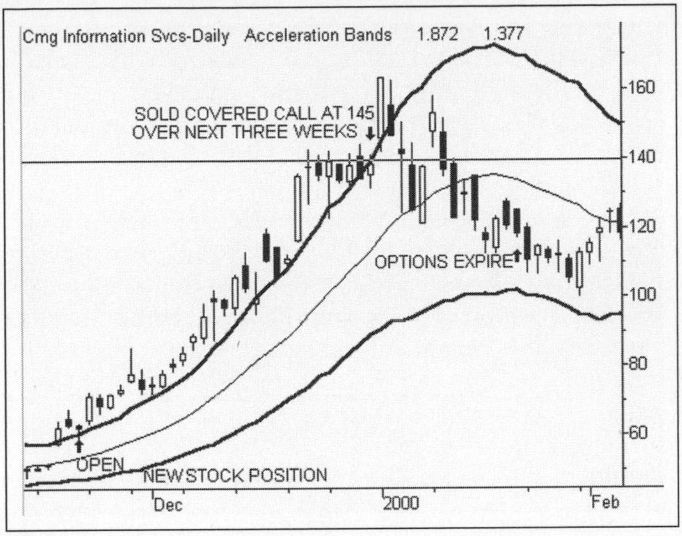

Chart created on TradeStation®, the flagship product of TradeStation Technologies, Inc.

falling, as there was apt to be a rush of investors who, like myself, were eager to lock in Internet stock profits once the new year hit. As you can see in Figure 11.1, that in fact did occur. The stock's first break was down to the 20-day moving average. In my daily stock service, subscribers actually bought more CMGI shares for a short-term trade when they touched the 20-day simple moving average as support. The rationale here is that the 20-day moving average as the mid-point of the Acceleration Bands often acts as support at first after a quick break back within the bands. The rewards were magnified as the stock bounced from the 125 area up to my short-term target at 150 in only two sessions, after which I unwound the pure stock position for a quick 20 percent gain while holding my covered call position since the stock was still firm. I could have bought back the covered call position by selling the stock and buying the option back for less than I paid for it. Instead, I rode out this position to the January options expiration, allowing the options to expire and selling the stock for 120.375. Since my option premium was fully collected, my effective sale price was another 13 points higher, at 133.375. This resulted in a 170 percent gain on the initial stock and covered call position. Obviously, I do not want to suggest that all situations should work out this well, but when you have a winning idea that you are getting nervous about, selling a covered call after much of the run-up can be the ticket to some nice incremental returns. (One caveat: Like collars, the covered call strategy is followed by the Internal Revenue Service near the end of the tax year. The general rule is that you should not sell calls more than one strike in-the-money or else you risk being classified as effectively selling your stock position in the prior tax year. I determined that I did not want to sell an in-the-money option, as I felt I could capture the time premium of the out-of-the-money call, plus give some room to let the stock run a little more to the upside.)

Buying puts on a stock is an alternative for investors with a low-cost basis who are seeking to avoid a taxable consequence on their stock. It also can make sense for an investor who believes in the stock long term and wants to ride out any short-term downturns. By buying a put and selling a call simultaneously, you can create what is known as a collar.

Collars

Zero-Cost Collar

A zero-cost collar will sell out of the money call and buy out of the money put the same distance away for the same premium on each side. The amount paid for the put for protection is offset by the amount collected for the call sale. The investor has gained a level of insurance in return for which the investor gives up the upside over a certain level. For example, if an investor bought a stock at 10 and it is now at 30, he could buy a 25-strike put and sell a 35-strike call both 5 points out-of-the-money, for zero cost. This would protect his gains if the stock fell under 25. In return, the investor gives up any appreciation in the stock above 35.

Put-Spread Collar

A put-spread collar will sell a low-strike price put, but sell a high strike price call. This approach offers more upside potential and keeps the hedge costless, but it does cause the investor to assume more risk.

There are tax implications to consider with collars. Your options should be out-of-the-money when you initiate this position. If you buy or sell in-the-money options, you will have to deal with the constructive sale rules. Here, the IRS considers that you effectively sold your stock if you sell a call more than one strike price in-the-money, which then creates the capital gain you were trying to avoid. There are two primary concerns with the tax rules here. You can lose your holding period on a short-term stock, and you cannot deduct your losses if one side of the position is still open.

If you collar a short-term stock, your holding period reverts to zero. So you would only want to consider this strategy for stocks you have held for at least 12 months. Once you collar the position, your holding period is considered frozen until you unwind the collared options position.

LONG-TERM EQUITY ANTICIPATION SECURITIES (LEAPS) AS A STOCK SUBSTITUTE

Long-Term Equity Anticipation Securities (LEAPS) are longer-term options, expiring as much as 39 months from the current date. LEAPS offer an investor a longer time frame to let a stock view play out, without being adversely affected by short-term market fluctuations that could temporarily delay and hurt shorter-term positions. Figure 11.2 shows an example of hypothetical stock ABC for a summary of the reward-versus-risk potential in using LEAPS as a stock substitute.

I recommended longer-term options in my NetLetter portfolio on April 5, 2001, for Household International (HI). The stock had given a longer-term buy signal on the monthly breakout above the Moving Average Envelopes, confirmed by the bullish Momentum Divergence indicator (see Figure 11.3). We discussed this powerful combination in Chapter 8, and it proved powerful again as HI steadily trended higher to allow me to capture a gain of 45 percent in the options position on a 21 percent gain in the underlying stock.

Figure 11.2   ABC LEAPS versus ABC Stock

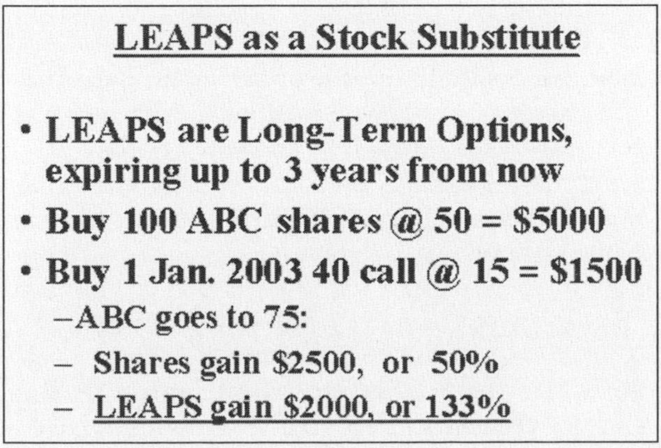

LEAPS as a Stock Substitute

- **LEAPS are Long-Term Options, expiring up to 3 years from now**
- **Buy 100 ABC shares @ 50 = $5000**
- **Buy 1 Jan. 2003 40 call @ 15 = $1500**
  - ABC goes to 75:
  - Shares gain $2500, or 50%
  - LEAPS gain $2000, or 133%

Figure 11.3   Household International Monthly 1994 to 2001

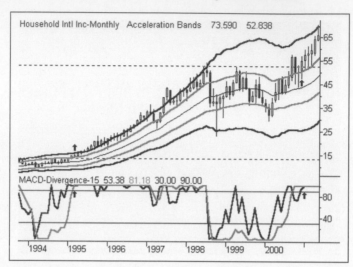

Household Intl Inc-Monthly   Acceleration Bands   73.590   52.838

MACD-Divergence-15 53.38 81.18 30.00 90.00

Chart created on TradeStation®, the flagship product of TradeStation Technologies, Inc.

IN-THE-MONEY OPTIONS AS A STOCK SUBSTITUTE

For a more aggressive way to use options as a stock substitute, consider In-the-Money (ITM) Options, as shown in Figure 11.4. With ITM options, you can reduce the effects of time decay, as the time premium of an option diminishes the deeper in-the-money that you buy your option. Let us look at a hypothetical stock XYZ in Figure 11.4 and compare buying short-term two-month options that are deep-in-the-money as a stock substitute.

I used this strategy in my NetLetter recommendation to buy May 30 calls on retailer Abercrombie & Fitch (ANF) on March 6, 2001 (see Figure 11.5). This buy signal occurred on the weekly chart based on three previously successful trades in a row once the stock broke above its Moving Average Envelopes and was confirmed by the Momentum Divergence signal. With the stock purchased at 32.01, I recommended May 30 calls at 4.00, and the position was sold when the stock reached 37.00 for a gain of 75 percent while the stock had gained just 15.6 percent.

DEVELOPING AN OEX OPTIONS STRATEGY

How to Profit from a Summer Sell Signal in the VIX with S&P 100 (OEX) Options

On June 13, 2001, I sent the following note to Erin Arvedlund, editor of "The Striking Price" options column in *Barron's* (she chose to publish parts of this strategy three days later):

Figure 11.4   XYZ In-the-Money versus XYZ Stock

In-The-Money's As a Stock Substitute

- **Buy In the Money Options to Get Rid of Time Value => Focus on Intrinsic**
- **Buy 100 XYZ shares @ 53 = $5300**
- **Buy 1-month 50 call @ 5.50 = $ 550**
  - –XYZ goes to 61 in 1 month or less:
  - **– Shares gain $800, or 15.1%**
  - **– ITMs gain $550, or 100%**

Figure 11.5   Abercrombie & Fitch Weekly 1999 to 2001

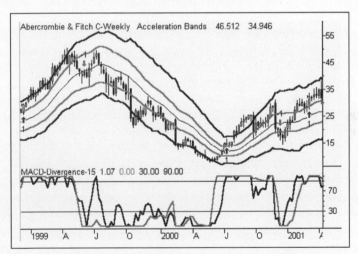

Chart created on TradeStation®, the flagship product of TradeStation Technologies, Inc.

Using the weekly CBOE Volatility Index (VIX) chart, I recently plotted 20-week Bollinger Bands around the VIX, with plus and minus one standard deviation—when the VIX sees a close outside these Bollinger Bands followed by the next week's close back into the band, then you have a contrarian buy signal (if coming from above the upper band back into the band, suggesting a peak in the VIX and a peak in fear to then buy the OEX) or a sell signal (if coming from below the bottom band back above it, suggesting a bottom in the VIX, or a sign that the greed/complacency period is ending).

The one caveat that improves performance significantly is to only take such signals when accompanied by technical price confirmation, which I used in the form of buy if the close this week is above the high of the prior week, or sell if the close this week is below the low of last week.

Based on these criteria, a sell signal for the OEX will occur at this week's close if below 647.64, the prior week week's low.

Past Performance

Historically, 11 of 16 prior signals have been profitable one week later, while maximum profitability over all sell signals is achieved by closing the short at the end of the third week (in which case 7 of 16 have been profitable, but total profits of 82.89 OEX points have been made on these shorts combined in three weeks).

In contrast, buy signals (the last occurring on April 13, 2001 at 608.26) are held until a sell signal reversal occurs, due to the uptrending nature of the market over time. Here the system has had 10 winners in 13 trades (77 percent) with a total of 510.80 points gained.

Adding up the total OEX points gained on both sides, the system has seen 593.69 points gained since the first signal on January 18, 1991 at 157.49 (so buy and hold has made 482.43 total points since that first signal, 111 points less than this system).

One interesting summer note is that summer sell signals have occurred in five of the last six years (including this week's signal). Only in 1997 did the market not get a summer sell.

The sells in 1996, 1998, and 1999 were profitable. The July 2000 signal was not profitable over the three-week holding period, but the early September 2000 signal was profitable.

Strategies

The odds of the OEX exploding to the upside are relatively low over the next several weeks, which makes me think first of call credit spreads on the OEX. Since I tend to find OEX options relatively expensive compared to the amount of movement you tend to get in the OEX, credit spreads and debit spreads make sense in this environment.

Selling the OEX July 660 (last night bid 8.80) and buying the OEX July 665 (last nite [sic] asked 7.80) for a net credit of $100 per spread looks like a good deal to me—of course, the goal here is to have the options expire worthless over the next five weeks (or buy them back after three weeks if the market really plunges hard), with any close at 660 or under making this position a winner at July expiration. That gives us 20 points of breathing room, which I believe is more than enough given the pending sell signal.

> OEX debit spreads would be a second choice—buying the OEX
> July 650 put and selling the OEX July 630 put for a net debit of $800
> looks reasonable to me with the potential to pocket $1,200.

As a follow-up, the credit spread position expired worthless, allowing the full $100 credit per contract (roughly an 18 percent return on margin after commissions) to be collected. The debit spread reached a peak of $1,180 for a 48 percent gain during the month, and closed up 28 percent at the July expiration (see Figure 11.6).

Option Charts: Predict Stock Price Movements with the Power of Option Charting

As an options trader these last 10-plus years, it always amazes me that options speculators are still doing much of their analysis off the stock chart, without much attention to options charts. Certainly there are traders who execute complicated options strategies who use options software to create diagrams of potential payoffs, but I am talking about actually tracking the option's day-to-day price movement in a chart to determine the trend of the option.

Option charts incorporate the elements of *time* and *volatility* relative to the price action of the underlying stock. If a stock was dead flat over a period of weeks, which direction would the options chart be headed? *Down!* Because the option is losing time—so that as time erodes and the stock does not move—the option becomes increasingly less valuable as it approaches its expiration.

Figure 11.6   S&P 100 Index (OEX) versus CBOE Volatility Index (VIX) June to July 2001

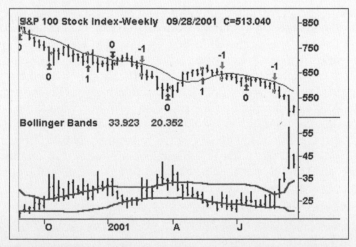

Chart created on TradeStation®, the flagship product of TradeStation Technologies, Inc.

Figure 11.7   Comverse Technology with 10-Day Exponential Moving Average

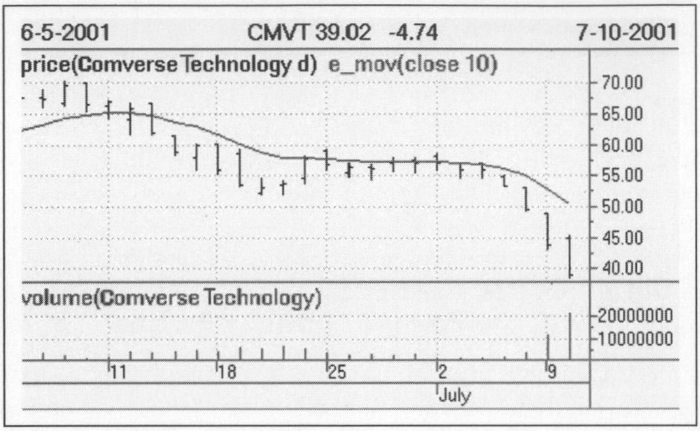

Chart created on TradeStation®, the flagship product of TradeStation Technologies, Inc.

Options charts also help sort out the developing trends from the increasing noise in today's price action. If a stock is truly breaking out, its option chart should be breaking out as well. This helps me find the situations I am truly looking for: where the stock price movement is more than overcoming the loss of time in the option. Thus, options charts can act not only as an options trading methodology, but also as a guide to pick only the best trending stocks.

Comparison of Comverse Technology July 60 Put (CQVSL) versus Comverse Technology Shares' Price Action

On June 27, 2001, I recommended the Comverse Technology July 60 put (CQVSL) in my Aggressive Options Trader service at an average entry price of 6.90. This entry was primarily driven by technical analysis, as the stock has been showing poor Relative Strength versus the Nasdaq Composite. In addition, the stock had held resistance at its 10-day exponential moving average (EMA) beautifully, and CMVT had broken prior technical support in the 58 to 60 area. I put the options trade on intraday when the stock was trading around 55, and I liked the 60 put better than the 55 put due to the five points of intrinsic value in the 60 put (meaning only two points of time value at risk in the 60 put). The stock subsequently shot down to my downside target at 45 on July 9th, leading to a 108.7 percent gain in the option position in only eight trading days (see Figure 11.7).

My options chart analysis shows how you can do even better by following the options chart as compared to the stock chart. The daily options chart is plotted just like a stock chart, capturing the high, low, and close for the actual options trades in a given day (we like to look at relatively active

Figure 11.8   Comverse Technology July 60 Put (CQVSL) with 10-Day
Exponential Moving Average

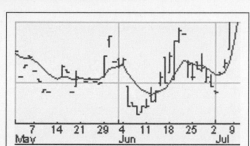

options contracts, since if an option does not trade, it will not offer any data points to plot for that trading session). I have plotted a 10-day exponential moving average (EMA) on the chart as well, seen in Figure 11.8.

As you can see from the chart, the option really takes off to the upside, or drops to the downside, once the 10-day EMA is broken. One methodology I use at BigTrends.com is to buy the option on a second straight close in a row above the 10-day EMA. For the Comverse Technology July 60 put, this occurred when the option closed at 6.60 on July 5th (since July 4th was a holiday). As you can see, the option then skyrocketed over the next three sessions to reach my initial target around 15. So the options chart actually allowed an options buyer to profit by a great amount in less than half the time that the stock chart analysis took to play out.

Clearly options charts are all about factoring in the elements of an option's price that are not related to normal stock chart analysis. The main element is time, and the other element is the change in volatility that the option will undergo during its life.

Open Interest

Another options indicator I follow is Open Interest, which is the number of options contracts open at a particular strike price. I often notice a key Open Interest level where a lot of options bets have been made, which proves to be a key support or resistance level. The Nasdaq 100 Trust (QQQ) had its last major August 2001 put open interest level at the 40 strike, where over 100,000 options contracts were open. Not coincidentally, the low on August 8 in the QQQ was 39.98 before it bounced in the late afternoon. This made the 40 level the final "line in the sand" for the market from an existing short-term support level. If the market closed under 39.50, it would confirm the final breakdown that I expected to lead to a more significant short-term decline for stocks.

Table 11.5   Nasdaq 100 Trust (QQQ) Open Interest Heavy at 40

	August Calls	August Puts	August Total
STRIKE			
37	3,351	41,168	44,519
38	3,928	27,242	31,170
39	19,046	53,915	72,961
40	63,205	120,915	**184,120**
41	99,033	60,022	159,055
42	113,809	54,781	168,590
43	21,017	90,717	111,734

Figure 11.9   Nasdaq 100 Trust (QQQ) Breaks Under 40 Support on a Closing Basis

Chart created on TradeStation®, the flagship product of TradeStation Technologies, Inc.

Table 11.5 and Figure 11.9 show the importance of this 40 level on the QQQ.

There are a number of other options strategies that traders use, including debit and credit spreads, strangles, straddles, and naked put or call selling. I do not focus on these strategies, as they do not give me the bang for my buck as a directional trader compared to the simple strategies previously listed. There are many excellent books for the non-directional trader if you want to learn these strategies also. See the Bibliography for more options strategy texts.

Figure 11.10   Growth of Account on $1 Doubled Every Day

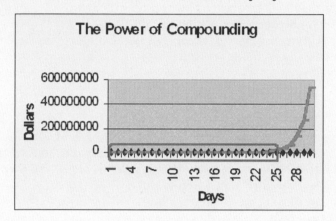

The Power of Compounding—Let Profits Run and Cut Losses Short

Let us say you were to double $1 every day for a period of 30 days as shown in Figure 11.10. In 10 days you would be up to $512, in 20 days you would be up to $524,288, and in 30 days you would be up to an amazing $536,870,912. But look further at the effect of daily doubling on the chart in Figure 11.10.

Once I charted the $1 doubling every day, I was blown away by the implications. At first thought, going up 100 percent per period shows no acceleration, and indeed if this chart were plotted based on a geometric basis in percentage terms, it would appear to be going up at a linear same rate of pace in every period. But when I plot the total dollar value, the chart shows the biggest dollar profits are made in the last five days of the 30-day period! In fact, the dollar gains in the final five days are so great that they make the prior 25 days of gains appear as almost a flat line near zero (though they are not, of course—remember, at 20 days, we are up over $500,000—it just looks this way relative to much bigger dollars that come later).

Let us now equate this to a trading principle: your best dollar gains will occur the longer you can hold a favorably-performing investment that is still compounding positively. While this may not sound like a revelation to some, let me ask you this: Have you ever sold one of your better-performing stocks, thinking it was "too high," only to cringe after watching it take off even higher soon after you sold it? I certainly have, and I think most investors have experienced this pain of "missing out." The important concept here is to give yourself the ability to stay with these big trends that carry your portfolio, perhaps for longer than you have previously been comfortable holding your position. At the same time, have a stop-loss discipline for positions that are not working, so that you can seek to focus your capital in better-performing ideas.

Since options involve the extra leverage that can really help (or hurt) compounding, let us focus on strategies to both reduce risk and still stay with the big winners.

Where Should Stops Be Placed on Options?

While most stock investors look for a stop rule around 5 to 8 percent on a stock, options traders need more room to breathe due to the extra leverage in the options position. My study of years of my own options purchases has revealed that when I start to lose 20 percent or more on an end-of-day closing basis, then the market is telling me that my options position is usually best exited, as it is not working out as I had expected. Notice in Figure 11.11 how much it takes to recover back to where the account value was before the loss. If a trader takes a $10,000 account and loses 20 percent down to $8,000, it will then take a $2,000 gain on the new $8,000 account value (a 25 percent gain) to get back to even. This is manageable, but as things start to slip below a 20 percent gain, a trader has to make back even more percentage points. For example, a 50 percent loss ($10,000 to $5,000) requires a 100 percent gain ($5,000 gain on a new $5,000 base) in order to get even. That is an extra 50 percentage points you have to make up (100 percent gain minus 50 percent loss) as opposed to the five percentage points a trader has to make up from a 20 percent loss to a 25 percent gain. Some then logically ask, "So why not take the 10 percent loss and only have to make up one percentage point?" Because that stop level is too tight with options in my experience. In some cases the bid/asked spread may be more than 10 percent. If you buy and option at the market at 1.20 when it is bid 1.00 and offered 1.20, you

Figure 11.11 Percentage Gain Needed to Break Even After a Loss

Percentage Loss	Gain Required to Breakeven
-10%	11%
-20%	25%
-33%	50%
-50%	100%
-75%	300%
-90%	900%

are already looking at a 16.7 percent loss if you turn right around and sell it at the bid of 1.00. That is why most of the options I buy are in the $3 to $8 range, where these bid/asked spreads are not so wide on a percentage basis. It also drives home the point that your entry level is critical, as it determines how much of a loss you are willing to accept before abandoning the trade. The closer you can get your entry to your "make or break" level, the lower your risk will be, and the higher your Reward-to-Risk ratio will be. The final point on the options stop/loss is that stops are even more critical for options buyers because of the impact of time. With stocks you do not worry as much about the stock going sideways— you just do not want to lose. The problem for the options buyer is that a sideways move in the stock means the option will decline in value due to the loss of time. Therefore, you are not only wrong if the underlying stock price is moving in the direction opposite of what you expected. You are also wrong and losing value if the stock is going flat over time as well. That makes quick stops all the more critical in options buying, to get your capital out of these non-movers and into a fresher situation with a better chance to move in your favor.

How to Stay with Big Options Winners

Give yourself a chance to stay with a Big Trend by taking *half* of your position profits at a 100 percent gain or higher (see Figure 11.11). This allows you to release the fear of giving up profits, as you recoup your initial investment and guarantee at least a breakeven on the entire position in the worst-case scenario, should the other half positions go to nothing. I call these remaining half positions No-Risk Trades, as you cannot lose if you take this first half out at a double (or slightly more if you want to factor in a small commission). Taking a double on half is very freeing emotionally, as you release the reference point issue that consistently vexes most traders. The market does not care where you bought or sold—it will do what it is going to do. By releasing the fear of letting a profit turn into a loss, you have much more emotional staying power on the other half position, and can really aim for the fences on this part of the position. You still need to apply sound money management rules. The rules I follow once I take half of my position profits at a double is as follows: on the upside, I will target to take out half of my remaining half position (one-fourth of the original position) if the position doubles yet again. Meanwhile, I place a closing trailing stop to exit the position if it gives back half of its profits from its high point. For example, say I trade 10 contracts in an option on XYZ. The position doubles, and I sell five at a 100 percent profit. My trailing closing stop/loss is now at a 50 percent gain. Any close at a 50 percent

Figure 11.12   How to Stay with Big Winners

> - Give yourself a chance to stay with a Big Trend by taking HALF of your position profits at 100% or more
> - This allows you to release the fear of giving up profits, as you recoup your initial investment and guarantee at least a breakeven
> - Ride the other half position until it gives back half its gains, or exit half again if it later doubles once more

gain or lower from my initial purchase price, and I will close the remaining position. It then goes to a 200 percent profit, so I sell another two contracts (I cannot sell partial contracts, so I round down to the nearest contract). I now raise my closing stop to a 100 percent gain as my stop point on a closing basis. Some may wonder if this 100 percent gap as a stop is too wide. I believe that you want to give your best ideas room to breathe, and as they go up dramatically, they tend to become more volatile as the trend progresses, so you want to have some leeway to stay on board. This approach gives you room to ride the big winners, while also still having a plan to exit at a healthy profit (see Figure 11.12).

Another Way to Look at Compounding—Shoot for Consistency

The Power of Compounding

The consistency of your gains over time can be very important in how your money grows. Many investors think in terms of averaging out gains arithmetically (by adding a gain and a loss and dividing by 2, for example +100 percent and −50 percent equals an average of +25 percent), when as an investor you really need to think geometrically (+100 percent and then −50 percent = zero total return). Let us look at Table 11.6, which shows what happens if you were to make 15 percent per year consistently, versus if you were to experience similar arithmetic results but with greater volatility every two years.

As you can see, the more consistent your returns are over time, the more your account will grow. Aim for consistency—keep stops relatively tight while seeking to squeeze the most gain out of your best trading ideas.

Table 11.6   The Importance of Consistency in Compounding

	6 Years	12 Years	24 Years	50 Years
+15% Per Year	131%	435%	2763%	108266%
+20%, Then +10%	130%	429%	2698%	103259%
+30%, Then 0%	120%	383%	2229%	70464%
+40%, Then −10%	100%	300%	1501%	32305%
+50%, Then −20%	72%	199%	792%	9440%
+60%, Then −30%	40%	97%	290%	1600%
+70%, Then −40%	6%	13%	27%	64%

THE 80/20 RULE IN TRADING

Ever heard of the 80/20 Rule, also known as the Pareto Principle? Dr. Joseph Juran, the total quality management guru, developed the Pareto Principle after studying the work of Wilfredo Pareto, a nineteenth century economist. The Pareto Principle states that a small percentage of situations (typically around 20 percent) will create a large percentage of the results (usually around 80 percent). Expanding Pareto to trading, it follows that roughly 80 percent of a trader's profits should come from only 20 percent of his or her trades. In options trading, the numbers can be even more dramatic. In Figure 11.13, I looked at all of my options purchases over a six-month period (January to June 30, 1999). Starting with a $50,000 account, investing 15 percent per trade, and including commissions, an investor finished the six-month period with a total value of $216,560. In contrast, I sorted out just those trades which managed to double or more in that period. Notice that there are a number of "half positions," per my earlier goal of selling half of my position at a double or more to create the No-Risk Trade. Adding up all these full and half positions, there are 8-1/2 positions out of 64 that doubled or more in that period. That is 13.3 percent of my trades, and they accounted for more than 100 percent of my profits, as these trades alone totaled an account value of $245,982! This is more like an 113/13 rule—113 percent of my profits came from 13 percent of my trades. The lesson here is that in options buying, a small percentage of your trades, the best trades, will carry your portfolio results if you let them. As you can see, if you exit these big profits too quickly, you would dramatically reduce your total profitability. What I have created is a "Success Profile" for my best winning trades (see the Trading Plan section for my Success Profile). At the same time, the remaining 80 percent of your trades that do not produce these big profits need to be evaluated for how quickly you can get rid of them. As soon as my Success Profile breaks down for a stock or options,

Figure 11.13   The 80/20 Rule Magnified in Options Trading

THE 80/20 RULE IN ACTION

S1 Corp. (1/2 position)	Apr. 90 call	$20,378	295.7%
Vignette (1/2 position)	Mar. 220 call	$33,878	240.4%
CMGI	Mar. 130 call	$9,470	214.5%
Nvidia (half-position)	July 120 call	$30,540	213.5%
S1 Corp.	May 55 call	$7,395	200.4%
Exodus Comm. (1/2 positi	Mar. 145 call	$21,915	184.9%
S1 Corp. (1/2 position)	Apr. 90 call	$12,278	178.3%
S&P 100 Index (1/2 positic	Feb. 760 put	$20,803	169.0%
Nvidia (1/2 position)	July 120 call	$25,855	136.2%
Nvidia (1/2 position)	July 120 call	$15,665	109.6%
Knight/Trimark	July 55 call	$4,420	104.9%
Exodus Comm. (1/2 positi	Mar. 145 call	$11,840	100.0%
Vignette (1/2 position)	Mar. 220 call	$14,078	100.0%
CommerceOne (1/2 positi	Mar. 220 call	$17,470	100.0%
8-1/2 (of 64 total) Positions		$245,982	
		$216,560	

I exit that position. This is the case even if the position is still profitable, because I am seeing that the pattern no longer holds. That capital will be better used in a fresher situation with a better opportunity to grow more quickly (see Figure 11.13).

We have covered plenty of ground here in the basic options strategies you should know to capture the best bang for your buck while still managing your risk appropriately in an options trade. Now that you understand the mechanics behind successful stock and options selection, let us move to the next section where I will review the aspects behind executing your trading plan, including money management concepts and psychological elements that you need to understand as you trade.

12

TRADING PSYCHOLOGY AND MONEY MANAGEMENT

I have covered in earlier sections the building blocks for methods that can create an edge for you, but now the challenge is to address several other areas that are quite often overlooked by most traders. These areas focus on building a trading plan that will fit your personality, psychological issues you may encounter when trading, and effective money management rules to minimize your risk of loss while maximizing your ability to profit from big trends.

CREATING AND IMPLEMENTING A TRADING PLAN

You may have heard the old saying, "Most people don't plan to fail; they just fail to plan." Planning how you will operate in the markets before you ever place a trade is critical, because this allows you to know how you will act in a variety of scenarios that can develop once you place the trade. This takes you out of a potentially emotional reaction to price action, and instead positions you to proactively take advantage of opportunities created by other emotional traders.

First you must define your trading process. My method focuses on a "top down" approach, focusing first on defining the overall market environment, then looking for relatively strong or weak stocks in the right sectors, and then defining an options strategy that fits my expectations where appropriate.

Definition of Goals

You must also define exactly what you want from your trading. Write out your specific goals. Once you define a dollar amount you will make for the year, break that goal down into what you need to make each month, each week, and each day on average. Your goals should not be just monetary. Your goals sheet should also list other areas like improving your percentage of winning trades, widening the size of your winners or reducing the size of your losers, and making sure to review your processes daily, to name a few.

177

Goals give us something to strive for, something to achieve. They focus our attention and our energy to give our efforts a clear direction. Setting goals gives the trader a feeling of control over what actions to take to accomplish a goal. This allows traders to grow beyond past limiting beliefs or fears that had previously held them back.

Performance or process goals (how well I followed my system) are better than outcome goals (how much money I made today). Try not to worry about the outcome, as that leads to a dilution of your energy. Focus on improving your performance and the outcome will be the result of meeting your performance goals.

1. Set specific, measurable goals, with a deadline date to completion. Personally, I like to set two deadline dates, a "want-to" completion date and a "need-to" completion date. This allows me to stay focused on the first "want-to" due date, while having some breathing room if an unexpected event temporarily delays me in my pursuit of the objective.

2. Set a long-term goal and define short-term goals needed to achieve your ultimate goal. Short-term goals have more focus than long-term goals, especially if deadlines are set. Individuals will lose motivation if it takes too long to reach a big goal without seeing progress along the way. Break long-term goals down into bite-size pieces that you can more easily focus on to track your progress. Monitoring your progress toward your goal gives you needed feedback.

3. Set challenging, yet attainable goals that will push you toward your limits.

4. Set performance goals as opposed to outcome goals. Every time you prepare to trade, and every day you are trading, you should be focused on a performance objective.

5. Monitor goals periodically and change your plan if you are not getting the results you expected. Many people are afraid of changing their initial plan, but I remember a valuable insight from former Chrysler chairman Lee Iacocca. He noted that some decisions are irreversible, and should be studied intensely before making a decision. But he also said that most decisions are not irreversible. Most decisions can be easily changed, and thus these decisions should be made quickly based on what you believe to be the correct decision at the time. You should not agonize or delay such decisions, but rather make the best decision with the data available at the time. If that is still not producing the results you want, then make another decision. The key element here is action. The hardest part of making changes for most people, myself included, is getting started. Once you can make a change quickly, then monitor it against your goals, you have the ability to powerfully change your financial future. The worst decision often is not making any de-

cision at all. Like Thomas Edison, who failed in thousands of experiments to finally get to an illuminated light bulb, you have to treat failure as evidence that you are one step closer to achieving your goal. If Edison had stopped part of the way through his process, and failed only half as much, he would not have become one of the greatest inventors of all time.

6. Keep your focus on your goal. Put a message to yourself on your computer monitor or in your journal, with whatever goal you want to focus on. Remember, you get what you focus on. Are you focused on any specific goal lately? As Yogi Berra said, "If you don't know where you are going, any road will get you there!" And usually the roads we take without a plan do not take us to the places we really want to be.

7. Once you accomplish a goal, celebrate—and then set a new goal!

You should also write out your trading edge. What do you do that generates a positive expectation in your results over time? Focus your efforts on that edge, and become an expert at a particular set of patterns in the markets that work for you.

Key Questions to Consider for Your Trading Plan

1. How will you enter trades?
2. How will you exit trades?
3. What type of orders will you use to enter and exit?
4. How much capital will you need to trade successfully?
5. What percentage of your capital will you invest in each trade?
6. How many positions will you focus on at once?
7. What will your Trading Journal look like?
8. What is your Position Review process?
9. What is your preparation process before trading?
10. What broker will you use?

I have a number of ideas to consider as you approach these key areas of your plan.

How Will You Enter Trades?

Entries should be defined by your system or method's signals. You should make sure you can make every new trade without losing focus. The key to good entries is putting on trades where there is relatively low risk compared to much higher reward. You should also write down a clear catalyst or "driver" for the expected stock move. You should have a written list of rules for entry, with your primary indicators defined precisely. Most traders enter trades with too little thought, on a whim or on a new piece of news, without doing the diligent homework required to make sure the odds favor their entry over time. The secret of great entries, in my experience, is in defining key points where you can be wrong relatively little before you have to exit the trade with a small loss, while having the potential to be right and win much bigger than you are wrong. This sets up what I call the Reward-to-Risk ratio, which preferably is 3-to-1 or higher and must be defined by objective analysis before you enter the trade. These low-risk entry points can occur at key support and resistance levels, and should include methods that alert you when these zones of opportunity are reached. When placing the trade to enter, the trader should already have defined specific exit strategies as well.

How Will You Exit Trades?

Exits are multi-faceted compared to entries. As some say, "entries are easy; exits are hard." It is easy to get into a trade but requires more effort to determine where you will get out of a trade. First, you have to have in place your plan for how you will take losses. Always worry about cutting losses first, and deal with the gains later. You should define an initial stop point for your trade before you enter the trade. This determines the risk you are willing to take. The whole purpose of a stop is to define the point at which the trend is invalidated. The potential reward should preferably be three or more times the risk you are willing to take. Next, you need to determine if a position is working for you, and how you will protect your profits. This is known as a trailing stop. In a good uptrend, I prefer to use a close under the 10-day exponential moving average as my trailing stop, unless I am using another method as my driver in the trade, such as a close back into a stock's Acceleration Bands.

At this point, let me explain my preferred stop method. I tend to use "closing stops," meaning I do not want to place my stop order intraday to be gunned by the floor or taken out by day-trader noise. I like to say that a lot of battles are fought during the trading day, but the war is won at the close. We want to wait to see who wins the war at the end of the session. If XYZ stock is going to close against my closing stop level, then I place a market order to close the position in the final minutes of trading. If the stock happens to be within a few cents of this level and it is unclear, I will wait for the close, and if my level breaks, I will make sure to sell it at the market on the next trading day's opening price. This has kept me from getting whipped out of a number of good swing trades during the day, while still giving me the ability to exit when the stock has proved me wrong by day's end. Some worry that a stock may move too far against them by the close compared to an intraday stop, and occasionally a stock will be filled well against our closing stop by the end of the day. But that risk is small compared to the bigger risk of getting whipped out of a position intraday, only to have it post a strong reversal in our favor and be off to the races. These situations are very similar to the "Bend But Don't Break" methods I highlighted regarding Acceleration Bands in Chapter 7. You want to wait for the end of that bar's close. If the chart is a weekly chart, wait until the end of the week's close to stay with the true trend while others will tend to get faked out.

The final exit issue we need to deal with here is how to take profits. Should we use a fixed target, or should we only use trailing stops on winning positions until the trend breaks? The answer depends on your risk tolerance. For conservative traders, I recommend sticking with price targets compared to defined risk levels, as you can lock in profits more safely that way. For more aggressive traders I usually recommend taking half of the position off at a price target, and then tightening your trailing stop to the breakdown of a fast moving average, like a five-day moving average. That way you give yourself a chance to stay with a winning stock, while keeping the profits given up from your initial target level to a minimum. In options trading, I am a big believer in using price targets to recapture my initial risk capital by taking a 100 percent profit on half of my position. Here are the simple rules I follow with options purchases:

1. If my position loses more than 20 percent on a closing basis, exit the position at the end of that day.
2. Allow a chance for a Big Trend by taking half the position off at a double, and let the other half ride. Exit the remaining half position if it gives back half its maximum profit on a closing basis, or scale out of the remaining half position every time it doubles again.

When your profit or loss is realized, are you done? No. Record your lessons learned in your Trading Journal at the end of each day, while your thoughts are fresh about that trade. Save any necessary confirmations for tax preparation.

What Type of Orders Will You Use to Enter and Exit?

I have a strong opinion about this subject, and it differs between entry and exit. When entering, I like to use limit orders, good for the day only, as opposed to market orders. Why? Because the limit price I choose sets the Reward-to-Risk ratio for my trades, relative to my stop and target levels for the trade. If I place a market order on a stock that closed at 51 that has a target at 55 and a closing stop under 50, and the stock gaps higher by two points the next morning on the opening to cause me to enter at 53, my Reward-to-Risk ratio has just flipped from 4-to-1 to now be at 2-to-3 (or 0.67-to-1)! Even a one-point gap higher would change the Reward-to-Risk ratio from 4-to-1 to 3-to-2 (or 1.5-to-1). Some may say that you might want to be riding a stock that was gapping higher at the opening. If it still fits my Reward-to-Risk parameters, preferably of 3-to-1 or higher, I may place a day limit order to buy a stock that is above its closing price for the next day's trading. If the stock opens below that limit, then the limit order is immediately converted to a market order to buy that stock. In these situations, you are not giving up these trades by placing a limit order. The runaway movers which no longer fit my Reward-to-Risk criteria can be left to other traders, as there will be another opportunity following very soon after any missed trades. This allows me to cultivate patience and remain disciplined in my approach.

On the exit, however, I generally prefer market orders if the market has not taken me out at my target or at my stop. If a trade is just sitting there and I see a better use for my capital, a market order gets the capital back into my account the quickest, making it available to be redeployed into better situations promptly. More importantly, while trying to "work" the trade with a limit above the market when my indicators said it was time to exit, I have experienced firsthand the pain of not getting filled at my limit, seeing the stock drop and placing a new limit back where I should have exited at the market. Then I have realized I was not going to get filled there, either, so I again kept lowering my limit until, in frustration, I placed a market order to exit much lower than I could have been out earlier in the session. Not only can it be draining to your financial capital, but here too you can be drained psychologically by the frustration of not getting filled. Plus you are wasting valuable time replacing orders if not filled, versus focusing your valuable energy on new opportunities instead of on old non-movers.

When seeking to lock in gains as the stock zeroes in on your target profit level, consider using "market if touched" (MIT) orders rather than limit orders. The difference between them is shown in that sometimes your price will be reached, but another trader is in front of you to exit, and then the price backs away from your target. With an MIT order, as soon as the stock trades at your specified price level, your MIT order is converted from a limit order to a market order. While you may give up a few cents by selling at the market rather than trying to work your limit order, you are guaranteed to avoid the unpleasant situation of missing your target exit and then seeing your position reverse sharply against you while you still hold it.

Exits on options purchased also involve another form of stop: the time stop. On underlying positions that are directionless and floating sideways, options buyers will feel the effects of time decay as the options get closer to expiration. In addition, my belief is that if you have not seen the options you bought move up by 20 percent or more within three trading days to no more than five trading days, then the market has not proven you correct in your timing. Not only do you risk the negative effects of time decay if you hang on in hope that the position will get moving, but you also have an opportunity cost that causes you to miss out on better options movers elsewhere. While most traders do not think to associate pain with a position until it is underwater, my thought process is to associate pain as soon as I realize that my capital can be more effectively put to work in another position. This quick pain threshold may make me seem impatient at times, but the ability to cut and run on non-movers, especially in options and even in stocks, is a valuable skill to cultivate.

In addition, I prefer chart-based stops just under support or just over resistance on a closing basis, as opposed to fixing my loss at a predetermined percentage or dollar amount. Certainly you want to place new trades right near key levels, where you can be taken out quickly if a key level or indicator does not hold while having a chance for three or more times as much reward for your risk. See Appendix B for a full definition of the different types of orders you can place.

How Much Capital Will You Need to Invest Effectively?

In today's markets, you should have at least $10,000, and preferably $20,000 or more, in risk capital to trade. If you try to trade with less capital, the economies of scale diminish. For example, if you traded once per day at $20 round trip in commissions, that is $5,000 in 250 trading days, or one year; so right away a $10,000 account needs to make 50 percent to cover these fees, while a $50,000 account needs to make just 10 percent to cover these commission costs. You should also factor in any other costs you incur to trade, such as quote vendors, trading software, and computer, if dedicated. You can see that the more you invest on the front end, the bigger your account should be to make these costs back more easily.

What Percentage of Your Capital Will You Invest in Each Trade?

The amount of capital I typically use is 10 percent per trade in my own accounts. I know traders who commit anywhere from 5 percent of their account per trade to 20 percent of their account per trade. As the amount you commit per trade goes up, the volatility of your portfolio will rise. As a result, I seek not to risk more than 2 percent of my total account equity on any losing positions, and I generally prefer not risking more than 1 percent of my total account equity on a losing trade. So if I invest 10 percent of my portfolio in a trade, and I want to keep my total portfolio risk at 1.5 percent, then I must stop the position if it reaches a 15 percent loss in the worst case (10 percent invested in a 15 percent losing position equals a 1.5 percent loss for the portfolio).

I also seek not to risk more than 2 percent of my total account equity on any losing positions, and I generally prefer not risking more than 1 percent of my total account equity on a losing trade.

The Kelly formula shows another way to determine the optimal percentage of capital to risk per trade:

The formula is: Kelly %= =W − (1−W) / V

W=Winning Percentage

(1−W)=Losing Percentage

V=Average Winning Trade / Average Losing Trade

If W=60 percent

If Average Winning Trade=500

If Average Losing Trade=250

Then Kelly % would=40 percent

The Kelly formula suffers from a drawback in that it assumes all profits and losses are equal, which is not the case. However, it can help a trader get an approximate assessment of the percentage to invest once he or she knows the system's winning percentage and the size of its average winner and average loser.

How Many Positions Will You Focus on at One Time?

I recommend you trade only a few stocks at a time. I like to concentrate my portfolio in my best ideas, plus I like to stay focused on how each stock is acting. If my portfolio is too big (I would say more than five to seven stocks is too many to focus on), then I will lose focus and invariably miss an exit on a trade that I should have previously exited. When looking for new opportunities, I will use computers to boil down thousands of stocks to ultimately keep the top three stocks I want to add to my portfolio at predefined levels. If my systems still leave me too many stocks and too many factors to look at, I will be unable to keep up with information overload. This will leave my mind overwhelmed, which will lead to an inability to pull the trigger. Famous analyst Richard Wyckoff suggested to look for signals you might need a break from trading: "The first is a technical warning—the situation in which your analysis gives unclear, confused signals. The other two are emotional—relying on 'instinct' rather than research and a growing or chronic indecisiveness about executing trades." Stay focused on a small number of top-performing stocks as an antidote to avoid burnout from information overload.

Information overload deserves additional discussion here, as the Internet age has spawned an endless amount of information, literally at our fingertips. Yet that can also lead to unproductive time and efforts being diluted as we get distracted by other information that interests us. How can we be sure to concentrate on our goal amid a sea of data and news?

We are constantly bombarded by an endless array of internal and external thoughts and emotions. We must develop the ability to focus on what is important while blocking out the rest. This process of directing our awareness to relevant data while ignoring irrelevant information is termed "selective attention." Concentration is the ability to sustain attention on selected stimuli for an extended period of time. Effective concentration has been described as effortless effort, being in "the zone" or in "flow" or being totally absorbed in the present moment.

Concentration is a difficult skill to master because our minds tend to lose focus when presented with new information. Here are some tips to improve concentration, adapted from John Murray's *Smart Tennis*, which can be useful to traders as well:

1. Avoid negative thoughts and feelings, as these are needless distractions which rob us of our limited attentional resources.
2. Remain focused on the present, attending to what is immediately important and blocking out past and future concerns. After a mistake, briefly write down any changes necessary, then move decisively to the next trade.
3. Recite key words or phrases to yourself prior to the trade to remind yourself to concentrate (e.g., "focus," "control," "good contact").
4. Be task rather than outcome-oriented. Thinking about dollars or whether you are right or wrong are common distractions. Your results will improve when you focus on your trading process and let the outcome flow from effective processes.
5. Slightly relax between trades while avoiding external distractions. Some traders achieve this by clearing their head of the emotions of a profitable or losing closed trade and visualizing the next low-risk trade set up needed to keep the odds of success.
6. Add a ritual, or consistent routine, to your trading process (e.g., writing and reviewing trading rules before and after a trade is placed) to help create a repeating pattern preventing distractions and keeping your mind focused.
7. Be particularly vigilant to be consistent and avoid getting too high or too low after a trade. Traders often lose their focus when coming off a big winning or losing trade. Review your rules and stay unemotional towards your next trade.

8. Attention and arousal are closely related. Avoid becoming overly excited or agitated while remaining focused on executing trades and consistently implementing your strategy. Breathing and relaxation exercises can help lower arousal and keep you calm and focused.

What Will Your Trading Journal Look Like?

It is critical to keep a Trading Journal. I ask myself at the end of every day, "Did I execute my trading plan properly?" If I did execute my plan correctly but I lost money, I give my trading that day a plus. If I did not execute my plan, even if I made money, I give my trading a minus. I also ask what caused me not to execute my plan. Was it lack of confidence in the system, fear, distractions, or something else? Then I write out a positive solution regarding how I can fix this in the future. I also write down if I overrode any of my rules—I have generally found that my ego-based decisions to tinker with my system added little value, and often hurt more than they helped. The ego wants to feel like it is adding value on top of the system, to make the trader feel important. I believe that trading for ego satisfaction is probably even more damaging than trading for entertainment or excitement, as the ego risks getting damaged by the financial fallout that can occur.

In my Trading Journal, I also note any insights I had on the current market, patterns that were working or not working, and other issues I encountered. I also list in my daily review any thoughts, feelings, ideas for improvement, strategies that did or did not work, and so on. Reviewing your entries in a Trading Journal helps you identify your strengths and weaknesses.

I trade not only to make money, which is the first goal, but also to learn about myself. Trading not only gives us lessons about what to do or not to do next time in a trade, but also life lessons about personality traits that could improve the rest of our lives—IF we are willing to work on them. Like all habits we form, change takes time, and we must commit to improving one element of our trading personality at a time, with total focus. For example, why do we let losses ride and cut profits short? I think part of the answer for me comes from experiences I recalled in my Trading Journal:

April 4, 2000

Why did I have trouble in the past taking losses? Because I was too much of a perfectionist, too concerned about looking good to others, and not wanting to admit I was wrong!

I have this tremendous desire to prove myself RIGHT! All of my school training says there is ONE right answer. In the stock market there are numerous right answers, many ways to win. The way to lose is to stick with your losers and have capital tied up in the dogs while better opportunities pass you by.

On stocks that rally sharply, I often have a sense that I have AL-READY missed out—in retrospect, many of these stocks go on to much bigger profits than the initial gain I missed. . . .

This goes back to my PERFECTIONIST tendencies, which have cost me too many great trades to recount in one sitting. The desire for the perfect entry, and the ego drive that says, "Dummy, you missed it . . . all is lost" is a big drag on my performance, as it is those huge winning trades which, while occurring less frequently, are the ones which CARRY my portfolio. This is even more true in options trading.

Perfectionism may help some people succeed in many other careers, but it can be fatal in trading. Ironically, it leads neither to higher performance nor greater happiness. Perfectionism can destroy your enjoyment of trading. Focusing on flaws and mistakes depletes energy. This may escalate to panic-like states prior to making the trade, impairing an objective performance. At some point perfectionistic standards get set too high, and trades are measured in units of accomplishment. The drive to be perfect becomes self-defeating, as the trader often places the intense pressure on himself or herself, which can become crippling. Perfectionists share a belief that perfection is required in order to be accepted by others. The reality is that acceptance cannot be gained through performance or other external factors like money or social approval. Instead, self-acceptance is at the root of happiness. Ultimately you must be the one who must live with yourself, so if others think you are perfect but you yourself are never happy, then you set yourself up to be disappointed. I have seen my performance suffer from perfectionism. I think the biggest obstacle to overcome that I have faced is fear of failure. If you have a perfectionist mentality when trading, you are really setting yourself up for failure, because it is a given that you will experience losses along the way in trading. You have to think of trading as a probability game. You cannot be a perfectionist and expect to be a great trader. Your losses (that you hope will return to breakeven) will kill you. If you cannot take a loss when it is small because of the need to be perfect, then the loss will oftentimes grow to a much larger loss, causing further pain for the perfectionist trader. The objective should be excellence in trading, not perfection. In addition, you should strive for excellence over a sustained period, as opposed to judging that each trade must be a winner. The great traders make their share of mistakes, but they are able to keep the impact of those mistakes small, while getting the most out of their best ideas.

In order to change long established behavior patterns and personality characteristics, it may be necessary to enlist the support and services of a qualified professional. Long established habits, beliefs, and traits never change overnight, but acceptance of a problem is a first step.

Here are a few tips consistent with attempting to become less perfectionistic:

1. Begin to appreciate the process as well as the outcome—set more achievable goals.
2. Realize that you are worthy no matter whether you win or lose on a given day.
3. Focus on achievement less and on enjoyment more—you may experience more favorable outcomes as you learn to cut losing trades more quickly while letting winners ride longer.
4. Do not be so critical of your errors—just learn from them.

Set one goal and make it focused on your trading process—forget about the outcome. If you achieve that goal to improve your trading, you win no matter the outcome. Perfectionists often seek to control uncontrollable factors in a trade (like waiting for all the risk to be out and everything to look perfect before they enter, the quality of the fill on the exit, hoping or "willing" a better outcome by doubling down on a loser, and many more). When a trader focuses on these uncontrollables, he or she is more likely to tighten up and not be able to pull the trigger to exit a losing trade or miss out on a new winner that has moved "too far."

Based on these perfectionist tendencies, I recommend the following entry strategy for perfectionists. Enter half a position as soon as you see an opportunity that generates at least three times the reward for the risk at the current market price, then place the remaining half at your desired "perfect" entry price. For exits, always place market orders, as the tendency for the perfectionist is to try to get a better exit price with a limit, and then keep missing the exit on the way down.

Here is an example of how this strategy can work: Buy just half of a $10,000 position in a stock as your initial order. If the stock goes down in price, do not buy any more of the stock. If it goes down to your stop price, sell the stock to take your loss. However, if the stock moves up in price from your initial buy point, and it is performing relatively well, you might add another $3,000 to your original $5,000 buy. You would have $8,000 of your $10,000 total position in the stock already committed. If the stock moves up another few percent, you can finish your $10,000 position by buying another $2,000. In this way you average up, not down. You only want to add money if your prior buys are working.

As far as cutting profits short, I am reminded of a quote from Edwin LeFevre's classic *Reminiscences of a Stock Operator*, reportedly based on the life of famed speculator Jesse Livermore. He said, "Men who can both be right and sit tight are uncommon." There is an ego need to feel like a winner when trading, by being able to say I made a profit on a trade. In my Trading

Journal I like to go back and look at my trades over the last month, to see how they subsequently performed. If I sold too soon, I want to find out why.

In my Trading Journal, besides the daily observations, I commit to doing a post-trade analysis at the end of every month. I note what I did right and wrong, and seek to learn from my mistakes to minimize future errors in similar circumstances, while also looking for winning patterns where I seek to repeat big successes. I call this a Success Profile. Be honest, and ask good questions: "What worked? What will I do differently next time?" Write about your thoughts, feelings, and trading behaviors to see if you can spot patterns. Also keep notes on the trades you liked but did not make. What held you back? Do you notice any patterns there that are causing you to miss opportunities? Look for patterns among your non-trades.

One of the daily notes I like to make is to ask myself, "How do I feel today?" in three primary categories: physical, emotional, and spiritual. I grade myself from 1 to 10, with 10 being best, and I write a note to myself about what I feel positively or negatively about in each category. There is no science in this case, but more of a personal "gut" sense of where my mind, heart, and soul are at on a given morning. Not surprisingly, some of my best days have correlated with scores of 26 or better, while I find that any total score under 24 is not very conducive to sharp, focused trading. The key if you score yourself low in an area is to then ask "Why?" and "What can I do to feel better now?" In some cases, if I feel sluggish physically, I have been known to get out of my chair and do jumping jacks and push-ups. This may sound silly to traders used to sitting for long periods, but I prefer to boost my self-esteem, even by marginal exercise, if I need it to feel better about myself. Both positive and negative emotions seem to translate into trading. I will journal to improve how I feel about an emotional issue, and if I feel spiritually malnourished, I will take time to pray and meditate. The bottom line is to find actions you can take to boost your self-esteem. If it works for you, incorporate that behavior into your trading process.

What is Your Position Review Process?

Have an end-of-day routine to close your day:

1. Review your trades—did you follow your method?
2. Log all trades—keep a record.
3. Have a comments section to make brief observations on the day.

What is Your Preparation Process Before Trading?

Self-confidence is directly correlated with the trader's perception of his or her level of preparation coming into the trading day, which leads to his or her ability to perform successfully. Good preparation also influences the skill level that a trader believes he or she possesses. You need defined time to prepare for the next trading day to build up your trading "feel" and confidence. After the close, I run my computer systems for new entries and exits, open positions first, then look at my plan and trading rules. The next morning I like to get in earlier than most, when things are quiet and peaceful. I find this leads to a more serene and calm effect on my trading for the rest of the day, versus getting in late and feeling like I am rushing. It is like the common metaphor of believing in abundance versus believing in scarcity. By getting in earlier without the rush into work, I preprogram myself to execute trade with visualization techniques, do my self-analysis described above to make sure I am ready to trade, then take action. After the close I review that day's trades, asking "Did I follow my rules?" Then I run my computer systems and the cycle begins again.

What Broker Will You Use?

Most traders mistakenly think that commissions are the number one factor they can control, so they go looking for the cheapest commissions on the Web. In reality, commissions are a small cost compared to the broker's effectiveness at executing the trade. If you place a market order on 1,000 shares that is filled at a price 10 cents worse than another broker, that costs you $100 on that trade, versus commissions which can be as cheap as $8 and should be under $50 at most discount brokers. You should also determine how you will be placing your orders. In this Internet age, most brokers are doing electronic transactions, but there are some brokers who can do phone trades even faster. Options transactions may require more complex orders to be placed on entry and exit, especially in the case of spreads or other combination positions. Make sure the broker either has the online capability to place your options orders, or that they can do it promptly over the phone. See Appendix C for recommended brokers you can consider for your options trades.

My Trading Rules

Here is a list of trading rules and reminders I review each day to keep me focused and to help me look for areas where I am executing or not executing my rules effectively.

PRICE'S PURPOSE: To continuously learn and grow to become the best trader I can be, by simplifying and focusing my energy to achieve a balanced, centered state that controls the emotions of fear and greed, allowing me to take action when my analysis says the time is now.

PRICE'S PHILOSOPHY: Big Trends—via Accelerations, Divergences, and Relative Strength—to define the best opportunities.

Consider these trading suggestions:

1. Focus on the three best new trades at any one time for each recommendation portfolio.
2. Take big profits and small losses—cut non-winners after three days (the best trades are winners from the start).
3. Options stops on:
   a. Close of −20 percent or more.
   b. Move stops to zero on a close of +25 percent or more.
   c. Time stop—exit after three days if not +20 percent or more.
4. Write down specific price levels for entry and exit—update trailing stops daily.
5. 3-to-1 Reward-to-Risk or higher.
6. JUST DO IT—take action after doing all the work!
7. Focus energy—identify energy drains (unfocused activities, distractions during the trading hours, worrying about open positions (close them)).
8. The less observed by the crowd, the better the trade.
9. 90 percent of profits come from 10 percent of my trades—follow my Success Profile.
10. It is OK to take a medium loss within my system (it is not OK to take big losses over 10 percent on stocks, or 33 percent on options).
11. I am a winner before I start the game of trading.
12. Go with the flow (the market is always right).
13. Preparation—Must plan BEFORE the opening (do charts at night, quick update of pre-open at 9:00 AM ET).
14. Recap the day—what I did well and not well. Did I execute my plan?
15. Boost personal assets—physical health (workout plan), family support, freely express emotions (write out emotions as they need to be expressed), dedication, flexibility, good judgment, patience, frustration tolerance, anxiety control (exercise and talking to vent).

Daily process:

1. Evaluate open positions.
2. Review rules.
3. Review daily plan.
4. Pre-program to carry out the trade.
5. Self-Analysis—am I ready to trade?
6. Take action on the plan.

ADDITIONAL MONEY MANAGEMENT CONCEPTS

Defining entry and exit levels, as well as the amount of capital to invest, are excellent starting points. If you write these key facts down before you place every trade, you are already ahead of 90 percent of all traders. However, there are many other points you need to consider in properly managing your money to further maximize your upside potential and minimize your risk.

1. Your method must have a positive expectancy to win over time.

This is a simple concept: even if you use sound money management in a system with a negative expectancy system, you will eventually lose over time. It is just a question of how much time. How do you think Las Vegas built all those billion-dollar hotels? They did it by having a "house edge." Let us take a look at the expectancy in the typical roulette payoff. For those not familiar with roulette, there are 38 numbers, and if you bet $1 on a specific number from 1 to 38 and your number hits on that roll, you win $36. If your number does not hit, the casino keeps your $1:

Expectancy = (W percent × AW) − (L percent × AL)

W percent = Probability of a winning trade

AW = Average gain

L percent = Probability of a losing trade

AL = Average loss

Roulette Expectancy = ((1/38) × $36) − ((37/38) × $1) = −0.052 or −5.2 percent

This suggests that for every $100 you bet over time, you will lose $5.20 on average after many trials. Think about this another way. You will lose 37 out of 38 times on average, so you need to win $38 on the one winning roll out of 38. Instead, the casino is only paying you $36. So you are effectively supporting a game that costs you $2 on average for every 38 bets made at $1 each ($2/$38 = −5.2 percent to play).

Let us look at a typical options buying system. Say it wins $900 just 40 percent of the time, while losing $300 the other 60 percent of the time. What is our expectancy now?

Options System Expectancy = (0.4 × $900) − (0.6 × $300) = $180 per trade, over time

This system has a positive expectancy. If you were investing $1,000 per trade, you would expect to see an 18 percent return on each trade on average over many runs of trades in the system. For more on positive expectancy, see Van Tharp's *Trading Your Way to Finacial Freedom.*

2. Gambling versus Trading

Too many people think of trading as one big gamble. They think that Lady Luck may or may not shine on them when they invest, and they figure their money is safer in CDs or an indexed mutual fund. For these people who attribute trading results to luck, they are probably better off elsewhere. However, this perception could not be further from the truth for those who treat trading as a business. There are two key aspects of proper trading that separate it from gambling Las Vegas style:

- Positive expectancy can be traded, while negative expectancy is gambling. If your system has a positive edge, then you can set up a trading business to capture that edge. It is only a question of having enough trades to let the probabilities play out in your favor. In contrast, when you are playing a negative expectancy game like those in Las Vegas, you are clearly gambling with the hope of getting lucky and then walking away. The longer you play at their tables, the more sure you are to lose. Consider the analogy of the house edge in Las Vegas. Companies have been built to exploit their edge over millions of bets per year. They run this gaming industry as a business, and they kick out individuals who do things that hurt the house's edge, like counting cards to improve the odds for the better. In addition, they set up table limits. If you play blackjack, you could theoretically never lose if you kept doubling down on every lost hand, assuming your bankroll was big enough. But if you are on a losing streak and you reach the table limit amount and lose, you cannot double your bet any more to get all of those losses back. These factors show you how the house cultivates their edge. A trading system where you have an edge can be run as a business, not as a gamble, if you use discipline and proper money management to realize your edge over a large sample of trades.

- Amount risked per trade—once you study the mathematical underpinning of most systems, you would generally not want to commit more than 1 percent of your trading portfolio as risk in any particular trade. But many traders will take a "go for it" attitude, betting far more on individual positions than is prudent. This excessive capital commitment per trade will eventually get to these gunslingers, as an individual betting 10 percent of his or her trading portfolio equity on every new position is setting himself or herself up for a fall. In many of the systems I have studied, most systems can expect a drawdown of 25 percent or more, with many giving up half their gains or more, due to at least five losers in a row and often 10 or more losers in a row. While we seek to minimize this occurrence by choosing the best systems, the reality is that losing streaks will occur, and individuals who risk too much of their portfolio on any one trade eventually get burned. I see traders get hurt most often by thinking they have a low-risk trade, and therefore allocating a heavy chunk of their portfolio to it, only to miss the stop and then get stuck with a big loser. For example, if a trader thinks a stock only has one point of risk versus 20 points of upside, the general inclination will obviously be to get excited and invest a larger amount than usual on a 20-to-1 Reward-to-Risk opportunity. So the individual bets 30 percent of his portfolio on a $20 stock, getting 1,500 shares. Let us say he invests $30,000 of a $100,000 portfolio, but then the stock gaps down overnight against him by four points, three points under his stop. As a result, the trader decides not to stop his position here (a critical mistake) as he is down $6,000 and figures he will get a bounce to exit back at his stop three points higher. Of course, the stock fails to bounce, and the shares now decline 10 points over the next four weeks. In frustration, he finally blows out the positions for a $15,000 loss, losing 15 percent of his portfolio on one trade. You can see the 20-to-1 Reward-to-Risk ratio was not a sure thing due to the gap, but even if the target was legitimately 20 points, the Reward-to-Risk dropped from 20-to-1 to 2-to-1 thanks to the inability to pull the trigger. You must exit when your stop gets violated. If your stop gets breached, you close it at the worse price and walk away. If you do not, you risk totally undercutting your plan to find low-risk trades with much more reward than risk.

3. Non-Self-Weighting Strategies

What money management concept really defines the winners from the losers? The ability to determine where a trader has a maximum edge and know how to capture more of that edge, via a non-self-weighting strategy. A self-weighting strategy involves implementing the same percentage of your capital into each trade, which is what I recommend for beginners to get more disciplined in their trading. But the next step, once you know all of the ins and outs of your method, is to be able to determine when you have the maximum edge in your method and then capitalize on it with a bigger financial commitment to that trade. One way to do this is to define very low-risk entries and then be willing to allocate a bigger portion of your porfolio, as long as your portfolio risk still does not exceed 1 to 2 percent on any one trade. This means if you know your stop is only 20 cents away, when it is usually $1 away, you could potentially put in five times more money than usual, and still be left with only a $1 loss on the trade if the stop was hit (20 cents × five units).

By the same token, most traders try to learn every different aspect of the markets: How to trade stocks in trends, but also how to trade stock in trading ranges. How to use oscillators in choppy markets, but also how to convert to trend-following once a breakout occurs. I submit that this is a tough proposition for most traders, to switch styles in the blink of an eye. Why? Because many traders get used to being conditioned to keep doing what they have recently been doing if it is working. If you are having success selling the tops of ranges on a stock bouncing between 20 and 30, and when you sell at 30 it breaks out to 35, are you now going to be willing to switch horses in mid-stream and say that selling at 30 was wrong and now you should buy at 35, five points higher? I doubt many traders could stop and reverse so effectively. If this does not sound like something you could do (for me, I have tried this and it creates incredible confusion for me in sticking with my method), you have to decide which factors to focus on when you cannot concentrate on everything. Instead of trying to maximize the largest quantity of trading elements, I suggest you look at the impact of each factor and maximize the quality of the largest impact areas. I have done better by focusing on only a few factors of major significance in finding the bigger trend, and sitting out markets that offer no Big Trends, waiting until the bigger trends start to reappear.

Most traders assume that their goal is to learn as many different strategies as possible, based on the assumption that more strategies will lead to more opportunities to profit. Yet you may know many different strategies but not play for the Big Trend, while a trader who sits back and stalks the market until he or she sees a Big Trend may make more money overall despite not making as many trades. I would take the quality and positive edge of a Big Trend any day over a large quantity of day trades that may only be generating a great deal of activity without producing the bigger net profits for the trader. I find that for most traders, it is far too easy for them to enter trades, when they need to cultivate patience until they have a greater edge which can allow them to trade with true confidence and conviction. Traders who overtrade may not have a big negative edge against them on any individual trade, but eventually this overtrading costs them a lot of money over time.

Winning traders also invest in stocks in a good sector, as opposed to buying a company in a poorly performing industry group. It is better to own the worst stock in a top-performing sector than to own the best stock in a downtrending sector. After all, I would rather be floating downstream without a paddle than going upstream with a paddle. Similarly, you have probably heard the saying, "A rising tide lifts all boats." In other words, you want to find out which sectors are performing well and search for good stock patterns within the leading groups, instead of rotating to the laggards. If you make a mistake and choose the third or fifth best stock in a good sector, that is a relatively small mistake, as your performance will likely still be healthy. If you make a mistake and buy a middle of the pack stock in a poor sector, this can be very hazardous to your financial health. Both *Investors Business Daily* and *Barron's* have excellent industry group summaries of relative performance among the key sectors of the market.

PSYCHOLOGICAL ISSUES WITH LOSSES

How you handle losing trades psychologically is a cornerstone to your ability to prosper in the markets. Losing properly (by losing small and continuing to take your trades) makes winning possible. You have to learn to accept your losses, because if you are not willing to take the chance that a trade could lose a pre-defined amount, you will be afraid to trade or will be scared out of a good position as soon as you get a small profit. This defeats the goal to score big when you are right. A successful trader's mindset must accept losses as a necessary and beneficial part of the trading process when handled properly.

Another vital aspect of knowing how to lose is that you must never give in to the temptation to ride your losses, which amounts to saying to yourself: "It will come back." That type of thinking has ruined many traders. In other words, you must have the discipline to always cut your losses or keep them small. This is the main thing that will allow you to stay in the game long enough to become successful.

Richard Thaler said, "Losing money feels twice as bad as making money feels good." That's why you must keep losses small and avoid the hoping or praying stage that a loser will come back to breakeven. Breakeven levels are deadly reference points on losers. Do not liquidate a winner to keep a loser. Start liquidating not when wrong, but when not right. This is an important distinction, as the implication to study is not just the level of a price move before you exit, but also if a position normally is profitable within a certain number of time periods, then you should exit non-movers at that time.

Developing the Confidence to Take Your Trades

You need good coping skills in order to be able to pull the trigger after a typical drawdown of 10 to 20 percent. The scars of past losses stay with us in trading, and the secret to success is being able to pull the trigger after a series of losers (assuming the methodology works over time, of course). Most amateur investors will bail out of an investment program after three straight losses. Yet many approaches that make excellent money in Big Trends and cut losses quickly on bad signals will often have winning percentages under 50 percent (though the size of the big win far outweighs the impact of the small losses). However, investors will see consecutive losses, which, while small, will scare them off from a method. Therefore, you should know the characteristics of any model, especially average drawdown, winning percentage, and size of average win to average loss, before you start trading that method. For a graphic example, let us say you have a method that wins 25 percent of the time, but it gains 10 times as much as it loses. So, in four trades, you could have a profile that looks like this:

$$-1, -1, -1, +10.$$

If you stay around for all the trades, you make seven points on the four trades, or an average gain of 1.75 points per trade. But many investors will be giving up on the method after the three straight losses, and not be around for the fourth trade. So their result will be -3 over 3 trades, or -1.00 per trade (a 2.75 points per trade swing). Another way to look at this is to say, "What are your odds of having three losers in a row in this method?" Since each instance offers a 75 percent chance of losing 1 and a 25 percent chance of winning 10, the odds of losing three times in a row are:

$$.75 \times .75 \times .75 = 42.2 \text{ percent}$$

If you are trading this method, you had better be ready to lose small for a while, but know that if you are an individual with some patience, the end result of sticking with it will pay off for traders who have discipline and patience.

Track Your Equity Curve to Minimize Your Drawdown

I track the equity curves of my various options systems, seeking to make trades which are experiencing positive equity curve trends, which are then overlaid on my market timing models to make sure the trends are likely to continue according to the market timing results which have worked well over time. My philosophy is that it is better to minimize risk by reducing trade frequency in tough times, since then I can get aggressive as the conditions for the models improve. As a result, I would rather not force trades just to trade.

Behavioral finance recognizes that human emotions and thought patterns play a greater role in investment decisions than previously acknowledged. One of the early advocates of behavioral finance, Robert Shiller, summarizes some key underpinnings of behavioral finance including:

1. Prospect theory
2. Regret theory
3. Anchoring
4. Overreaction and underreaction

Prospect theory shows people are more upset at the idea of losses compared to their level of pleasure from comparable gains. The tendency toward loss aversion implies that investors will take more risk to avoid a loss while being too satisfied with small gains. Investors will take a sure payout if positive, even over a less certain opportunity to receive even more on average but with a chance of receiving nothing. When it comes to losses, investors will take a bigger risk on average rather than admit they were wrong and take a guaranteed smaller loss.

Regret theory focuses on investors' emotional responses to making a mistake, whether buying shares that have declined or missing out on one they considered which has since gone up. Investors avoid selling a stock that dropped to avoid the regret of making a poor investment or the shame of showing a loss. Investors often find it less painful psychologically to follow the herd and buy a popular stock: if it later declines, it can be rationalized that everyone else lost too. Contrarian investing, betting in the opposite direction of the crowd is more difficult since the investor feels more alone if wrong.

Anchoring involves investors assuming that recent prices are a good form of reference for making new investment decisions. Investors will be at great risk when they give too much weight to recent stock prices when those prices may be much higher or lower than historical norms.

Similarly, investors overemphasize recent news compared to other information, causing the phenomenon of market overreaction or underreaction. Investors will become more hopeful when the market rises and more fearful when the market drops. Therefore, prices plunge too much on bad news and surge too much on good news. This can lead to a boom and bust cycles. (See Charles Kindleberger's *Manias, Panics, and Crashes*, which gives an excellent overview of many such extreme events.)

Two psychological theories underpin these views of investor behavior. The first is known as the "representativeness heuristic"—where investors tend to see patterns in random sequences and they react excessively to random changes in stock prices. The second, "conservatism," suggests that people remain slow to change their opinions despite new data that conflicts with their current belief. I have noticed investment analysts fall prey to conservatism, as they are often changing earnings estimates relatively slowly, allowing companies to continue the trend to keep beating or missing estimates in subsequent quarters.

Psychological Traps to Avoid When Trading

1. Trading defensively after a loss.
2. Trading only once everything looks "perfect."
3. Not following initial reasons during trade.
4. Not following price stop or time stop.
5. Not taking action after analysis complete and opportunity presents itself.
6. Not keeping a Trading Journal on all trades and lessons learned.

7. Trading an old uptrend that is too obvious.

8. Having too much exposure on either the call or put side at one time.

9. Letting others' opinions affect your analysis of the trade's actionability.

10. Taking a 100 percent loss on an options trade.

11. Taking three losses in a row totaling -100 percent or more on options trades.

12. Feeling out of control while trading.

13. Fear of missing out.

14. Fear of losing.

15. Fear of leaving money on the table.

EXECUTION ISSUES

The biggest trades are winners right from the start. But what if you have trouble getting into an idea you are right about?

1. The hard trades to enter are the ones you most want to get filled. Competition for sought-after shares makes execution difficult at a desired price. Yet these are the stocks you want to own. If you instead think these leaders have run too far, and start to pick laggards you hope will catch up, you are likely to be left with poor performers. The saying, "If you lie down with the dogs, you get up with the fleas" is very true here. If you do not fight to get on board the leaders, and instead let the market pick your stocks, you get only the bad ones.

2. The most expensive trade is the one never done. Impact can be expensive, but failure to complete usually costs more. If you do not track the undones, you will believe you are doing a good job when you are not. Think like a principal broker calculating his or her P&L position.

3. The best way to improve your trading is to record what you tried under what conditions and how well it worked. You cannot learn by looking only at your successes—or only at your failures.

Ego

You must trade without ego as much as you possibly can. Ego decisions create the desire to take winners too quickly and take losers too slowly. The need to protect the ego version of the self must be let go in order to rid ourselves of the desire to lock in profits too early and erase the expensive hope that our losers will come back to breakeven. In addition, you need to be aware that any contest or competition will raise your level of ego naturally, as you want to perform well not only for yourself, but also in front of others.

You must reframe trading so that you do not see the market as a competition with others, but instead as a constant opportunity flow that you can tap into at any time.

Some of my subscribers have sent me messages over the years that they successfully held on to positions that I had stopped out previously per my rules, as if to say that they could add more value to determine when to stop out or not stop out of my recommendations. While I understand this ego need for the individual to add value, this is a very dangerous approach as the ego is then rewarded for not following rules. That invariably leads the ego-driven trader to wind up with positions that continue to drop well below the stop, which leads to unacceptable drawdowns and capital being tied up in under-performing positions. Trading without stops implies the ego never wanted to be held accountable to admit that a position was a mistake if a certain level is breached or a certain set of circumstances play out in an unexpected manner.

Let the market take you out. This takes your ego out of the decision on what stop level to exit, which should be calculated before entering the trade. Again, you want to prevent your mind from playing tricks by rationalizing a new reason to hold on to a poor performer (this relates to the importance of reviewing your Trading Journal each day in order to remind yourself of your #1 Entry Driver and key stop levels. If any of these are broken, you have lost the edge you projected and you should exit such busted trades immediately.

Too many moves end with panic selling or panic buying, driven not only by greed to jump aboard the (now-obvious) trend, but also driven by fear from those rushing to exit positions going against them. We often can see that the relief felt by many to be out of the position later turns to horror when we realize we took our loss near a panic low, or had to cover a short amid a final buying panic that created a top.

Part of the secret of making truly extraordinary profits is spotting the early warning signs of a new trend developing when *it is not yet obvious!* By the time the trend becomes obvious (which can often be seen by national press coverage), you should be looking to cash in some of your chips and force yourself to take some of your profits off the table.

I often knew when it was time to take some profits by evaluating the magnitude of *pride* in my gut of how right I had been to select such an outstanding investment. Another common feeling was the dream scenario, where this stock was on just the beginning of a run that would make me rich beyond my wildest dreams, or be publicized at the end of the year as the Stock of the Year (which would be a stroke for my ego for being such a phenomenal analyst).

What my experience with stops taught me was that I needed to have a relatively wide berth in the first few days of a trade, in order not to get whipped out of the volatile stocks in which I was seeking big new trends, but that I needed to then tighten stops to my entry level quickly thereafter and follow with a trailing stop.

The nutshell version says that when my trades lose 10 percent on a closing basis (intraday stops whipped me out of too many good trades) after five trading days, it is time to get out. Why 10 percent on any closing basis? It seems that my odds of initially being wrong are greater even on eventual winners, while the big winners should recover by the close on the fifth day. Part of this is my contrarian nature, as I like to place trades when sentiment is especially fearful, as this is where I have found the biggest profits over short periods of time. The hazard of this method is that trying to find the climax in fear can result in initially being wrong as sentiment gets even more fearful before it peaks. I am usually relatively close to the bottom with this method, as the five-day rule tells me that the big profits I stop out in the first five days cost me more than the trades I have to exit at a 10 percent or greater loss on the fifth day or later.

Lessons I Have Learned in Trading

One of the lessons I have learned is that trading is a mirror of other elements of my life. If I am behaving in an undisciplined way outside of trading, my trading shows undisciplined behavior, such as not following stops. If I feel depressed about something in my personal life, my trading observations will not pick up as many opportunities, as I cannot see the possibilities that I see when I am in a positive frame of mind.

Some of the other lessons I have learned include:

Treat every trade as both a potential loser and a potential winner. Know how to tell the difference when you are in it.

Think positively. Have confidence in yourself. If you do not feel good about what you are doing, change it immediately.

Never make a trade on a market that just completed a major move if the only reason for making the trade is that you just saw a major move and missed it. (Warning—those most susceptible to this are the ones who did expect the move but made the trade earlier.)

To relate this to trading, winning traders and losing traders experience the trading environment differently. It makes them feel different and, as a result, their actions consistently vary. In psychological terms, they interpret the market differently because they have a separate belief system in the way that they see themselves relative to the stock market.

Know when to play offense and defense. There are times when growth stocks outperform, which is where I often play most aggressively. Such phases require a more proactive, offensive approach. In contrast, when growth stocks underperform, I will adopt a more defensive approach, trading less and waiting for conditions to improve if the market is directionless.

Know when not to trade—this skill is just as important as knowing when to pull the trigger. Part of being a great trader is being a keen observer of what a stock is telling you.

Accept total responsibility for the results of your trading. Even if you authorized someone else to trade on your behalf, it was you who made this decision—nobody forced you. Remember, losers always look for somebody else to blame. Winners look to themselves, particularly if they have to take a loss on some trades—as is inevitable for all traders and all systems.

In addition, do not trade for excitement or entertainment. Avoid the highs that come from quick profits or the lows that can appear after losses. If you have a sound system it does not matter whether any particular trade makes a profit or a loss. What matters is that the probabilities over time are in your favor. You must remember that no system is perfect, and prepare for losses along the way. You should measure yourself on whether you followed your rules and executed your system for both winning and losing trades. The process of trading is much easier when you focus on execution of a system rather than on whether each individual trade was right or not, because you take your ego out of the process. This makes you more rational and less emotional, which leads to better investment performance.

It is critically important to protect your psychological capital by not overtrading or playing for excitement instead of profits. This can cause you to be emotionally "drawn down," and then force you to sit out, usually as a move just begins that could have been a big opportunity. However, you will miss the new Big Trend because you were financially and emotionally exhausted by overtrading in a tough market. As a result, you cannot see through the negative emotions because you feel beat up by the markets. Managing your psychological state of mind is equally important as managing your financial position.

The desire to buy at the low or sell at the high is not what will make you the most money over time. More important is the psychological damage that comes from taking too big of a loss or a long series of small losses. I unfortunately see too many circumstances where a trader gets involved with a hot trading method after it has run-up, then takes the pain of the drawdown and gives up just before a run to a new high in that method. While the system shows great overall performance, the trader shows a good-sized loss. The usual cause of this is excessive optimism about getting rich too fast, which leads the trader to put too much capital into each trade and thus magnify the pain of the drawdown. You must position yourself to be able to still be part of the gain after a system's drawdown. Therefore, make sure you study the system's historical drawdown tendencies, then multiply the worst drawdown by a factor of two to determine the percentage of capital you could allocate and still handle a worst-case drawdown, both financially and psychologically. In most systems, you would prefer to see maximum drawdowns of no more than 20 to 25 percent from the peak in the equity curve. So could you handle it if the drawdown was twice that (40 to 50 percent)? If this is unacceptable to you, then you need to define a drawdown point based on past history where you would be able to pull the plug on the system. If maximum drawdown was under 20 percent, you might say that if drawdown exceeded 25 percent, then you would pull the plug. Just make sure you define your risk tolerance in advance, so that you avoid emotional decisions in the heat of the trading process.

Affirmations

This self-analysis can be accomplished in precisely the same way the tracks were created: by using self-talk or, more specifically, affirmations. An affirmation is a statement of fact or belief—positive or negative—that will lead toward the end result you expect. Anything that follows the phrase "I am," such as "I am a peak performance athlete" or "I am quick and agile," is an affirmation. The simplicity of affirmations often causes them to be overlooked. Nonetheless, affirmations are regularly used by professional athletes and successful business people.

The process for changing a limiting belief to a resourceful one using affirmations is simple. First, identify the areas of your life which are not working to your satisfaction. Next, write out the affirmations that represent things the way you desire them to be. They will be the vehicle for creating new pathways for success.

Your affirmation must be short and to the point—simple enough that a child will understand it—and should always be stated in the positive. Further, your affirmation should be stated in the present tense—as if it has already happened, for example, "I am a well prepared trader."

Now you are ready to begin your daily (minimum) reprogramming process:

- Sit upright in a comfortable chair.
- Close your eyes and take a few minutes to gradually relax.
- Release your body's focus on the physical world physically to allow yourself to reach a deeper level of relaxation.
- Speak your affirmation aloud from up to twenty times (depending on the time available—the more you can repeat, the more ingrained the new belief can become).

By speaking your affirmation aloud you are down-stepping your thoughts to the brain's electrical network to speech, and you are involving more of your brain by involving more of your senses: auditory, kinesthetic and visual (if you write out your affirmations on cards and look at them as you read them). It is important that you trust this process and give your affirmations time to achieve your desired goal. Worry or self-doubt as to whether your affirmations are working only conveys to your subconscious worry and the belief that your desire may not come to pass or the affirmation may not succeed. Be patient; success is on the way.

I am a big believer in affirmations. Here is a list of positive statements I use to remind myself where I need to focus in my trading, and also to take note of any areas requiring more attention and focus:

1. When I am trading, I find it relatively easy to control my anger and quickly release any negative thoughts that may occupy my mind.
2. My trading objectives are perfectly clear, and I truly believe I will achieve these goals.
3. I take time to create a plan to achieve my trading goals.
4. I prepare my plan before the trading day starts.
5. I regularly monitor my trading results to measure my progress toward my goals.
6. While I have a back-up plan for difficulties, I visualize my trading success in every detail.
7. I use positive self-talk and affirmations to perform at my highest level.
8. I use relaxation tactics to stay calm under pressure.
9. I quickly discard negative emotions that can hurt my trading results.
10. When I lose, I try to learn from the experience, then put it behind me. I rarely dwell on a loss once the trade is complete.
11. I can raise my energy level whenever I need extra focus.
12. I have a specific method of preparing before the trading day.
13. I am focused on the market during the trading day, and not easily distracted by non-market activities during trading hours.
14. I regularly read instructional materials on trading or work with a trading coach.

Do not think when implementing your system's trades. Yogi Berra said, "You can't think and play baseball at the same time." If you are thinking too much, you cannot get into a good rhythm and flow with the markets. If you play golf, you may have a key swing thought in the pre-shot routine. However, when swinging the club, just swing it. You cannot be thinking "Left arm straight! Head down! Bring club back inside to out . . ." or you will produce a very forced swing that will not hit the sweet spot of the club in most cases. The mind will be clouding the body's ability to take action. Similarly, if you are about to place a trade, thinking about all that can go right, all that can go wrong, and many "what ifs," then you will undoubtedly not be in the moment with the market. The likely outcome is that you will miss your proper entry point, which if the market goes in your direction you now must chase, hurting your Reward-to-Risk ratio; or, if the market goes opposite your signal and you figure you saved yourself a bad trade, you will be second-guessing every future trade. Neither scenario positions you for trading success over time.

The learning curve in any endeavor involves four stages:

1. Unconscious incompetence (where the trader has no idea how much he or she does not know about trading).
2. Conscious incompetence (where the trader realizes after initial losses that he or she has a lot to learn).
3. Conscious competence (where the trader has developed and is now doing well as long as he or she works in his or her system and its rules).
4. Unconscious competence (where the trader has mastered the rules and also knows when to break the rules as conditions change, in a complete flow with the markets based on great experience).

The way you avoid thinking too much during the trade itself is to practice consistent execution of your system's trades. This takes you from the conscious incompetence stage, where the trader has not learned how to execute, to the conscious competence stage, where you know that if you just focus on consistent execution of your plan, you can expect to win more consistently over time.

Every trader who wishes to improve his or her bottom-line results must decide what area most needs attention immediately. The trader must start by taking an honest self-assessment of strengths and weaknesses, prioritize the highest impact areas, and then focus on changing one behavior at a time. Most ambitious traders (myself included) have at one time tried to tackle too many issues at once, only to not produce the desired change in any of those areas. Change takes time. Just as a golfer hitting a drive or a basketball player shooting free throws has developed a certain "muscle memory" for success by repeated practice, so too is your mind a muscle that you have created a muscle memory for in trading (and in all areas of your life). The hardest part of the process is changing that memory from one that has not worked to one that will produce consistent results. Once your mind starts to recognize and get comfortable with these new procedures, maintenance of the change will be much easier.

You must commit to one objective and focus on it. Give yourself a month to work on a given issue, focusing on it each day in your Trading Journal. Set up potential solutions and then try them out to see if they fit your personality. Create a method to measure your progress. Do you have trouble taking a loss at your predefined stop objective? Trade very small for a month, and just work on following your system and taking each loss. The financial impact will be small for a month, but the discipline you instill will last you for years if done properly. You can take this approach with any issue you face. Just remember to stay focused on one at a time until you are confident you have mastered it.

One of the most difficult things to do is to abandon the game plan that you have practiced so hard to attain. Yet there is a time to be offensive and a time to be defensive. Trading success in 1999 came by being offensive, while the two years thereafter in 2000 and 2001 were won by defensive investing. Sometimes just surviving through the tough periods in the markets separates the eventual winners from the losers.

How can one expect that one game plan will be successful in every market, when the markets are constantly changing? The smart trader will never trade with just one game plan. He or she will always be able to switch from offense to defense. My benchmark for changing game plans is to monitor the market's mood in my sentiment data. This tells me if people are getting too extreme in their emotional views towards one side of the market. That is often when I will become more concerned about the current trend ending and start to scale out of that trend, gradually increasing my bet that a major turning point will soon occur.

A quitter's psychology has a large influence on his or her performance. Defeat often stems from the inability to manage anxiety, fear, anger, or despair. The ego of the trader will not want to admit flaws or weaknesses. Yet this lack of honesty with the trader's strengths and weaknesses is exactly what holds the trader back from being honest during his or her trades, admitting losses quickly, and getting out with minimal pain.

When traders are too focused on an end goal instead of the process, they tend to consider any increased arousal as stress or fear. However, when a trader loves the process of trading, and knows that by following each step of the process the end goal should be achieved, the trader will be more likely to consider heightened arousal as excitement. Sometimes this stress can be a good thing, but the key is how you interpret it. If you use the anxiety created by a losing trade, or another area to develop, as a positive sign of action needed to improve, you are using stress as a positive factor. If you interpret anxiety as a sign you are "never" going to win or some other negative frame of mind, then your interpretation of this anxiety blocks you from advancing to a higher level of growth and self-esteem. It is by tackling these issues that we build ourselves up. Therefore, find an area to work on and go tackle it! You can always start with what you consider an easy area that you know you can improve, and then you can work your way up to bigger challenges as your confidence grows. How you experience trading is very much determined by your level of enjoyment of all aspects of trading versus viewing trading only as a means to make a lot of money. While money is important, the best traders truly love the game.

The Mental Games

Here are some of the mental games one has to master:

1. *Expectations*—Your expectations create the potential for a "disappointment gap" relative to what you hoped to achieve as a trader. You must learn to accept what the market gives you in your trading method.
2. *Trading Slumps*—Any trader, whether professional or novice, will experience slumps in trading.

In slumps, do you ever find yourself blaming something outside yourself? One of my favorites used to be blaming "the system"—for example, the system is rigged against me, the brokers are the only ones getting rich, the market makers are killing me on these bid/asked spreads, the guys getting in pre-IPO are getting the best prices, and so on. When you blame an external situation, you are giving up control, and instead letting yourself be controlled by outside events. This converts you from a proactive trader into a reactive trader. If you are reacting after the fact in the markets, you are in turn letting your emotions start to rule you, instead of planning how you will react to any set of circumstances. You know how letting emotions control you turns out in the markets—badly. Justifications and excuses are the hallmark of traders who consistently lose. Successful traders seek total responsibility for all of their actions and outcomes.

The great middle distance runner Joaquim Cruz said: "We are responsible for our actions. You are what you informed your mind you wanted to be. If you want to limit your mind . . . that's what you're going to become, and you will have limited results. Focus on what you want." You should *not* focus on what you do *not* want! The mind seems to only hear the beginning and end of your desire, not the middle. If you say "I must not fail" to yourself, that last word is what you leave in your mind. Consider the alternative: "I will do whatever it takes to succeed."

Excuses seek to diminish the trader's responsibility for a losing trade, creating what psychologists call an "External Locus of Control." This means that the trader is acted upon by events beyond his control. In comparison, a trader with a heavy Internal Locus of Control believes he is responsible for every reaction that happens to each action he takes. When the trader feels external circumstances control his results, he will not tend to set goals (why should he?—the market will create the result for him), and the controlled trader will not apply as much effort to prepare or trade. This makes it nearly impossible for a trader to build self-confidence. How can you believe that your actions will succeed when events are totally out of your control?

Great traders take total responsibility for each action they take. They do not carelessly take actions to buy or sell just for the heck of it. Such impulsive moves can destroy the trader's confidence. The successful trader knows that every action taken will produce a reaction, and actions taken with the probabilities on the trader's side will increase the odds of favorable reactions over time. You must believe that you control your own destiny. If you are not getting the results you expect of yourself, look inside yourself. Start analyzing your actions and behaviors: are you hanging on to losses too long? Are you cutting profits too soon? Are you not able to pull the trigger, leaving you to watch helplessly as the stock roars on without you? These or other frustrations should clue you in that you need to fix some element of your trading personality, and you should make decisions and act immediately to find a proactive solution after evaluating your situation.

BUST OUT OF A SLUMP

Trying too hard to pull out of a slump makes it even worse, as a trader's mental focus is often further disrupted. For example, I see traders losing confidence (even though this is completely controllable), becoming overly intense, obsessing on irrelevant thoughts, and setting unreasonable goals. The bottom line is that a losing streak often builds a self-perpetuating momentum, and this continues the pattern of losing. It is a vicious cycle of negativity.

Why does a slump happen in the first place? Momentum plays a large part. It may be that you simply lost focus on a few trades and now think your next trade must be held after a decent gain to make up your losses. Then, when you had a winner, you lose again! Momentum takes over.

Expectations have a great impact on performance, too. Just as it helps to remain confident (always expecting the best), the reverse also holds true. Expecting the worst usually gets you there. Negative self-talk leads to negative performance and results. The mind cannot focus on the bad and the good at the same time.

How then do you dig yourself out of a slump? The first thing to do is take a break. Reduce the intensity of the slump you have experienced with something totally unrelated to trading that you find relaxing.

Here are some suggestions to create a slump-busting process:

Is the Slump Driven By Something Outside of Trading?

Sometimes traders get into a slump because they are preoccupied or distracted by family problems or personal issues. Sometimes a slump is one of the only ways an athlete can cope with too many performance pressures. The trader may not be aware of the problem, as it is often occurring at the subconscious level.

Reframe the Slump

Slumps and failure in trading are to be expected. To be successful you must learn to deal with and master losing trades. The slump occurs as the trader gets down on himself and uses negative self-talk. This in turn becomes a self-defeating prophesy. Reframe the meaning of those bad trades in terms of their necessity in order to have good trades.

Visualize What You Want (Instead of What You Don't Want)

A slumping athlete has a tendency to always "see" what he or she does not want to happen instead of what he or she wants to be the result. Help your athletes "change the channel" and begin to focus on making that play or getting that hit rather than focusing on what they are afraid of. The more internal practice of the right images, the more chance the ball player will have of quickly snapping out of his or her performance difficulties.

Restore Proper Concentration

Yogi Berra once said, "A full mind is an empty bat." A slumping trader thinks too much. When he or she is on, all reactions should be automatic and reactive. It is the faulty focus that is the main cause of the slump which prevents the ball player from trusting the hits to just happen. Being too conscious causes the athlete to try too hard. Help refocus the athlete and distract his or her conscious mind from the at-bat or play.

Get in the Flow of the Present Moment

When you play well you are mentally in the "here and now." The slumping trader is either stuck in the past, thinking about past bad trades; or in the future, dreaming of potential riches without thinking of the process to get to the goal. Traders need to identify when they leave the "now" moment when trading, and reframe to get in the present promptly.

Separate Your Self-Worth from Your Net Worth

At every level, traders get stressed out when they attach their self-worth to the quality of their trading that day (i.e., "I played well so therefore I am a winner," "I was awful and therefore I am a not a good person"). Do not make the mistake of equating your performance with how you feel about yourself as a person. If your ego is on the line every time you place a trade, you have a lot to lose. When you trade with a lot to lose, you will most likely get stressed out and trade poorly.

Act Like a Winner to be a Winner

If you are slumping "act as if" you are trading well. Sit up straight (where do you think the term "slump" came from?). Smile. Relax. And think about your next winning trade. What will the setup look like? What do you need to do to spot it and get on board?

Change a limiting belief to a positive one. We have up to 50,000 thoughts a day. The danger is when inner dialogue takes on a negative connotation such as, "I will never be as good an athlete as he is," "I do not have the mental toughness to compete at this level," or "I will never be that fast." The ongoing negative reinforcement created by habitual negative self-talk results in the creation of a limiting belief(s) that goes on to become a self-fulfilling prophecy.

Unsuccessful traders construct a fantasy in which the market provides them with future riches. They transplant these fantasies onto the individual stocks that they purchase and have difficulty confronting the reality of being wrong. When events do not match their illusions they simply ignore them. If a stock they bought drops below their purchase price they refuse to reject the fantasy that their decision to purchase the stock will make them money and instead convince themselves that it is a winner that is merely not in favor yet.

Beliefs of Successful Traders versus Unsuccessful Traders

Beliefs of Successful Traders	Beliefs of Unsuccessful Traders
The markets provide a constant stream of opportunities.	I must trade every day.
If I miss an opportunity, another one will soon follow.	If I lose on this trade, I will feel like a loser.
If the position is stopped out, then I need to reconsider the trade.	I must catch today's hot stock, though my system gave no signal on it.
I trade one trade at a time, and stay in the present moment.	I cannot afford to lose anything on this trade.
I seek a standard of excellence, not perfection.	I cannot go broke taking small quick profits.
Losing small is part of my trading plan to maximize profits.	When this loser gets back to even, I will dump it.

As a trader, you have to move from a fearful mindset to a mental state of confidence. You have to believe in yourself and you must use a strategy that builds confidence by taking healthy profits and small losses. The toughest part is continuing to take the trades after a string of losing trades, even if they are small. Psychologically that is where many traders will give up, because they are usually too quick in judging consecutive small losers as a system that is not working. What you may want to do is practice trading your system with what you consider a small amount of capital, where you care about the money but not so much that you will give up on the plan. This is in contrast to paper trading which, while fine for starters when doing initial testing, cannot simulate the psychological aspects of trading with real dollars. Your goal in this exercise is to take your system's trades, even through what may appear to be painful losing streaks. Just experience what it is like to keep trading through that drawdown and how good it feels to follow your rules through the good, the bad, and the ugly days. You will instill in yourself a confidence to take trades that you never knew you had. You will foster both consistency and discipline as you progress through this exercise. You will know when it is time to move up to the real dollars you intend to commit, once your psyche is battle-tested through several drawdowns. Giving up is the only way you can lose. You win as long as you execute your trades, whether they make money or lose money in this exercise.

You have to move away from a mindset that stocks will make you rich and instead believe that your trading method will make you money. Being right or wrong on each individual trade does not matter. You have to be able to move through the adversity of losing trades and hold the faith that you will make money in the long run. This is why people find it so difficult. People focus too much on the individual trades and hold unrealistic fantasies about them, while they cannot take responsibility for the decisions that go wrong. The worst ones take it personally.

I have always been a fan of Mark Douglas' work, as my copy of his initial book on trading psychology, *The Disciplined Trader*, is thoroughly marked up thanks to Douglas' many innovative ideas about mastering the internal challenges we all face with trading. His latest book, *Trading in the Zone*, is full of more great insights. Here are the following key points I took out of Douglas' groundbreaking insights:

1. *Develop consistency.* Douglas focuses on how we can create a mindset of consistency by developing beliefs which support us in obtaining this result. In order to develop consistency, Douglas emphasizes beliefs such as objectively identifying the trader's edges, defining the risk in each trade in advance, accepting the risk to be able to exit a position when a defined loss level is realized, and many other key mindsets that

help traders work through the issues they face in taking a trade, making the trade, and executing an exit from the trade.

2. *Jumping in too soon or getting in too late.* These mistakes come from traders not having a well-defined plan of how they will enter the market. This positions the trader as a reactive trader instead of a proactive trader, which increases the level of emotion the trader will feel in reacting to market movements. A written plan helps make a trader more systematic and objective, and reduces the risk that emotions will cause the trader to deviate from his or her plan.

3. *Not taking profits on winners and letting winners turn to losers.* Again, this is a function of not having a properly thought-out plan. Entries are easy but exits are hard. You must have a plan for how you will exit the market, both on your winners and your losers. Then your job as a trader becomes to execute your plan precisely.

4. *Great traders do not place their own expectations onto the market's behavior.* Poor traders expect the market to give them something. When conditions change, a smart trader will recognize that, and take what the market gives.

5. *Emotional pain comes from expectations not being realized.* When you expect something, and it does not deliver as expected, what occurs? Disappointment. By not having expectations of the market, you are not setting yourself up for this inner turmoil. Douglas states that the market does not generate pain or pleasure inherently; the market only generates upticks and downticks. It is how we perceive and respond to these upticks and downticks that determine how we feel. This perception and feeling is a function of our beliefs. If you are still feeling pain when taking a loss according to your plan, you are still experiencing a belief that your loss is somehow a negative reflection on you personally.

6. *The four major fears: Fear of losing money, being wrong, missing out, and leaving money on the table. All of these fears result from thinking you know what will happen next.* Your trading plan must approach trading as a probabilities game, where you know in advance you will win some and lose some, but that the odds will be in your favor over time. If you approach trading thinking that you cannot take a loss, then take three losses in a row (which is to be expected in most trading methods), you will be emotionally devastated and will give up on your plan.

I recently read a great book on trading psychology called *Mind-Traps*, by Roland Barach (this book is recommended by trading psychologist Van Tharp).

MindTraps focuses on how the average person tends to think, compared to how we need to think to make money over time in the markets. Here is a summary of points that can benefit you as a trader:

1. Before entering any trade, you should consider the other side of the trade and state the reasons you would take the other side of the trade. This helps you objectively enter a trade with a full understanding of the major risks involved.

2. Analyze your behavior from the beginning to the end of the trading process (from idea generation to entry and finally to exit). What are the areas you can improve to help your trading profitability the most?

3. Keep a Trading Journal of your thoughts on open positions and new ideas. Writing things down helps you objectively look back and see where you went right and wrong.

4. Fear blinds us to opportunity; greed blinds us to danger—emotions cause "perceptual distortion" where we only see the part of the picture that our beliefs allow us to see.

5. We are likely to continue doing things for which we are rewarded. This can cause us to get too bullish after the bulk of the uptrend has occurred, or get too bearish near the lows.

6. Fear of regret slants stock market behavior toward inaction and conventional thinking. The person who is afraid of losing is usually defeated by the opponent who concentrates on winning (an analogy for sports fans is the Prevent defense in football—playing "not to lose" only prevents you from winning).

7. You cannot have a personal agenda to prove your self-worth in the markets. The focus must be on following your plan to maximize the ability to make money.

8. Do not get overly attached to any one view on a stock or market. Do not talk to others about open positions; it just makes it that much harder to exit when your plan says you should.

9. Our predictions are only as good as the information available to us. Objectively look at the indicators and data you use to get the best quality of information and focus available.

10. People prefer gains to be taken in several pieces to maximize their positive feelings about their ability, while they prefer to take all their losses in one big lump to minimize the pain they feel.

People prefer a sure gain compared to a high probability of a bigger gain, so they can say they made a profit; in contrast, people will speculate on a high probability of a bigger loss over a sure smaller loss, because they do not want to feel like a loser. In trading, we must flip around the conventional emotions to allow us to let profits run while cutting losses shorter.

The Psychology of Trading

After reading Dr. Robert Rotella's excellent book, *Golf Is Not A Game Of Perfect*, I was drawn to the similarities sports psychology had to the psychology of successful investing. Like golf, trading is not a game of perfect. You will be faced with numerous possible outcomes in trading, and must be prepared to deal with the majority of cases that do not fulfill the best-case scenario. In this section we will discuss a number of psychological challenges, as well as the desired psychological state we all strive for, known as "the zone."

In the Zone

When I am in the zone as a trader, I am totally focused and absorbed in the moment. Time seems to expand, my mind is clear, and I know what is coming next. My assessment of the chart seems as if it is in slow motion, and I can see where the market wants to go easily. This is where my intuition feels in perfect harmony with the market. I can already envision what will happen next—a breakout fits my Success Profile and moves easily, and I ride it. Another breakout starts to turn into a fakeout, and I close out for a small but inconsequential loss. Any ego dreams about my trading greatness disappear—I am just along for the ride, and my indicators speak clearly to me. I look for the Big Trends and seek to follow my rules for low-risk entry points along the way, while lightening up at profit target levels of resistance or new divergences. I have already planned to let nothing take me out of this zone—no phone calls, no other duties or deadlines—just intense focus on what the market is doing in this present moment. And being a part of this "now" moment is what makes me, as a trader, perform at the highest level. Not worrying about bills to pay or other future obligations, nor fretting over missed opportunities from the past.

How many times have you looked back at a stock you just sold to see if it is lower than you sold it? Or kicked yourself when you looked back at the stock having risen higher than you sold it? This is your ego wanting to be proven right! The more you do this, the more your ego is influencing your trading and also pulling you back into the past, instead of focusing on the current moment and what you will now do to position yourself for a new profit. When you leave the zone like this, your ego will not admit that you are out of the zone. Then you begin to overtrade, trade for revenge to get back at the market, or average down because you are 100 percent convinced that the losing stock you bought will eventually recover. That is when you can implode as a trader.

Think about this—when you average down on a stock, why are you doing this? The term "average down" says it all: you are trying to lower your average cost basis compared to the current lower stock price, so your ego can reduce the amount of pain that it feels for your prior mistake (face it, you bought a stock that went down, and in retrospect it was a mistake). Such ego-based decisions are invariably the wrong thing to do. What I find is that such downtrodden stocks may occasionally recover, but it will often take more time than expected. Prior buyers are relieved to get a better price to reduce their loss and move on, and so selling pressure occurs on each rally in a downtrend. So the reality in most circumstances is that the new money that goes to average down the stock could be better utilized in a new idea with a chance to be a better opportunity (not to mention the old capital that is still tied up in the underperformer that could also be freed up). It is compounding an error doubly by throwing new money at an idea you were wrong on.

Ask yourself "What would a trading coach observe about my trading?" Step outside your own body. For me, a mentor would say "Price, you're in this for results, right?" I nod. "Well, your trend-following systems show a high degree of accuracy as you stretch out to weekly and monthly time frames, while your intraday and many times daily systems are full of noise. This reduces your confidence and your conviction level as you reduce your time frame. You need to focus on weekly and monthly time frames to maximize your total returns, while using daily and especially intraday charts as counter-trend opportunities." This effort to be objective brings out the best in all of us as traders, as many of us often know the answers if we only will look inside ourselves and get our ego out of the way to hear the truth.

My ego thinks that this sounds boring, as I want to be "in the game" every day, all day. But the return on investment (ROI) on my time diminishes, both absolutely and on a per-hour basis, the shorter the time frame on which I focus.

We are raised with certain beliefs that we inherit as young children. The big part of maturing is learning which beliefs serve us, and which beliefs need to be modified. Growth occurs as we monitor our results, and the underlying beliefs that create them, and then make changes to see how we can get better results in our lives. Socrates said, "The unexamined life is not worth living." Yet I know a lot of individuals who will complain to me that they are not getting the results they want, although they are not willing to look at themselves. You do not have to be experienced to do this. Rather, you have to have the courage to honestly evaluate what is going on inside of you. Then you have to have the discipline to take one behavior at a time that you want to change, and create a plan to replace that belief with a new, more empowering value. But there are some people who simply will not do this. It either hurts too much, or they value comfort and security over the prospect of improving with effort. The bottom line is that only you can set the standards for your life—the truly great individuals have set a standard of excellence of which many have never even dreamed. The champions do not reach the pinnacle overnight. They do it through years of incrementally boosting their goals. Once you accomplish one goal, you celebrate that success and then replace it with a bigger goal. Peak experiences seem to occur often in what many individuals have called "the zone."

Some athletes report experiencing a state of focused energy, or a transcendent state of well-being, or an altered sense of time, or being on a high. The "runner's high" is now well known, and it offers my first recollection of the idea of being in a zone, or a euphoric state of optimal performance. This euphoric state is believed to be caused by the release of endorphins during physical exertion. On a more spiritual plane, runners have described this sensation as euphoric, with a greater sense of well-being and a transcendence of both time and space.

The zone describes a spiritual experience, a transcendent state, going beyond the self, or a mystical experience with exceptional feats of strength and endurance. Some refer to the zone as an exhilarating, uplifting event, with a sense of mastery and control, or a sense of invincibility. Others express the zone as radiant happiness, laser-sharp intuition, life unfolding in slow motion, and an out-of-body experience. Mihaly Csikszentmihalyi in his ground-breaking book *Flow* named this experience "flow," described as total absorption in the present moment, with no self-consciousness or distractions. He also called it a state of mind that is "intrinsically rewarding." He discusses the component of doing something for its own sake, much like I have mentioned that the great traders all seem to have a love of the game itself, rather than the outcome.

The zone is a rarely achieved psychological state, but once you have been there, you will want to return to the zone again. Csikszentmihalyi offers six key traits that precipitate entrance to the zone: confidence, focus, visualization, pleasure, relaxation, and the ability to handle excitement.

1. *Confidence*—applied to trading, confidence means you take trades with a positive expectancy that the odds are in your favor. You truly believe you are a capable and skilled trader.
2. *Focus*—the zone is achieved by having a narrow focus on the task at hand, or by being completely in the present moment. Fears about the outcome in the future and regrets about the losses from the past are non-existent.
3. *Visualization*—in total focus, a trader gets in the zone through visual processing of data in a focused manner. Verbal cues can take an individual out of the zone.

4. *Pleasure*—having fun at what you do in life increases the odds that you will participate with all your being. This increases your chances at achieving mastery which further enhances your enjoyment of any activity. It works the same way for traders. Those who view trading as work will grind through the day and struggle to find great trades, while those who love trading will immerse themselves and increase their odds of being in tune with the markets.

5. *Relaxation*—once you get to the zone, you may start to get nervous that you have never gone this far before. Stay relaxed to let yourself go deeper in the zone. Some traders will get scared, although fear will bring you back out of the zone.

6. *Excitement*—a certain level of tension is helpful to performance, but too much intensity will create undue stress and negatively impact performance.

One of the keys as a trader is that you must spend the time necessary to make trading skills "automatic" and create winning trading habits. If you wish to be immersed in total focus, you cannot be thinking about technique or strategy. Preparation and practice make for proper skill development. By making these actions automatic, the mind can be totally absorbed within the zone.

There are numerous traits that help keep individuals in the zone. They include focusing on the present moment, loss of personal ego, a sense of control, and an intrinsic reward system. Other useful traits include relaxation, calmness, high energy, optimism, enjoyment, effortlessness, alertness, focus, and self-confidence.

What is the key to success? Dedication. The more you practice, the better you get. Also, the level of emotion you put into what you do, and the intensity of your emotions and the ability to transform your feelings play a role. The trader needs to learn to change his or her feelings by transforming pain into an intense, positive emotion.

Believe in yourself and your ability to succeed. Successful people take credit for their successes and failures, while unsuccessful people tend to blame fate or circumstances. Our beliefs about ourselves influence the tasks we undertake, the efforts we make, and the results we achieve. Keep your thoughts and behaviors positive, and you will increase your odds of a favorable outcome in your trading.

CONCLUSION

These days it seems most market gurus are polarized in either the bull or bear camp. Perhaps one of the contrarian conclusions that would most surprise the majority would be a longer-term trading range over the next several years. This certainly would fit the pattern of the market after the last two major bear markets in 1973–1974 and back in the 1930's.

Yet whether the market resumes an overall uptrend or downtrend, there will always be opportunities on both sides of the markets in individual stocks and options. The one constant is that change continues to accelerate, forcing investors to be quicker to make decisions if they wish to capitalize on the increased volatility in today's market.

Trading success boils down to several simple, yet critical, elements. Clearly, you must have an investment method that gives you an edge over time. This book has spent a great deal of its focus on providing you with indicators and systems that have tested positively to effectively assess the overall market and then select the best individual stocks and options. In addition, you must utilize sound money management rules to capture your edge over time, and this book discussed some simple and effective methods to both cut your losses quickly and stay with your best ideas for the truly big trends. In addition, the importance of the proper trading mindset cannot be underestimated in placing you in a position to not only find the next big trend, but also manage your risk to stay in the game during choppy or otherwise difficult market conditions.

Mastering these disciplines provides you the framework to be successful. Now you must create a process to execute your plan. The execution stage is made easier if your plan helps to take your emotions out of the entry and exit process. The more systematic you can be in executing orders, the more objective and balanced you will remain through the market's highs and lows. I believe the most important factor to execute consistently is discipline. Disciplined trading means that your system only takes trades that offer acceptable reward-to-risk levels, and the system will not chase trades not fitting such criteria. That's how many traders get hurt. They chase into a position and then take a financial hit when the stock reverses, and more importantly, these traders take an emotional hit that damages their confidence. While we all want to preserve and grow our financial capital, successful traders know that each day they must protect their emotional capital as well. If you avoid emotional decisions in your trading and investing, you will take your ego out of the game and increase your odds of success.

I have also included additional information in the appendices to help you get started in options trading if you need a launching point. I share with you my favorite web sites for options traders and a selected list of options brokers, as well as information on various types of entry and exit orders you can place.

As you develop your trading plan, while you should make sure your plan addresses any weak areas, I encourage you to focus on your strengths and fit your plan to your unique personality. There is no holy grail to trading, nor can an investment approach be applied in a "one size fits all" fashion. You must factor in your level of risk tolerance to determine whether stocks, options, or perhaps mutual funds are most suitable for your trading personality. By matching your trading approach to your particular comfort level, you will be much more likely to stick to your trading plan through thick and thin. Many investors tend to think they have a more aggressive risk tolerance than they actually have, only to later find out in the heat of the battle that a drawdown is too much for them to handle. This invariably leads to the investor giving up at an adverse time, often right at the point where performance then starts to improve. If you are not sure if a method is right for you, consider receiving a trial subscription to evaluate it before throwing hard dollars behind it. Paper trading is no substitute for the greater intensity of actual trading, but this can give you a better understanding of how long you hold trades, what type of risk and reward you incur, and whether the general philosophy fits with your trading personality.

One of the challenges in this Information Age is that I can guarantee that you will be overwhelmed with information if you do not proactively seek to filter news and data down to only the most important trading opportunities into your trading method. I find most traders are too eager to trade every day, and in turn throw their capital rather indiscriminately at the next stock or options with promising news that comes across the web. This serves to distract investors from the bigger trends when they occur, and it also tempts traders to scalp the eventual home run stocks for a small profit and move on to the next news the next day. That can prove costly based on the themes of opportunity cost and compounding discussed earlier. Filtering information to what is truly important is a major focus for me, and I encourage you to use sources of information that get your portfolio concentrated in the best potential movers as opposed to being spread too thin in too many issues that you can't monitor properly.

THE FUTURE OF TRADING

While the bear market of 2000–2001 has brought with it a perception that the active traders have been mauled, I see evidence of the opposite phenomenon: more investors who previously would only buy and hold now want to learn how to profit from volatility while being able to exit more quickly to reduce their risk. In particular, many investors ask me about options strategies to reduce their dollars at risk while still being able to participate in the trends on both the upside and the downside.

I think you will see a boom in options trading in the years ahead, as well as more growth in active stock trading. The heightened volatility of today's markets will persist in the coming years, thanks to electronic trading and the quicker information flow to investors and traders alike. In addition, more competition for options business should lead to tighter spreads and increase the use of options as a substitute for stock for traders with relatively short-term time horizons. Investors will continue to utilize options in greater numbers as well, to both protect their portfolios and to lessen their dollars at risk in volatile times.

I wish you great success in your search for investment profits, and I hope this book serves as an ongoing resource to help you spot and profit from tomorrow's big trends.

Appendix A

STOCK PICKING CHECKLIST

Stock Picking Checklist

Stock Symbol: ; Price, Today's Change: ; Date: ; Time:
Option Symbol: ; Bid: ; Ask: ; Volume: ; Open Interest:

Does the idea fit with the current sector view? Best alternative in sector:

Is it compelling right now? Why?

What is the No. 1 driver?

Have I traded options on this stock before? How was the performance and fills?

Earnings Trend—What has been the reaction?

A. Last quarter.

B. Previous two to three quarters.

C. When is the next quarterly earnings report due?

D. Are you reasonably comfortable with any earnings event risk?

E. Is the expectation level for upcoming earnings high/low or average?

Technicals:

A. Are Moving Averages in your favor?
   20 day?   50 day?   200 day?

B. Location of Acceleration Bands?
Upper   Lower

C. Location of Moving Average Envelope?
Upper   Lower

D. Any Momentum Divergences?
15 minute   Daily   Weekly   Monthly

E. Any technical support or resistance?

F. Breakout points?

G. Is there a channel forming or breaking?

H. What is the rally potential versus pullback risk?

I. What is your target based on past history?

J. If in a trading range, why do you believe it will breakout?

K. Short interest level? How many times average daily volume?

Option Pricing:

A. Historical volatility?

B. Theoretical value versus actual asked?

C. Liquidity.

D. How do second-month options compare to first month in pricing, delta, and targets needed (mainly for lower-risk trades)?

Is there any other noteworthy news?

Appendix B

TYPES OF ORDERS

Entry and Exit Orders—when to use Market, Limit, Buy-Stop, Market-if-Touched, and more.

MARKET AND LIMIT ORDERS

A market order is an order to buy or sell a stated number of option contracts and is to be executed at the best price obtainable when the order reaches the post. A limit order is an order to buy or sell a stated number of option contracts at a specified price, or better.

Execution of Market and Limit Orders

CONTINGENCY ORDER

A contingency order is a limit or market order to buy or sell that is contingent upon a specific condition being satisfied while the order is on the trading floor.

1. Market-If-Touched Order (MIT)

A market-if-touched (MIT) order is a contingency order to buy or sell when the market for a particular option contract reaches a specified price. A MIT order to buy becomes a market order when the option contract is at or below the order price. A MIT order to sell becomes a market order when the option contract trades at or above the order price.

2. Market-On-Close Order (MOC)

A market or limit order may be designated a market-on-close order to be executed as close as possible to the closing bell and should be executed near to or at the closing price.

3. Stop (Stop-Loss) Order

A stop order is a contingency order to buy or sell when the market for a particular option contract reaches a specified price. A stop order to buy becomes a market order when the option contract trades or is bid at or above the stop price. A stop order to sell becomes a market order when the option contract trades or is offered at or below the stop price.

4. Stop-Limit Order

A stop-limit order is a contingency order to buy or sell when the market for a particular option contract reaches a specified price. A stop-limit order to buy becomes a limit order when the option contract trades or is bid at or above the stop-limit price. A stop-limit order to sell becomes a limit order when the option contract trades or is offered at or below the stop-limit price.

NOT HELD ORDER

A not held order is an order marked "not held," which gives discretion as to the price or time at which such order is to be executed.

ONE-CANCELS-THE-OTHER-ORDER (OCO)

A one-cancels-the-other order consists of two or more orders treated as one. The execution of any one of the orders causes the other to be canceled.

ALL-OR-NONE ORDER (AON)

An all-or-none order is a market or limit order which is to be executed in its entirety or not at all.

FILL-OR-KILL ORDER (FOK)

A fill-or-kill order is an order which is to be executed in its entirety as soon as it is represented in the trading crowd, and such order, if not so executed, is to be treated as canceled.

Appendix C

FAVORITE WEB SITES

Price Headley's Favorite Options web sites include:

For Options Information

www.bigtrends.com—For directional options trading on stock and index options.

www.cboe.com—Options quotes and daily market statistics on the VIX and put/call ratio.

cbs.marketwatch.com—For easy-to-expand options chains.

www.freeoptionpricing.com—Options pricing models.

www.ivolatility.com—For options volatility data.

www.optionstrategist.com—For volatility rankings and various options strategies.

www.option-wizard.com—For options pricing information.

For Options Brokers

www.americanoptionservices.com

www.mansecurities.com

www.optionsxpress.com

www.optiontraders.com

www.ptisecurities.com

www.wallstreetaccess.com

For Charts

www.stockcharts.com

www.tradestion.com

Appendix D

FAVORITE QUOTES

"Have an opinion on what the market should do but don't decide what the market will do."

—Bernard Baruch

"There is only one side of the market and it is not the bull side or the bear side, but the right side."

—Edwin Lefevre, *Reminiscences of a Stock Operator*

"It was never my thinking that made the big money for me. It was my sitting. Got that? My sitting tight. . . . Men who can both be right and sit tight are uncommon. I found this one of the hardest things to learn. . . . It is literally true that millions come easier to a trader after he knows how to trade than hundreds did in the days of his ignorance."

—Edwin Lefevre, *Reminiscences of a Stock Operator*

"The speculator's deadly enemies are: Ignorance, greed, fear and hope."

—Edwin Lefevre, *Reminiscences of a Stock Operator*

"Trade the structure and not the money."

—Mark Douglas, *The Disciplined Trader*

"Excellence can be attained if you Care more than others think is wise, Risk more than others think is safe, Dream more than others think is practical, and Expect more than others think is possible."

—Anon

"Press on. Nothing in the world can take the place of persistence. Talent will not: nothing is more common than unrewarded talent. Education alone will not: The world is full of educated failures. Persistence alone is omnipotent."

—Calvin Coolidge

Referring to the relationship between the position and the momentum (mass times velocity) of a subatomic particle, it basically states,

"The more precisely the position is determined, the less precisely the momentum is known in this instant, and vice versa."

—Warner Heisenberg

"Knowing and not doing are equivalent to not knowing at all."

—Fortune Cookie

GLOSSARY

American Association of Individual Investors (AAII) This not-for-profit organization conducts investor surveys showing the percentage of their members polled who are bullish, bearish or neutral on the stock market's outlook. AAII helps educate investors and offers numerous local chapters across the United States, where investors can meet and hear well-known speakers.

American Option An option that allows the holder (buyer) to exercise anytime prior to expiration. All equity options are American Style as is the S&P 100 Index (OEX). Generally, call options should not be exercised early (except perhaps to capture a dividend) and put options should be exercised early once the put is sufficiently in-the-money (where delta = 1 and time value no longer exists).

AMEX An abbreviation for the American Stock Exchange. The AMEX is home to the second largest options exchange in the world.

Ask Price Is the lowest price that a stock is being offered for sale. Also called the "offer price". The *ask price* is higher than the *bid price*.

At-The-Money "At-the-Money" describes an option with a strike price equal to the market price of the stock. Because it is rare to see a stock trade exactly at one of the strike prices, the term is loosely used to mean the strike nearest the current stock price.

Average Directional Movement (ADX) ADX measures the degree of trend or direction in a market. A rising ADX suggests a strong trend; a falling ADX reflects a reversal or non-trending conditions in a market.

Bear (Bearish) An investor who believes a stock or index will fall. The term gets its name from the way a bear attacks; it raises it paws and swipes down simulating a high to low motion. If you think stocks are moving from high to low, you are bearish.

Behavioral Finance Behavioral finance focuses on the belief that stock prices are greatly influenced by investors' behavior and emotions.

Such behaviors include fear and greed, as well as the existence of self-reinforcing behavior, which leads to trends which last longer than most expected.

Bid   The price a buyer is willing to pay for a particular stock.

Bid/Ask Spread   The difference between the asking price and the bid price. For example, if the bid is $5 and the ask is $5 1/2, then the spread is 1/2 point. Spreads tend to widen when there is more risk or less liquidity (which is a form of risk). Because of this, it is not uncommon to see for months, out-of-the-money, or deep in-the-money options trade with very wide bid/ask spreads. The market (not the market makers) determines the spreads, which is contrary to what most traders believe.

Black-Scholes Option Pricing Model   Developed by Fisher Black and Myron Scholes, the model produces the theoretical value of an American call option with the following five inputs: stock price, exercise price, risk-free interest rate, volatility and time. Myron Scholes was awarded a Nobel Prize for his contributions in 1997.

Breakout   A technical analysis term, used to indicate a rise in a stock's price above its resistance level (such as its previous high price) or drop below its support level (commonly the last lowest price.) The assumption is that the stock will continue to move in the same direction following the breakout, which generates a buy or sell signal.

Bull (Bullish)   An investor who believes a stock or index will rise. The term gets its name from the way a bull attacks; it lowers its horns and raises its head high. If you think stocks are heading from low to high, you are bullish.

Call Option   A contract between two people which gives the owner the right, but not the obligation, to buy stock at a specified price over a given time period. The seller of the call has an obligation to sell the stock if the long put position decides to buy.

Candlestick Charts   A form of Japanese charting that has become very popular in the US. A narrow line (shadow) shows the day's price range. A wider body marks the area between the high and close. If the close is above the open, the body is white; if the close is below the open, the body is black.

CBOE   An abbreviation for the Chicago Board Options Exchange. This is the largest options exchange in the world.

Closing Price   Is the last price at which a stock transaction takes place on any given day. This is the price quoted in the newspapers and in chart services as the last trade of the day in regular-hours trading.

Closing Stop   Instead of stopping out a position at any point during a particular bar of trading (whether intraday, daily, weekly or monthly bars), the stop is only applied if the stop level is broken at the close of that bar.

This method seeks to avoid the noise generated during the bar, while still quickly exiting at the end of the bar if the level is violated at the close.

Consensus Inc. An organization that provides weekly sentiment data on the percentage of Bulls across all the major futures markets, including Stock Indices.

Contrarian The process of betting against the prevailing market mood. At BigTrends.com we believe you must define an extreme in investor fear or greed upon which you should then look to be a contrarian.

Covered Call A short call option position in which the writer owns the number of shares of the underlying stock represented by the option contracts. Covered calls generally limit the risk the writer takes because the stock does not have to be bought at the market price, if the holder of that option decides to exercise it.

Day Order A buy or sell order that is automatically cancelled at the end of the trading day, if it has not been executed as instructed.

Directional Movement This indicator, called DMI, plots a +DI line measuring buying pressure and a −DI line measuring selling pressure. The pattern is bullish as long as the +DI line is above the −DI line. The formula utilized the past 14 time periods. The ADX line is derived from this system and is based on the spread between the +DI and −DI lines.

Earnings Surprises Positive or negative differences from the consensus forecast.

Efficient Market Hypothesis (EMH) The EMH in its strongest form suggests that the stock markets are completely efficient, because all information that is known about a company's stock is believed to be acted upon as of that point in time. EMH thus believes future price action is completely random, based only upon new information that may be released and acted upon at some future date. EMH is a key assumption of traditional options pricing models. Contrast to *Behavioral Finance*.

Expiration Technically, option expiration (for equities) is always the Saturday following the third Friday of the month. If a trader has an October call option, it can no longer be exercised after that point. But, for trading purposes, the last day to buy or sell an option will be the third Friday of the month. Equity options trade until 4:02 EST, while index options trade until 4:15 EST.

Expiration Cycle In addition to options having a "front month" and "second month" options series, options are listed in one of several cycles, rotating in 3 month increments. Stock options in a January cycle will be listed and expire in January, April, July and October. Stock options in a February cycle will be listed and expire in February, May, August and

November. Stock options in a March cycle will be listed and expire in March, June, September and December.

European Option   A style of option that allows the holder (buyer) to exercise only at expiration. Most index options are European style with the exception of the S&P 100 Index (OEX).

Exponential Moving Average (EMA)   An exponential moving average is calculated by applying a percentage of today's closing price to yesterday's moving average value. Contrast to *Simple Moving Average*.

Fundamental Analysis   The opposite of visual or technical analysis. Fundamental analysis relies on economic supply and demand information, as opposed to market activity.

Good 'Til Canceled (GTC)   Sometimes simply called "GTC", it means an order to buy or sell stock that is good until you cancel it. Brokerages usually set a limit of 30–60 days, at which the GTC expires if not restated.

Implied Volatility   The volatility calculated by the Black-Scholes Option Pricing Model to provide the current option quote. It is the future volatility of the underlying security *implied* by the current market price.

Index Option   An option on an existing index, such as the S&P 100 Index (OEX).

International Securities Exchange (ISE)   The ISE is the newest exchange to open for options trading, seeking to revolutionize options trading via pure electronic mechanisms as opposed to the traditional options trading floors.

In-the-Money   A call option with a strike below (and a put option with a strike above) the current stock price are said to be in-the-money. This is also the intrinsic value of the option—the amount received if exercised immediately. For example, if the stock is $102.50, a $100 call is $2.50 points in-the-money. Any amount above $2.50 in this example is called time value.

Intrinsic Value   An option's intrinsic value is the amount by which it is in the money.

Investors Intelligence   A firm which has surveyed investment advisers for over 30 years on a weekly basis regarding their outlook for the stock market going forward. Investors Intelligence reports its survey respondents as Bullish, Bearish or Correction. When only 25 percent of professionals are bullish, the market is considered oversold. A reading of 55 percent or higher is overbought.

LEAPS®   Long-Term Equity Anticipation Securities (LEAPS®) are longer-term options with expiration dates as much as 3 years into the future. LEAPS® give investors a way to invest in a stock for the next 1-3 years at a reduced cost relative to owning the underlying stock. LEAPS® also do not experience time decay as quickly as shorter-term options. The longer time frame allows an options investor to create additional strategies with LEAPS® that are not possible with shorter-term options.

Leverage   The use of borrowed capital to increase the return of an investment. Or the use of vehicles like options, which provide financial leverage. The leverage factor is usually calculated by taking the stock price divided by the option price. For example, if the underlying stock is trading for $50 and you purchase a call option for $2, the leverage is $50/$2 = 25. You control stock worth $50 for only $2, so you are leveraging the stock by a factor of 25. Some also examine leverage by taking the strike price of the option divided by the option's price. If our option is a $60 strike, some consider the leverage as $60/2 = 30. This approach reasons that since you have a right to buy at 60 and paid $2, the leverage factor has risen from 25 to 30.

Limit Order   An order that guarantees the price but not the execution. If a trader places an order to buy 10 contracts at a limit of $3 (the limit), the only way the order will fill is if it can be filled for $3 *or lower.* Similarly, if a sell order is placed for $6, the only way it will fill is for $6 or *higher.* Because of these restrictions, limit orders are not guaranteed to fill.

MACD (Moving Average Convergence Divergence)   A powerful trending indicator consisting of two simple lines. When the lines cross, it can indicate a change in trend. The first (MACD) line is the difference between two exponential moving averages (usually 12 and 26 periods) of closing prices. The second (signal) line is usually a 9-period average of the first (MACD) line. Signals are given when the two lines cross.

Market Order   An order to buy or sell at the best available quote *when the trade reaches the floor* (or market maker). It is guaranteed to execute because the price is allowed to fluctuate. Also, there is no need to designate "day" or "good-til-cancelled" with a market order because it is sure to fill (unless it is a short sale with no "uptick"). See also *Limit Order.*

Market Vane   A company based in Pasadena, California, which polls investors each day to determine a percentage who are bullish on the various futures markets, including stocks.

Momentum Divergence   When a new high (low) in Price is not confirmed by a new high (low) in Momentum, this lack of confirmation creates a Momentum Divergence.

Money Management   The process of determining appropriate entry and exit rules to both maximize potential reward and minimize risk. Includes rules on the size of initial positions and increasing or decreasing the size of open positions.

Multiply-Listed Options   Options for a security which are available for trading on more than one options exchange.

(Nova+OTC)/Ursa Ratio   BigTrends.com tracks asset flows in several key RYDEX funds on a daily basis to measure bullish/bearish sentiment. RYDEX Nova tracks the S&P 500 with a leverage factor of 1.5. OTC tracks the Nasdaq 100 Index 1-to-1. Ursa inversely tracks the S&P 500 1-to-1 (meaning a 10% drop in the S&P 500 should result in a 10% gain if you own the bearish Ursa fund). These assets flows have historically proven to be a useful contrarian indicator at extremes.

Open Interest   The net long and short positions for any option contract. If a trader "buys to open" and another "sells to open," then open interest will increase by the number of contracts. This is because both traders are opening. If one "buys to open" and the other "sells to close," then open interest will remain unchanged. Finally, if one "buys to close" and another "sells to close," then open interest will decrease by the amount of the contracts.

Options Contract   An option contract gives the holder the right to buy or sell a security at a pre-determined price over a limited time period. Investors can use them to generate income, protect an existing investment or leverage new investments with a dramatically reduced outlay of capital compared to purchasing the underlying security.

Out-Of-The-Money   A call option with a strike above and a put option with a strike below the current stock price are said to be out-of-the-money. Also, an option with no intrinsic value is said to be out-of-the-money. For example, if the stock is $100, a $105 call and a $95 put are out-of-the-money. See also *In-the-Money and Extrinsic Value.*

Premium   The total cost of an option. The option's premium consists of intrinsic value and time value.

ProFunds   A mutual fund family offering leveraged fund trading in both bullish and bearish funds.

PSE   The Pacific Stock Exchange, one of the options exchanges.

Put Option   A contract between two people which gives the owner the right, but not the obligation, to sell stock at a specified price over a given time period. The seller of the put has an obligation to buy the stock if the long put position decides to sell.

Put/Call Ratio   The ratio of volume in put options divided by the volume of call options is used as a contrary indicator. When put buying gets too high relative to call buying (a high put/call ratio), the market is over-sold. A low put/call ratio represents an overbought market condition.

Relative Strength   Calculated by dividing the performance of a stock's price over a period by a market index. Used to determine a stock's performance relative to the market and other stocks.

Resistance The opposite of support. Resistance is marked by a previous price peak and provides enough of a barrier above the market to halt a price advance.

Reward-to-Risk A term used by BigTrends.com to define the level of upside compared to the level of down side in your position. Look for Reward-to-Risk ratios of 3-to-1 or higher for the most favorable trading opportunities.

RYDEX A mutual fund family offering leveraged fund trading in both bullish and bearish funds.

Selling Short An initial sale of stock by an investor who believes that a stock will go down in price. The investor borrows the stock from a broker, sells it, and eventually hopes to buy it back at a lower price and then return the new shares to the broker. If the stock declines in price between the time the investor sells the shares and buys them back, a profit is realized. If the stock rises in price by the time the investors buys the stock back, a loss is realized.

Sentiment Analysis The study of sentiment involves indicators focused on measuring investor emotions like fear and greed, in an effort to assess when the crowd has over-reacted in a particular direction. Generally used for contrarian strategies at major market extremes.

Sentiment Survey A survey of the prevailing bullish or bearish opinions of those surveyed. Generally expressed as a percentage of those surveyed who are bullish or bearish. See *American Association of Individual Investors, Consensus Inc., Investors Intelligence*, and *Market Vane*.

Simple Moving Average A trend-following indicator that works best in a trending environment. Moving averages smooth out price action but operate with a time lag. A simple 10-day moving average of a stock, for example, adds up the last 10 days' closing prices and divides the total by 10. A buy signal is given when the price closes above the average. When two averages are employed, a buy (sell) signal is given when the shorter average crosses above (below) the longer average.

Split The dividing of a company's shares, creating a greater number of shares, while halving the price per share. The most common is a 2-1 split. Sometimes this creates more opportunities for a buyer, due to being less expensive. For example, you own 100 shares at $20 each the invested amount equals $2,000. The company announces they are splitting the shares "2-for-1." This means the price per share is now $20/2=$10. The 100 shares you own equal 100×2=200 shares now owned. The dollars invested are the same: 200 shares times $10 = $2,000. Companies like to split their growing stocks to keep the perceived cost per share low, which attracts individual investors who want to own more shares at a lower price.

Standard & Poor's 100 Index (S&P 100–OEX)   The S&P 100 Index (OEX) is a market-capitalization weighted index of 100 large capitalization stocks. Options on the OEX options are traded on the Chicago Board Options Exchange (CBOE).

Stop Order   A limit order that becomes a market order if the stock trades at that limit. For example, say a stock is trading for $10. A trader placing an order to sell the stock at a stop price of $9.50 wants to make the order a market order if the stock trades at $9.50 or *lower*. Stop orders do not eliminate losses, since a market order will occur at any price below $9.50. The stock could open for trading at $7, and the trade will be exited at this price instead of the $9.50 he expected.

Strike Price   The pre-determined price per share for which underlying stock may be purchased (in the case of a call) or sold (in the case of a put) by the option holder upon exercise of the option contract.

Support   A price area below the current market price, where buying power is sufficient to halt the price decline. A previous reaction low usually forms a support level.

Target   The anticipated profit level at which partial or full profits can be realized on an investment.

Technical Analysis   The study of market action on price charts including the use of volume and other indicators. Also called chart analysis, market analysis and visual analysis.

Time Decay   The steady erosion of the option's value as time passes, as other factors hold constant. An option seller will typically prefer to sell short-term options with greater time decay, while option buyers will seek to buy more time to minimize the impact of time decay.

Time Stop   Exiting a position based on a pre-determined number of bars if the position is not profitable by that time. Especially useful for options buyers.

Time Value   The portion of the premium that is based on the amount of time remaining until the expiration date of the option contract, and the underlying components that determine the value of the option may change during that time. Time value is generally equal to the difference between the premium and the intrinsic value.

Trading Range   The difference between the high and low prices traded during a certain time period. The high end of the range is known as Resistance, while the low end of the range is known as Support.

Trailing Stop   A regularly-adjusted order to sell a stock when the price falls to a specified level. As the price moves up, you keep moving up the stop loss order—trailing it under the share price—to avoid giving up all of your profits if the stock pulls back.

Underlying Security   The security subject to being purchased or sold upon exercise of an option contract. For example, General Electric (GE) stock is the underlying security for GE options.

VIX   The CBOE Volatility Index (VIX) produces an anticipated volatility reading based on the prices of 8 OEX options (4 calls and 4 puts) with an average expiration date of 30 days. A good contrarian indicator, as spikes in fear produce high VIX readings near significant market bottoms.

Volatility   This describes the fluctuations in the price of a stock or other type of security. If the price of a stock is capable of large swings, the stock has a high volatility. The pricing of options contracts depends in part on volatility. A stock with high volatility, for example, commands higher prices in the options market than one with low volatility. Volatility may be gauged by several measures, one of which involves calculating a security's standard deviation.

BIBLIOGRAPHY

Adler, Robert J., Feldman, Raisa E., and Taqqu, Murad S. *A Practical Guide to Heavy Tails* (Boston: Birkhauser, 1998).

Appel, Gerald. *The Moving Average Convergence-Divergence Method* (Great Neck, NY: Signalert, 1979).

Appel, Gerald and Hitshcler, Fred. *Stock Market Trading Systems* (Homewood, IL: Dow Jones-Irwin, 1980).

Arms Jr., Richard W. *The Arms Index (TRIN)* (Homewood, IL: Dow Jones-Irwin, 1989).

Arms Jr., Richard W. *Trading Without Fear* (New York: John Wiley & Sons, 1996).

Balsara, Nauzer J. *Money Management Strategies For Futures Traders* (New York: John Wiley & Sons, 1992).

Barach, Roland. *Mindtraps* (Homeood, IL: Dow Jones-Irwin, 1988).

Baruch, Bernard M. *Baruch* (New York: Henry Holt & Company, 1957).

Bernstein, Jake. *The Complete Day Trader* (New York: McGraw-Hill, 1995).

Bernstein, Peter L. *Against the Gods* (New York: John Wiley & Sons, 1998).

Beyer, Andrew. *Picking Winners* (Boston: Houghton Mifflin, 1975).

Bittman, James B. *Options for the Stock Investor* (Chicago: Irwin Professional Publishing, 1996).

Blau, William. *Momentum, Direction, Divergence* (New York: John Wiley & Sons, 1995).

Brown, Constance. *Aerodynamic Trading* (Gainesville, GA: New Classics Library, 1995).

Brown, Constance. *Technical Analysis for the Trading Professional* (New York: McGraw-Hill, 1999).

Cassidy, Donald L. *It's When You Sell That Counts* (New York: McGraw-Hill, 1997).

Chande, Tushar S. and Kroll, Stanley. *The New Technical Trader* (New York: John Wiley & Sons, 1994).

Chisholm, Michael. *Games Investors Play* (Winchester: B&B Publishing, 1981).

Cohen, A. W. *How to Use the Three-Point Reversal Method of Point & Figure Stock Market Trading* (Larchmont, NY: Chartcraft, 1984).

Conners, Laurence A. and Hayward, Blake E. *Investment Secrets of a Hedge Fund Manager* (Chicago: Probus Publishing, 1995).

Cooper, Andrew. *Playing in the Zone* (Boston: Shambhala Publications Inc., 1998).

Coppock, Edwin Sedgewick. *Practical Relative Strength Charting* (San Antonio: Trendex, 1960).

Csikszentmihalyi, Mihaly. *Flow: The Psychology of Optimal Experience* (New York: Harper Collins, 1991).

Dalton, James F. *Mind Over Markets* (Greenville, SC: Traders Press, 1999).

Darvas, Nicholas. *How I Made $2,000,000 In The Stock Market* (Secaucus, NJ: Carol Publishing Group, 1998).

Deel, Robert. *Trading The Plan* (New York: John Wiley & Sons, 1997).

Dembo, Ron S. and Freeman, Andrew. *Seeing Tomorrow* (New York: John Wiley & Sons, 1998).

Dent Jr., Harry S. *The Great Boom Ahead* (New York: Hyperion, 1994).

Dent Jr., Harry S. *The Roaring 2000's* (New York: Simon & Schuster, 1998).

Dobson, Edward D. *Understanding Fibonacci Numbers* (Greenville, SC: Traders Press, 1984).

Douglas Mark. *The Disciplined Trader* (Upper Saddle River, NJ: Prentice Hall, 1990).

Douglas, Mark. *Trading in the Zone* (Upper Saddle River, NJ: Prentice Hall, 2001).

Edwards, Robert D. and Magee, John. *Technical Analysis of Stock Trends* (Boston: John Magee Inc., 1992).

Elder, Alexander. *Trading for a Living* (New York: John Wiley & Sons, 1993).

Embrechts, Paul, Kluppelberg, Claudia, and Mikosch, Thomas. *Modeling External Events* (New York: Springer, 1997).

Eng, William F. *The Day Trader's Manual* (New York: John Wiley & Sons, 1993).

Fosback, Norman G. *Stock Market Logic* (Fort Lauderdale, FL: Institute For Econometric Research, 1976).

Frost, A. J. and Prechter, Robert. *Elliott Wave Principle* (Gainesville, GA: New Classics Library, Inc, 1985).

Galbraith, John Kenneth. *A Short History of Financial Euphoria* (New York: Penguin Group, 1990).

Gallacher, William R. *Winner Take All* (New York: McGraw-Hill, 1997).

Gehm, Fred. *Quantitative Trading & Money Management* (Chicago: Irwin Professional Publishing, 1995).

Goodspeed, Bennett. *The Tao Jones Averages* (New York: Dutton/Plume, 1983).

Granville, Joseph E. *New Strategy of Daily Stock Market Timing Form Maximum Profits* (Englewood Cliffs, NJ: Prentice Hall, 1976).

Haugen, Robert A. *The Inefficient Stock Market* (Upper Saddle River, NJ: Prentice Hall, 1999).

Hurst, J. M. *The Profit Magic of Stock Transaction Timing* (Englewood Cliffs, NJ: Prentice Hall, 1970).

Jones, Ryan. *The Trading Game* (New York: John Wiley & Sons, 1999).

Jorion, Philippe. *Value At Risk* (Chicago: Irwin Professional Publishing, 1997).

Jurik, Mark. *Computerized Trading* (New York: New York Institute of Finance, 1999).

Kiev, Ari. *Trade To Win* (New York: John Wiley & Sons, 1998).

Kindleberger, Charles Poor. *Manias, Panics and Crashes* (New York: John Wiley & Sons, 2000).

Koppel, Robert. *The Intuitive Trader: Developing Your Inner Trading Wisdom* (New York: John Wiley & Sons, 1996).

Koppel, Robert and Abell, Howard. *The Inner Game of Trading: Creating the Winner's State of Mind* (Chicago: Probus Publishing Company, 1993).

Koppel, Robert and Abell, Howard. *The Outer Game of Trading: Modeling the Trading Strategies of Today's Market Wizards* (New York: McGraw-Hill, 1994).

Kritzman, Mark P. *Puzzles of Finance* (New York: John Wiley & Sons, 2000).

LeBon, Gustave. *The Crowd* (Atlanta: Cherokee Publishing Company, 1982).

LeFevre, Edwin. *Reminiscences of a Stock Operator* (New York: John Wiley & Sons, 1993).

Livermore, Jesse L. *How To Trade In Stocks* (Greenville, SC: Traders Press, 1940).

Lowenstein, Roger. *When Genius Failed: The Rise & Fall of Long-Term Capital Management* (New York: Random House, 2000).

Mackay, Charles. *Extraordinary Popular Delusions & the Madness of the Crowd* (New York: Crown Publishing, 1995).

Mandlebrot, Benoit B. *Fractals and Scaling in Finance* (New York: Springer, 1997).

Marder, Kevin N. and Dupee, Marc. *The Best* (Los Angeles: M. Gordon Publishing Group, 2000).

May, Christopher T. *Nonlinear Pricing* (New York: John Wiley & Sons, 1999).

McClellan, Sherman and Marian. *Patterns for Profit: The McClellan Oscillator and Summation Index* (Lakewood, WA: McClellan Financial Publications, Inc., 1989).

McMillan, Larry. *Options as a Strategic Investment* (New York: New York Institute of Finance, 1983).

Murphy, John. *Technical Analysis of the Futures Markets* (Upper Saddle River, NJ: Prentice Hall, 1987).

Murphy Jr., Joseph E. *Stock Market Probability* (Chicago: Irwin Professional Publishing, 1988).

Murphy, Michael and White, Rhea A. *In the Zone* (New York: Penguin USA, 1995).

Murray, John F. *Smart Tennis: How to Play and Win the Mental Game* (New York: Jossey-Bass, Inc., 1999).

Najarian, Jon. *How I Trade Options* (New York: John Wiley & Sons, 2000).

Natenberg, Sheldon. *Option Volatility and Pricing Strategies*, revised edition (Chicago: Probus Publishing Company, 1994).

Neill, Humphrey B. *The Art Of Contrary Thinking* (Caldwell, ID: Caxton Printers, 1985).

Niederhoffer, Victor. *The Education of a Speculator* (New York: John Wiley & Sons, 1997).

Nison, Steve. *Japanese Candlestick Charting Techniques* (New York: McGraw-Hill, 1991).

Nison, Steve. *Beyond Candlesticks* (New York: John Wiley & Sons, 1994).

O'Neil, William J. *How to Make Money in Stocks* (New York: McGraw-Hill, 1994).

O'Neil, William J. *24 Essential Lessons for Investment Success* (New York: McGraw-Hill, 2000).

Peters, Edgar E. *Fractal Market Analysis* (New York: John Wiley & Sons, 1994).

Peters, Edgar E. *Chaos and Order in the Capital Markets* (New York: John Wiley & Sons, 1996).

Pirsig, Robert M. *Zen and the Art of Motorcycle Maintenance* (New York: Bantam Books, 1984).

Plummer, Tony. *The Psychology of Technical Analysis* (Chicago: Irwin Professional Publishing, 1993).

Pring, Martin J. *Technical Analysis Explained* (New York: McGraw-Hill, 1991).

Pring, Martin. *Martin Pring on Market Momentum* (Los Angeles: International Institute For Economic Research, 1993).

Robbins, Anthony. *Awaken the Giant Within* (New York: Simon & Schuster Trade, 1992).

Robbins, Anthony. *Unlimited Power* (New York: Simon & Schuster Trade, 1997).

Rotella, Robert. *Golf is Not a Game of Perfect* (New York: Simon & Schuster Trade, 1995).

Rowntree, Derek. *Statistics Without Tears* (New York: Allyn & Bacon, 1981).

Rubenstein, Lorne. *Links: An Exploration into the Mind, Heart and Soul of Golf* (Collingdale, PA: DIANE Publishing Company, 1994).

Schaeffer, Bernie. *The Option Advisor* (New York: John Wiley & Sons, 1997).

Schiller, Robert J. *Irrational Exuberance* (New York: Broadway Books, 2001).

Schroeder, Manfred. *Fractals, Chaos, Power Laws* (New York: W. H. Freeman and Company, 1991).

Schumpeter, Joseph A. *Business Cycles* (New York: McGraw-Hill, 1939).

Schwager, Jack. *Market Wizards* (New York: Harper Business, 1993).

Schwager, Jack. *The New Market Wizards* (New York: Harper Business, 1994).

Schwager, Jack. *Stock Market Wizards* (New York: Harper Business, 2001).

Schwartz, Martin, Morine, Dave, and Flint, Paul. *Pit Bull* (New York: Harper Business, 1998).

Shapiro, Alan. *Golf's Mental Hazards* (New York: Simon & Schuster, 1996).

Shefrin, Hersh. *Beyond Fear and Greed* (Boston: Harvard Business School Press, 2000).

Sperandeo, Victor. *Trader Vic 2: Principles of Professional Speculation* (New York: John Wiley & Sons, 1998).

Sperandeo, Victor and Brown, T. Sullivan. *Trader Vic—Methods of a Wall Street Master* (New York: John Wiley & Sons, 1993).

Steidlmayer, Peter J. *Market Profile Workshop* (New York: John Wiley & Sons, 1990).

Thackrey Jr., Ted. *Gambling Secrets of Nick the Greek* (Chicago: Rand McNally & Company, 1968).

Thaler, Richard H. *The Winner's Curse* (New York: The Free Press, 1992).

Thaler, Richard H. *Advances in Behavioral Finance* (New York: Russell Sage Foundation, 1993).

Tharp, Van K. *Trading Your Way to Financial Freedom* (New York: McGraw-Hill, 1999).

Train, John. *The Money Masters* (New York: Harper & Row, 1980).

Tzu, Sun. *The Art of War* (Oxford: Oxford University Press, 1984).

Urbach, Richard M. A. *Footprints Of Chaos in the Markets* (London: Financial Times, 2000).

Vince Ralph. *Portfolio Management Formulas* (New York: John Wiley & Sons, 1990).

Vince, Ralph. *The Mathematics of Money Management* (New York: John Wiley & Sons, 1992).

Wilder, Welles J. *New Concepts in Technical Trading Systems* (Greensboro, NC: Trend Research, 1978).

Williams, Larry. *Long-Term Secrets to Short-Term Trading* (New York: John Wiley & Sons, 1992).

INDEX

Page numbers followed by f indicate figures.
Page numbers followed by t indicate tables.